THEORETICAL DEVELOPMENTS IN HISPANIC LINGUISTICS
Javier Gutiérrez-Rexach, Series Editor

Interfaces and Domains of Quantification

Javier Gutiérrez-Rexach

THE OHIO STATE UNIVERSITY PRESS · COLUMBUS

Copyright © 2014 by The Ohio State University.
All rights reserved.

Library of Congress Cataloging-in-Publication Data
Gutiérrez-Rexach, Javier, author.
  Interfaces and domains of quantification / Javier Gutiérrez-Rexach.
    pages cm — (Theoretical developments in Hispanic linguistics)
  ISBN 978-0-8142-1255-4 (cloth : alk. paper) — ISBN 0-8142-1255-7 (cloth : alk. paper) — ISBN 978-0-8142-9358-4 (cd-rom) — ISBN 0-8142-9358-1 (cd-rom)
  1. Spanish language—Quantifiers. 2. Spanish language—Syntax. 3. Spanish language—Semantics. 4. Grammar, Comparative and general—Quantifiers. 5. Grammar, Comparative and general—Syntax. 6. Semantics, Comparative. I. Title.
  PC4171.G88 2014
  465—dc23
                          2013040907

Cover design by AuthorSupport.com
Type set in Adobe Minion

∞ The paper used in this publication meets the minimum requirements of the American National Standard for Information Sciences—Permanence of Paper for Printed Library Materials. ANSI Z39.48–1992.

9 8 7 6 5 4 3 2 1

Contents

Acknowledgments		*vii*
	Introduction	1
1	The View from the Syntax-Semantics Interface	5
2	Scope Parallelism and the Interpretation of Ellipsis	21
3	Indefinites and Sentential Modality	50
4	Existence and Beyond: Varieties of Having	75
5	Free Relatives and Quantificational Variability	100
6	Correlatives and Degrees	119
7	Concessive Conditionals and Scalarity	143
8	Superlatives, Degrees, and Focus	170
9	The Dimensions of Modal Discourse Particles	190
	Final Thoughts on Quantity, Structure, and Meaning	210
Bibliography		*215*
Index of Abbreviations		*231*
Index		*233*

Acknowledgments

THIS BOOK is the result of several years of research on different topics in the structure and interpretation of Spanish quantificational structures of various sorts. I have benefitted enormously from interaction with audiences at conferences and venues where materials related to different chapters have been presented: the Linguistic Symposium on Romance Languages (LSRL), the Hispanic Linguistic Symposium (HLS), Going Romance, the Linguistic Society of America (LSA), Sinn und Bedeutung, the Chicago Linguistics Society, and others. I have also benefited from comments and observations by several colleagues at institutions where earlier drafts of chapters or research related to them have been presented: Georgetown University, Michigan State University, Rutgers University, Universitat de Barcelona, University of Illinois, Chicago, University of Michigan, and the University of Ottawa.

Introduction

THE LINGUISTIC STUDY of grammatical categories, features and expressions has experienced a series of rapid and radical advances in the last forty years. This progress can be attested not only in all linguistic disciplines—phonology, phonetics, syntax, semantics, etc.—but also, and more importantly, in the analysis of phenomena and data belonging to languages other than English. Although the advent of generative grammar marked a milestone in the application of scientific methodology and theory production, progress has been uneven across different areas. Obviously, obtaining and analyzing empirical evidence in the realm of sounds seemed to be more easily conducive to a series of uniform heuristics and protocols, given the discrete and measurable nature of phonetic data. On the other hand, analyzing the structure and meaning of expressions seemed to be dependent on performing several abstraction steps which were sometimes the focus of intense theoretical debate.

The linguistic analysis of Spanish has mirrored this progress path to a great extent. We have gained a great deal of knowledge on phonetic and morpho-phonological patterns, dialectal variation, social determinants of linguistic behavior, etc. If we look at the syntactic side of this emerging picture, it is obvious that a great deal of work has been done on a number of significant structures and constructions: clitics and pronominal doubling, the indicative/subjunctive alternation, tense and aspect, etc. Nevertheless, only during the last decades of the twentieth century and the beginning of the new

Millennium we have reached milestones leading to a more comprehensive understanding of several phenomena that can be covered under the generic label of "quantification." The analysis of such phenomena requires a genuine interdisciplinary approach, with insights coming from syntactic theory but also from semantic and logical analyses as well as pragmatic approaches.

Quantification is an intrinsically complex phenomenon, covering several structural and semantic domains. Looking at the structural domain first, it seems obvious that quantification takes numerous shapes whose inventory and particular properties have not been completely charted to date. In this book, we explore several linguistic forms associated with the expression of quantification in Spanish, from indefiniteness to the quantificational properties of adverbial particles, all of which have idiosyncratic edges and peculiarities that have been traditionally overlooked or not well understood. Another important benefit of looking at quantification with a magnifying glass is that it quickly becomes apparent that it does not associate only with one semantic domain. The most prominent domain with which quantificational expressions are associated is the domain of individuals, but there are also quantificational expressions ranging over entities of a different nature, such as times or degrees. In sum, only if we look at the different syntactic and semantic domains of quantification in natural language, it is possible to truly understand its multifaceted nature. This analysis thus requires considering a wide range of structural forms and also different semantic and pragmatics properties. This peculiarity is what has brought to the fore the centrality of quantification for the study of the interface domains of grammar.

In chapter one, quantification is characterized as belonging to several interface areas of research. Linguistically, an interface is a cognitive domain associated with an area of inquiry belonging to a border territory where several linguistic disciplines and approaches converge. The recent history and problems associated with the emergence of the notion of an interface are described, as well as the advances that have emerged in this research territory with respect to the analysis of quantification.

In chapter two, one of the most intriguing phenomena belonging to the syntax-semantics interface is considered: ellipsis resolution and its impact on how quantificational order or scope is determined. Elliptical constructions trigger scope asymmetries and parallelism effects whose analysis has led some researchers to posit powerful constraints such as Global Economy. In this chapter, it is argued that an interface approach exploiting several well-known semantic operations can explain all the relevant data and does not require look-forward constraints, such as those based on economy considerations.

Chapters three and four explore two difficult issues in the expression and interpretation of indefiniteness. First, the impact of sentential mood is described with novel data not previously analyzed in the literature. More specifically, the indicative/subjunctive alternation is considered in the emergence of different readings associated with indefinite expressions. The interface approach advocated here combines several well-known syntactic constraints with the semantic analysis of indefinites as choice functions. Second, a somewhat overlooked element is considered: the interpretation of the verb *tener* 'have,' in its light or bleached form. This variant has been normally associated with indefinite complements, but the consequences are shown to be far reaching. A comprehensive semantics for *tener* is provided in which this verb is claimed to express the attribution of essential properties. This approach clears the path for deriving the complexities and varieties of readings associated with this verb.

Chapters five and six explore quantification in relative clauses. In chapter five, a new approach to the semantics of free relatives is proposed, which is critically based on Spanish data. It is argued that the fact that relatives can express several types of quantificational force shows that these constructions clearly instantiate the phenomenon of quantificational variability. These differential quantificational properties are linked to the structural make-up and composition of the free relative. In chapter six, correlativization is characterized as a structural mechanism used to express quantification over degrees. Spanish correlative constructions can take several shapes, which might lead us to the wrong prediction that they do not instantiate a unique pattern. It is argued that a syntactic analysis based on movement of the degree term needs to be coupled with a semantic explanation of how degree-related features are associated with quantificational structures instantiating well-known patterns in other domains.

Conditional sentences have attracted the attention of traditional grammarians and logicians, given their unique grammatical and logical peculiarities. Semantically, the analysis of conditionals has mostly focused on standard material-conditional constructions, given their significance for the logical and semantic analysis of connectives. Nevertheless, concessive structures seem to be of special interest because some of them also express quantification over degrees and have properties that belong not only to the syntax/semantics interface but also to the semantics/pragmatics interface. Chapter seven looks at two types of Spanish prepositional conditionals—conditionals headed by prepositions—, which can be described as having a concessive meaning. An exhaustive analysis of their properties is presented and it is also shown how quantification over degrees interacts with the pragmatics of scales and scalar reasoning.

The study of superlatives has received a great deal of attention recently, mostly because certain semantic peculiarities seem to be systematically associated with an interface property, namely focus, as shown in chapter eight. This dependence is argued to go beyond a mere prosody-form correlate. It is at the core of several interpretive possibilities and impacts the way in which superlatives are structured.

Finally, chapter nine also explores a form of quantification which is deeply rooted in the interface between semantics and pragmatics. Discourse particles and markers have commonly been characterized as rhetorical or pragmatic devices used for the expression of several user-based discourse relations. This chapter shows that there is an important subgroup of particles that have a quantificational core. This core is not only apparent in their morphological composition but also in the fact that they share many properties with other tripartite quantificational structures of an adverbial origin. Adopting this line of analysis seems to be not only appropriate for understanding the properties of certain classes of discourse particles—for example, those expressing contrastive or reiterative content—but also paves the way for an extension of this approach to rhetorical particles in general.

Summarizing, the wide array of constructions considered in this book is ample proof of the fact that structure and meaning do not interact in a unique fashion in the expression of quantification. Taking a detailed look at the different forms, patterns and structures associated with several quantificational domains seems to be the only fully explanatory way to advance our knowledge of the syntax, semantics and pragmatics of quantificational structures.

1

The View from the Syntax-Semantics Interface

1. In search of a notion

The development of linguistic theory during the sixties and seventies led to a separation of linguistic subdisciplines in the eighties, especially syntax and semantics. These subdisciplines were sometimes associated with cognitive domains or modules corresponding to them in a psychodynamic fashion: A domain A would be in charge of the tasks belonging to grammatical module A, and a different module B would be associated with a separate cognitive domain B, etc. Whereas such separation was productive in isolating certain phenomena and in establishing heuristic and methodological tools belonging to different domains, it also brought in an artificial compartmentalization of linguistic objects, which lost their unitary nature. Nevertheless, the points of convergence between syntax and semantics are numerous, highly debated and analyzed, and are now emerging as an important field of research. In this chapter we explore the notion of an interface between syntax and semantics and how it has been characterized in linguistic theory. Several possible approaches are considered. The cornerstone of the syntax-semantics interface is the study of quantification, which has numerous empirical ramifications on related subjects. In this chapter some of the most promising prospects and developments in this research area will be reviewed.

The notion of a linguistic interface is not one that seems immediately natural to grammatical analysis. Whereas the awareness that grammatical phenomena should be characterized differently as a function of the material domain they belong to has been present in grammatical theory for a long time, the connecting notion of an interface seems to be more elusive (Ramchand and Reiss 2007). Thus, one can find insightful considerations about categories and linguistic objects belonging to different domains in classical and pedagogical grammars. For example, in the work of Greek grammarians or in the grammars of Andrés Bello and Salvador Fernández Ramírez, it is not uncommon to find descriptions listing properties of linguistic objects belonging to the separate realms or domains of sound and meaning, or sound, meaning and form. On the other hand, the idea that certain phenomena belong to one of more of these domains, although not completely uncommon, is probably more difficult to grasp or present as a characterizing hypothesis. This might explain why several phenomena lacking a clear adscription or having characteristics belonging to more than one domain of inquiry have received less attention in the grammatical tradition. Such is the case, for example, of focus constructions. The notion and varieties of 'stress' and 'intonational contours' have been traditionally described more or less accurately from a phonetic point of view (cf. the classic Navarro Tomás [1918] 1982). Nevertheless, an accurate characterization of the relationship between several prosodic or intonational properties and their syntactic, semantic and pragmatic correlates is more difficult and has escaped a unified analysis for a long time. One of the main reasons, if not the most important one, for this scenario is the lack of a framework unifying the relevant properties in a cogent fashion.

This intrinsic difficulty or evasiveness of phenomena belonging to more than one domain is also a contributing factor explaining why not only the properties associated with focus and focus constructions but also several word classes, expressions or phenomena have received scarce attention in the grammatical literature. For example, certain non-standard quantificational terms; constructions making reference to abstract entities such as degrees; non-declarative sentences; etc. have not enjoyed widespread attention from formal linguistic theories until relatively recently. This assessment probably has to be understood in not completely-strict terms, but it seems fair to make it, especially if we compare the situation with other well-established research subjects in morpho-syntax and/or semantics, such as the analysis of tense, aspect, extractions, the position of adjectives, etc.

2. Syntax, semantics and the architecture of grammar

Intuitively it seems that we could benefit from having a theory, heuristic tool, or hypothesis applying to phenomena whose analysis does not fit well-established domains of linguistic inquiry, seems to fall between them, or belongs to more than one of them. Nevertheless, we have to wonder whether such analytical constructs would just be convenient but not well-founded explanations for something that we need but we do not know how to characterize. In other words, since we do not know how to characterize phenomena seeming to fall through the cracks of established domains of linguistic inquiry, we might be tempted to create a vague area mediating them, like a safety net that will allow us to catch everything. I believe that the answer to this objection can be made without hesitation and in a positive fashion. The development of the notion of an "interface" is partly an answer to this issue. Interfaces are not catch-all artificial constructs. Interfaces and their properties are claimed to be grounded in psychological reality, have neurological correspondences in the brain, and have become of increasing interest in linguistics and in the cognitive sciences in general during the last two decades (Jackendoff 2007; Roeper 2011). In sum, their empirical and theoretical foundations are strong.

The initial period of generative grammar, during the 50s and 60s, witnessed the development of several generative-transformational models in which the presence of certain central assumptions made difficult for researchers to realize that there are genuine interface phenomena and interface domains. The most important obstacle for this realization was the prevalent idea that syntax was independent or autonomous. The Autonomy of Syntax Hypothesis (Chomsky 1957, 1965) has been one of the cornerstones, probably the essential one, in the development of generative grammar until the mid to late 90s. Methodologically, it entailed the assumption that not only syntactic phenomena had to be dealt within syntactic theory *per se*, but also that other neighboring phenomena, such as those related to morphology (word formation) or semantics (quantifier scope), should receive a syntactic explanation. Thus, interface phenomena were explained by reduction to a strictly syntactic explanation.

Although such a strategy paid important dividends and allowed for bringing to the fore realms of data not considered so far, it also triggered an increase in the complexity of design of the theoretical model. The linear derivational models of the 50s and 60s required mappings between a hypothesized deep structure and several corresponding surface structures through a variety of transformations, differing in nature and complexity (Chomsky 1957, 1965). Alternative models within generative semantics (Lakoff 1971, among others), which were designed precisely to improve the explanatory potential in accounting for phenomena deemed to be more semantic in nature, were not substantially satisfactory either.

The "linguistic wars" between generative semanticists and interpretivists were resolved with an apparent victory of the interpretivist camp (Harris 1995). Nevertheless, the theoretical models that emerged during the 80s— most prominently the Government and Binding (GB) paradigm (Chomsky 1981)—attempted a new strategy to deal with interface issues. This strategy was to compartmentalize what was a uniform and probably rigid derivational engine until then. Starting with the idea of the modularity of the human mind (Fodor 1983), the GB paradigm proposed a radically modular model of grammar. Modularity in grammar, in combination with the Autonomy of Syntax Hypothesis, entailed the assumption that the syntactic component of grammar was divided into several modules of a heterogeneous nature. Some modules were clearly syntactic: bounding theory, or the theory of the limits or boundaries to constituent extraction. Other modules had an interface flavor: binding theory, or the theory of the association between dependent expressions and their antecedents. Finally, others had a clearer semantic foundation: theta theory, or the theory of the thematic content of verbs. The connections and interrelations between such modules were never worked out in full detail, although several constraints were claimed to apply across the board: locality constraints, restrictions based on the notion of "government," etc. Interface phenomena were displayed in a mixed fashion. Some were viewed as belonging to a syntactic module, others—mostly quantificational phenomena—were ascribed to Logical Form and the semantic component.

The Minimalist Program (Chomsky 1995; Hinzen 2012) advocated a radical transformation in the conception and analysis of the interfaces and interface phenomena. First, the multi-leveled representational structure of previous models is discarded in favor of a fully derivational engine with only two representations or derivational endpoints: Logical Form (LF) and Phonetic Form (PF). These levels are viewed as genuine interface levels, in the sense that they only include legibility conditions or instructions for the performance systems. These systems are the conceptual-intentional system, which interfaces with Logical Form, and the sensory-motor system, interfacing with Phonetic Form. This narrow view of the interfacing systems mostly reflects Chomsky's own internalist views about semantics, namely, the hypothesis that semantic interpretation should be stated in conceptual or internal terms, making referential or externalist semantics not desirable since there appears to be less cognitive evidence supporting it (Pietroski 2008).

Nevertheless, the interface model for the connection between syntax and semantics does not necessarily favor or exclude one view of semantics or other. It is possible to have an internalist or conceptual view of meaning in combination with a construction-style syntax, as in Jackendoff's model (Jackendoff 2002; Culicover and Jackendoff 2005). On the other hand, Heim and Kratzer (1998) present a model which is more strictly based on the Frege-Tarski externalist view of semantics but pays very close attention to interface issues. It assumes the importance of syntactic derivation for semantic interpretation, advocating a connection between semantic external reference and a cognitive internal property (syntactic computation). Thus, the issue of the precise nature of the syntax-semantics interface and its place in grammar does not seem to decidedly favor one view of semantics or other—cf. Gutiérrez-Rexach (2004) for an extensive compilation of fundamental texts from different perspectives.

This conclusion is not completely accurate, though. An assumption that seems to be shared by several current approaches to the interfaces is the centrality of compositional derivation and interpretation. The GB model was based on postulating syntactic processes with a derivational end-point: Logical Form (LF). Such a post-output arrangement or sequence of labeled terminals would then be mapped to semantic interpretation. Thus, although the interpretation of LF would be compositional, syntactic operations taking place before this level were exclusively syntactic and, as such, not subject to a compositionality requirement. This not only allowed for non-compositional derivations but also sidestepped the issue of compositionality entirely, since semantic computation is assumed to start only after the syntactic derivation is complete, namely when the syntactic object has been mapped to the semantic component. In the Minimalist Program, this view has been progressively eliminated, although it was still presupposed in the initial models (Chomsky 1995). An interesting trend that has emerged, following minimalist assumptions, is the idea that syntactic structure is the result of a "multiple-spell out" process (Uriagereka 1999), with different stages or phases (Chomsky 2001). In other words, the products of syntactic derivations are spelled out or interpreted at different points. There is no need to wait for a terminal point in order to achieve an interpretable structure. A very similar idea would be to claim that syntactic and semantic derivations go in parallel (Gutiérrez-Rexach 2000; González-Rivera 2010). Linguistic objects are always meaningful entities and it is not possible to separate form from meaning. Interface issues would arise as a consequence of apparent mismatches in derivations or computations. They could also emerge as the by-product of the interplay of the two grammatical computations (syntactic and semantic). This allows for a more abstract perspective on grammatical invariants, i.e. expressions with syntactic and semantic fixity (Keenan and Stabler 2003, 2009). Those would be the expressions that remain stable or invariant independently of the grammatical operations they might be subject to.

In other grammatical frameworks, the idea that syntax and semantics go in parallel or "interface" in a continuous fashion is not new and, to a certain extent, it can be claimed that it has been around for a while. For example, the Curry-Howard isomorphism in categorial grammar (Carpenter 1998) explicitly proves the equivalence between categorial (syntactic) derivations and the computation of meaning, which is represented via formula derivation in a lambda-language. In sign-based theories of syntax, such as Head-Driven Phrase Structure Grammar (HPSG) (Sag, Wasow, and Bender 2003), syntax and semantics are integral parts of the feature specification of a sign. Thus, the constructional composition of meaning and form, through feature unification, affects the syntactic component or features of the sign and its semantic specification, formulated using the situation-semantics formalism in the earlier versions of the theory, or in minimal-recursion semantics in latter models (Copestake et al. 2006). A more direct instantiation of the Curry-Howard isomorphism and a parallel architecture is the convergent model advocated by Pollard (2008)—cf. Morrill (2012) for general issues in logical grammar. As it was previously the case with derivational frameworks, it is extremely difficult to assess whether there would be a real critical advantage depending on the choice of one interface model or other, or even if one is more predictive than other from an empirical point of view.

In functionalist models of syntax and in frameworks based on theories of grammaticalization (Hopper and Traugott 2003), researchers focus on changes in structure or construction use. This "change in progress" is viewed as a by-product of the increased frequency of use of a certain pattern. Change is associated with the mechanism of grammaticalization in that those patterns that are more frequent tend to become part of the grammar, i.e. they "grammaticalize." In a majority of instances, grammaticalization processes are driven by pragmatic motivations, so researchers working within this framework conclude that speakers' attitudes and intentions have a critical role in shaping grammatical constructions. Thus, interfaces are explained away by intentionality-driven reasoning of a Gricean nature (Grice 1989).

Other theories of a semantic or pragmatic nature also have implicit or explicit assumptions about the interface of semantics and/or pragmatics with syntax. For example, in Discourse Representation Theory (Kamp and Reyle 1993) rules constructing Discourse Representation Structures (DRSs) operate on and take their input from syntactically parsed structures. Interface issues can be tackled at the level of DRS-representation in that properties of words and constructions are able to trigger or block the application of a certain DRS-construction rule (Lascarides, Calder, and Stenning 2006). Finally, Relevance Theory, and other pragmatic approaches based on similar hypotheses, work with the assumption that logical forms are cognitively motivated or grounded. Such logical representations are pragmatically or contextually enriched to derive explicatures (Sperber and Wilson 2004). In general, the level of commitment to the significance of syntactic mechanisms and the compositional methodology varies a lot among these frameworks, which partly explains why they have been less productive in interface areas. Another factor associated with theoretical and methodological divergences is the significance of differential views on the semantics/pragmatics interface and the borders drawn between these two disciplines (McNally 2013).

3. Quantifiers: From logic to grammar

A standard subject-predicate sentence such as *John is happy* attributes the property P of being happy to the individual j denoted by *John*. When the subject is a full noun phrase containing a determiner, this element plays a crucial role in the attribution process that we have described. The contrast between the sentences *Some students are happy* and *Every student is happy* is due to the different nature of the determiner that expresses the number of individuals to which the property P applies. We say, then, that these sentences differ in quantificational force. The first one states that there is at least one student who is happy in the situation under consideration. The second one states that every individual under consideration is happy. This semantic contrast can be expressed as a contrast in the logical form that captures the truth conditions of these sentences, as defended by the philosophers G. Frege and B. Russell. In first order logic, the determiners *some* and *every* are respectively translated as the existential quantifier and the universal quantifier. In general, quantifiers are treated as propositional operators which bind a variable in an open proposition. Going back to the above sentences, the paraphrases of their respective logical forms are: *There is at least one individual x such that x is a student and x is happy* and *For every individual x if x is a student then x is happy*. For more details on the issues described in this section, see Szabolcsi (2010) and Gutiérrez-Rexach (2012).

One of the limitations of the first-order logic analysis of quantification is that the semantic contribution of a noun phrase is not uniform. The determiner is a propositional operator and the noun is part of the open proposition. Another limitation is that this analysis is not designed to capture the content of the extensive variety of natural language determiners. For example, it has been shown that the natural language determiner *most* is not expressible in first order logic. Generalized Quantifier Theory developed during the 1980s after the initial contribution of the philosopher Richard Montague. In Generalized Quantifier Theory (Barwise and Cooper 1981; Keenan and Stavi 1986; Peters and Westerståhl 2006), a noun phrase is taken to denote a function from properties (predicate denotations) to truth values (*True* or *False*). Thus, we can represent the sentences in the previous paragraph compositionally as *some students (happy)* and *every student (happy)*, where *some students* and *every student* are functions that take the property (the set of individuals) *happy* as an argument and map it to a truth value (*True* or *False*). A determiner denotes, in turn, a function from sets of individuals to generalized quantifiers. Given a universe of individuals E, and P, Q subsets of this universe, the determiner *some* denotes the function *some* defined as follows: *some(P)(Q)* is *True* if and only if (iff) the intersection of the sets P and Q is not empty. Similarly, we can characterize other determiner denotations; *every (P)(Q)* is *True* iff the set P is a subset of the set Q; *no(P)(Q)* is *True* iff the intersection of the sets P and Q is empty; *more than three(P)(Q)* is *True* iff the cardinality of the intersection of the sets P and Q is greater than three; *most(P)(Q)* is *True* iff the cardinality of the intersection of the sets P and Q is greater than the cardinality of the complement of P with respect to Q, i.e. the number of those Ps who are Qs is greater than the number of those Ps who are not Qs; etc. Applying these definitions we say that the value of *every(student)(happy)* is *True* in a situation iff the set of students under consideration in that situation is a subset of the set of happy individuals in that situation. In sum, a natural language simple or complex determiner denotes a function with two arguments. The first argument corresponds to the head noun and the second argument to the content of the sentence verb phrase.

Natural language determiners also satisfy a series of constraints setting them apart from their logical counterparts. For example, all natural language determiners are conservative or "live on" their first argument. The sentence *Some sailors left* is equivalent to the sentence *Some sailors are sailors who left*. If we substitute any other determiner for *some* in this sentence, the equivalence still holds. What this means is that for any determiner function *Det,* and properties *P, Q,* the function *Det(P)(Q)* is equivalent to *Det(P)(P and Q)*. The effect of this constraint is to make natural language quantification inherently restricted to the first argument of the determiner. In checking whether *Det(P)(Q)* is *True* we do not have to consider those individuals in the universe *E* who are not *P*.

Determiners are also characterized by the type of inferences that they license, namely set to subset inferences or set to superset inferences. The inference patterns licensed by a determiner, in this particular sense, are called its monotonicity properties. For example, the sentence *No students smoked* entails the sentence *No students smoked cigars*. We say then that ***no*** is a decreasing determiner function in its second argument because for any verb phrase denotations *P, Q, Q'* if *Q'* is a subset of *Q* and ***no(P)(Q)*** is true, then ***no(P)(Q')*** is also true. In the previous sentence, since the property *smoke cigars* is a subset of the property *smoke,* the described entailment follows. The determiner *no* is also decreasing in its first argument. In other words, for every property *P, Q, Q',* if *Q* is a subset of *Q* then ***no(P)(Q)*** entails ***no(P)(Q')***. The sentence *No students smoked* entails the sentence *No female students smoked,* given that the property ***female students*** is a subset of the property ***students***. The determiner function *some* has the opposite monotonicity pattern and is increasing in its two arguments. Thus, we predict that the sentence *Some female student smokes cigars* entails both *Some female student smokes* and *Some student smokes cigars*.

Quantifiers can also be partitioned depending on whether they can occur in an existential construction. Consider the sentential pattern *There is/are Det student(s) in the garden*. The determiners *some, three, no, fewer than five,* and *many* can be substituted for *Det* and occur in this construction, whereas the occurrence of determiners such as *every, most,* and *all but three* would make the sentence ungrammatical. The determiners that can occur in an existential construction satisfy the property of intersectivity: their denotations depend on the intersection of their two arguments. On the other hand, those determiners which cannot occur in an existential construction are characterized by being inclusion quantifiers, such as *every,* or proportional quantifiers, such as *most.* Definite simple and complex determiners (*the, the ten,* etc.) and other quantifiers headed by demonstrative and possessive determiners do not occur in existential sentences either. These determiners are all inherently context dependent.

When more than one quantifier occurs in a sentence, a form of semantic interaction called scope arises. Scopal relations are determined by the different order of quantifiers in the semantic representation of a clause. In the logical prefix [Q_1, Q_2, . . .], we say that the outermost quantifier Q_1 has scope over the innermost quantifier Q_2. For example, the sentence *Every student read a book* is ambiguous. Under one interpretation, every student read a different book. Under the second, there is a unique book such that every student read it. This ambiguity is a genuine scope ambiguity. In the first reading, the scope order of the quantifiers is the one that respects the linear order of the noun phrases. Using > to represent precedence in scopal order, we represent such order as: *every student* > *a book.* The universal quantifier scopes over the existential quantifier. The second reading is an inverse scope reading in that the scopal order of the quantifiers differs from the surface linear order. The existential quantifier scopes over the universal quantifier to generate this reading (*a book* > *every student*).

Some linguistic theories argue that the existence of this class of ambiguities constitutes evidence for the existence of a level of representation called Logical Form, as described above, where the scopal order of quantifiers is disambiguated. We use capital letters to differentiate this syntactic level of Logical Form from the semantic representation proper or logical form. The level of Logical Form is derived from the surface syntactic representation of a sentence by the application of a rule that displaces noun phrases from their original position and moves them to the positions where they take scope. This rule is known as Quantifier Raising. Hence, in the inverse scope reading of a sentence the noun phrase in the object position would end up in a position which is structurally higher than that occupied by the noun phrase in subject position. In the scope reading that preserves the linear surface order both noun phrases are displaced to positions at the level of Logical Form that preserve the linear surface order. Quantifier Raising has, thus, the purpose of deriving the input to the semantic representation of a sentence from its surface structure. As suggested in the previous section, recent and current research in this area focuses not only on the semantic properties that affect scopal relations but also on other issues: how syntactic restrictions seem to block the application of the Quantifier Raising rule; whether such a rule really exists or its effects are derived from other types of movement; and, finally, whether displacement is needed to derive scopal effects.

So far, we have considered only nominal quantification, namely that type corresponding to the meaning of noun phrases. Nevertheless, other elements may also contribute to the quantificational force of a sentence. Adverbs such as *always, sometimes,* and *often* are not merely temporal adverbs. In the majority of contexts, they behave as adverbs of quantification. For example, the sentence *Peter always drinks coffee* does not mean that Peter drinks coffee at every moment, but rather that whenever Peter drinks, he drinks coffee. Adverbs of quantification can be taken to express quantification over situations. The sentences in which these adverbs occur have the same tripartite structure proposed for generalized quantifiers: ***Adv(Q)(P)***. The main difference with nominal quantification is that there seems to be a process of semantic partition that derives the semantic representation of these structures from their respective Logical Form.

Interrogative generalized quantifiers are *wh*-phrases such as *who, what, where,* and those headed by *wh*-determiners, such as *which* and *what*. An interrogative determiner Det_{int} is a function mapping a property to an interrogative generalized quantifier. The functional denotation corresponding to an interrogative sentence is also tripartite: $Det_{int}(P)(Q)$. Interrogative determiners are also conservative. The interrogative sentence *Which students are rich?* is equivalent to *Which students are students who are rich?* Determiners belonging to this class are also intersective, since the denotation of an interrogative determiner depends on the intersection of its two arguments. For example, a complete answer to ***which(students)(rich)*** specifies in a situation the intersection of the set of students and the set of rich individuals in that situation. Interrogative determiners and existential determiners such as *some* have a majority of their properties in common. From this point of view, the fact that there are an important number of world languages which use the same lexical expressions for interrogatives and existential determiners becomes unsurprising. It is just a manifestation of the common semantic core of these determiners.

Sometimes, the quantificational force of a sentence cannot be associated to any overt element in the clause. The sentence *Lions are fierce* is usually interpreted as stating that most lions are fierce or that lions are normally fierce. In order to characterize the semantic properties of this sentence, the existence of hidden or non-overt operators of diverse quantificational force has to be postulated. In the example under consideration, there is a hidden operator of generic force **Gen**, so the tripartite representation of this sentence would be: ***Gen(lions)(fierce)***. A function with the form ***Gen(P)(Q)*** is *True* iff it is generally the case that *P*s are *Q*s.

Nominal and adverbial quantification interact in apparently unexpected ways. This interaction arises mostly when an indefinite occurs in the scope of an adverb of quantification in relative constructions, conditional sentences, etc. In the sentence *Every farmer who has a donkey beats it,* the indefinite lacks its typical existential force. The sentence does not mean that every farmer beats one donkey or other (at least one) that he has. Rather, the correct interpretation is that for every pair consisting of a farmer and a donkey owned by that farmer, it is also the case that the farmer beats the donkey. The indefinite seems to have universal force here, so we may conclude that there is a binary universal quantifier that associates both with the restriction of the universal noun phrase and the indefinite. The same pattern can be observed in the sentence *Always, if a farmer owns a donkey, he beats it,* where both indefinites seem to inherit the universal force from the adverb of quantification. Some theories have concluded, based on this type of data, that indefinites lack quantificational force and inherit their apparent force from other surrounding elements in the clause. In general, adverbs of quantification are taken to transmit their quantificational force to all the indefinites that appear in their scope. This phenomenon is known as unselective quantification.

4. Interface issues: Problems and prospects

It seems clear that the nature of the syntax-semantics interface and its place in grammar has been the object of debate in recent grammatical theorizing. An immediate consequence has been not only the increased attention to topics that were dealt with mostly within semantic theory, but also the incorporation of their properties as central in grammar design. This has been the case cross-linguistically, and also in the Romance languages. Traditionally, the subject that seems to pertain most centrally to the syntax-semantics interface is quantification. This is so because quantifiers have very precise syntactic and semantic characteristics. They are functional words and they are subject to strict co-occurrence restrictions, but they also behave as logical elements. Although the notion of logicality has received a great deal of attention in the philosophical literature (cf. Sher 1991), its impact is also significant for grammatical analysis. Logical words are expressions with an invariant interpretation that contribute substantially to the logical (semantic) content of a proposition (Keenan and Stabler 2003). In this sense, their content has to be separated from that of other lexical elements. For example, the study of the meaning of nouns or adjectives belongs to the lexical domain—the dictionary or the study of the lexical competence—and is incrementally acquired over time. The meaning of quantifiers is logical (permutation invariant; cf. Keenan 1996). The acquisition of such content is linked to that of other functional elements (Grinstead 2009) and it is considerably more stable over time and across dialects.

Whereas the study of quantifiers has enjoyed the attention of numerous logicians and philosophers, the study of these expressions has not been systematic in grammatical analysis and linguistics until relatively recently—see Szabolcsi (2010) and Keenan and Paperno (2012) for an exhaustive survey. There are several issues that led to this state of affairs. First, the functional category of quantifiers is not one that is marked morphologically or syntactically in a uniform fashion. Determiners and articles are normally viewed as standard quantificational elements, but other elements also play a quantificational role, such as *wh*-expressions, degree words, certain adverbs, etc. Even if it is debatable whether quantifiers are a uniform word class or grammatical category, they are certainly a uniform category at the syntax-semantics interface (Bosque and Gutiérrez-Rexach 2009). Their most significant unifying property is that they participate in scope interactions with other quantificational elements. The nature of these interactions is broader than expected. A nominal quantifier interacts not only with other quantifiers of the same type, but also with other operators, such as verbs, modal expressions, etc. Thus, not only quantifiers of the same type interact, but also quantificational elements from different domains (individuals, times, events, etc.).

Scope interactions are pervasive and play a significant role in the interpretation of a sentence, and, more importantly, in the emergence of sentential ambiguities—the association of more than one meaning to a given expression. Typical ambiguities that have been addressed in the logical literature are those involving the interaction of *some* and *every* in English. In the semantic tradition, such ambiguities have been spelled out as a difference in logical form. One interpretation or sense of the ambiguous sentential expression corresponds to one translation (translation 1) in a logical language, and the other interpretation corresponds to a different one (translation 2). What makes translations 1 and 2 different is the order of the quantifiers involved in the scopal interaction. The linguistic implementation (or not) of this idea has been the subject of ample debate (cf. López Palma 1999). In the generative models of the 60s and 70s such differences could be viewed as contrasts at the level of Deep Structure (generative semantics position) or as the result of different transformation (interpretive semantics position). In the late 70s, a linguistic level of Logical Form (LF) was postulated, which was different from the levels of Surface Structure and Deep Structure. Scopal order was considered to be equivalent to c-command order at the level of Logical Form: If a quantifier Q_1 c-commands Q_2 at LF, then Q_1 has to be interpreted as having scope over Q_2 (May 1977). This model was refined (May 1985), allowing for a relaxation of this requirement: At LF, all the quantifiers are attached by adjunction to the sentential node in order to take scope over the clause forming a quantificational prefix, in a mutual c-command relation. Scope asymmetries are derived *a posteriori*, and not as a by-product of c-command (cf. Bosque and Gutiérrez-Rexach 2009, chap. 8).

In Minimalism, as we stated above, Logical Form becomes the central linguistic interface for the interplay between structure and meaning. Nevertheless, the elimination of the representational model and the concomitant notions of government, c-command and tree-related relations required a modification of the way in which scope relations are represented. For Hornstein (1995), scopal asymmetries are the by-product of the asymmetrical landing of quantifiers in subject/object agreement projections. For Stowell and Beghelli (1997) a more refined model is required within a feature-checking model. Quantifiers target one landing site or other as a result of their checking-requirement needs. For example, a distributive quantifier such as *each* in English or *cada* in Spanish would check such a feature under a DistrPhrase; a referential quantifier would check its feature on a RefP, the Referential Phrase, etc. The same applies to focal expressions (landing on FocusP), narrow scope elements (landing on ShareP, etc.) Landing sites are hierarchically arranged to render the relevant scope relations. For example, RefP and DistP are higher than ShareP, etc.

A problem with a generalized hierarchical or asymmetrical approach to syntactic projection is that there are elements that seem to get scope in a different fashion. For example, indefinites may have not only wide and narrow readings, but also intermediate readings, so scope assignment via feature checking seems problematic in this case, unless we embrace mechanisms of variable lexical or syntactic encoding. Thus, certain authors have proposed that such elements are assigned scope via different mechanisms—cf. Gutiérrez-Rexach (2003) and references therein. If we assume that they contribute a choice function to Logical Form, then—by Skolemization mechanisms (Winter 1997)—scope options multiply depending on where the function is quantified over (the scope of the function). Unfortunately, this cannot be a general solution either, since indefinites seem to come in more guises cross-linguistically, and their scope is also a by-product of interaction with other features. For example, in Spanish it has been argued that other factors that interact with the scope of indefinites include thetic/categorical structure, focus, and distributivity/collectivity entailments (Gutiérrez-Rexach 2010). Some of these factors will be considered in the remainder of this book.

Other approaches, especially within the non-transformational tradition, dispense with the notion of a level of Logical Form or anything similar to it, either as a level of grammatical representation or as an associated semantic representation in a logical language. Those advocating surface interpretation and direct compositionality (Barker and Jacobson 2007) postulate that scope is assigned *in situ*. There are no displacement operations involved or additional levels of representation needed. Narrow scope/wide scope asymmetries can be derived via type shifting (Montague 1975) or by associating quantifiers with different extensions as a function of their grammatical role (subject/object, nominative/accusative) (cf. Keenan 1989). Finally, new developments in the semantics of computer languages have been applied to the interpretation of scope via the use of continuations (Barker 2002).

An issue that makes matters even more complex is the influence of epistemic factors (Alonso-Ovalle and Menéndez-Benito 2003), implicatures and implicature generation (Chierchia 2004). A recent debate centers on the status of implicatures, whether they are independent and belong to pragmatics exclusively or whether they are incrementally processed and dependent on grammatical computation. Vargas-Tokuda, Grinstead, and Gutiérrez-Rexach (2009) show that the latter is the case and that differences in the lexical specification of elements trigger measurable contrasts and diverging outcomes in the acquisition of interpretation, implicature generation, and blocking. These properties are acquired earlier, in tandem with other interface issues.

The interpretation of focus is also critical to the syntax-semantics interface. Jackendoff (1972) made focus-based arguments a cornerstone of his ideas on semantic interpretation. More recently, Reinhart (2006) addresses the relevance of focus computation for minimalist analyses. In a similar fashion, Zubizarreta (1998) views focus as a syncretic category, which can be computed in association with other features/projections. Lopez (2009) also addresses the importance of focus in syntactic computation.

Reference to and quantification over degrees has also been a hotly debated topic in the interface literature, from the nature and determination of what a degree is to its instantiation across categories (Kennedy 2007). Degree expression is evident in comparatives, certain relatives (Gutiérrez-Rexach 1999e), predicative structures and gradable adjectives (Pastor 2008), and exclamatives (Castroviejo 2008; Gutiérrez-Rexach 2008). Further research is needed to determine whether uniform explanations can be reached for all these constructions.

5. Conclusion

The syntax-semantics interface is a border territory of difficult delimitation and analysis. This helps explain why it has been the subject of critical debates that have shaped the development of grammatical theory, but also why many problems remain undecided, independently of their status in grammatical theory. A wide array of very insightful and fruitful research has been carried out in the last two decades on phenomena that cannot be reduced either to syntax or to semantics and that critically touch upon both areas. See also Suñer (2009) for an overview of additional topics. Nevertheless, a strategy that has been taking shape in the last years is to approach the interface problem following a bottom-up strategy. Whereas past approaches attempted to propose a grand overarching theory that was then applied to different phenomena, it seems more advisable to start with a detailed analysis of interface phenomena and only later reach conclusions about common mechanisms and strategies. In this book, we follow this micro-based strategy and pursue the analysis of a complex array of Spanish phenomena that have been attributed to a variety of interfaces: syntax/semantics or semantics/pragmatics. Our answers, even if preliminary, are presented with the hope of helping to develop a more precise cartography of the interface landscape in all its complexity.

2

Scope Parallelism and the Interpretation of Ellipsis

1. Introduction

A widespread characteristic of natural languages is the ability shown by numerous constructions to retrieve the content of missing fragments of a sentence from material occurring in the preceding discourse. Consider the following examples from English and Spanish:

(1) a. Jill will come to the party but Jane will not.
 b. I have bought many books recently, but I will only read some.
 c. Bill invited two candidates. I can't remember which ones.
 d. Juan se quitó las gafas y María no lo hizo.
 'Juan took his glasses off but María did not.'
 e. Yo compré un libro y Pedro también.
 'I bought a book and Pedro too.'
 f. He leído tus libros y los de Pedro.
 'I have read your books and Pedro's.'
 g. Sé que desayunaron algo pero no sé el qué.
 'I know they had something for breakfast but I don't know what.'

The above examples are instances of the class of phenomena commonly called ellipsis and illustrate several different sub-types, such as Verb Phrase ellipsis (VP ellipsis), N' or N deletion, and sluicing. Several syntactic analyses of these constructions have attempted to identify the conditions under which ellipsis takes place and the elements that determine differences or similarities in interpretation—see Brucart (1986) and Gallego (2011) for excellent surveys of ellipsis phenomena in Spanish. A standard syntactic solution within the Government and Binding paradigm would be to postulate the existence of empty categories in the elliptic segment and to study the licensing conditions of those empty elements. The emergence of the Minimalist Program (Chomsky 1995, 1998, 2000) demanded a stricter solution doing away with unnecessary empty categories and X-bar related notions such as government or the Empty Category Principle. The elimination of empty categories follows Chomsky's (1995) "Inclusiveness Principle", which requires that only lexical elements drawn from the initial numeration be participants in grammatical derivations. This principle is obviously reminiscent of similar criteria in other frameworks. In categorial grammar and unification-based formalisms, empty categories and representational notions such as the above mentioned ones are not present—see Gutiérrez-Rexach (2000) and González-Rivera (2010) for a generalization of a formalized minimalist framework that takes into account some of these considerations.

In this chapter, the syntactic and semantic properties of a group of scopal restrictions that arise in ellipsis constructions are studied. An explanation of these restrictions that has gained widespread acceptance is the one proposed by Fox (1995, 2000). His theory is based on a global principle of Economy, which favors derivations that are less complex or consist of fewer derivational steps. Such a principle applies at the interfaces in a generalized or global fashion. Alternatively, it can be argued that the proper explanation bears heavily on semantic operations closely related to the general process of ellipsis resolution and that global Economy criteria have undesired consequences and should be dispensed with, as argued by Johnson and Lappin (1997, 1999) and Chomsky (2000). An explanation of the latter type will be defended in this chapter, which is structured as follows. In the first section, the received view on the interactions between scope and VP ellipsis is described and, in section two, Fox's (1995, 2000) Economy-based analysis is presented. In the next two sections, it is shown how this approach faces some empirical and theoretical problems and, finally, in the last sections an alternative analysis based on parallelism and higher-order unification is developed. This analysis successfully accounts for the data discussed in the previous sections. It is also more parsimonious, since it does not rely on powerful unrestrained principles operating at the interfaces.

2. Scope asymmetries and VP ellipsis

Sag (1976) and Williams (1977) noticed an interesting contrast surfacing in the interaction between VP ellipsis and scope interpretation. Sentence (2a) is ambiguous, but (2b) is not.

(2) a. Some boy admires every teacher.
    b. Some boy admires every teacher and Mary does too.

There are two quantifiers involved in the above sentences and two possible scopal orders. One corresponds to the surface linear order (*some* > *every*). In the second one, the quantifier in the object position may scope over the quantifier in the subject position (*every* > *some*). In a coordinate construction in which the second VP is elided, as in (2b), there is no ambiguity. The object wide-scope reading is not available. The only possible reading is the one in which there is a unique boy who admires every teacher (*some* > *every*). Within May's (1985) theory of Logical Form (LF), the two potential Logical Form representations (LFs) for (2a) are as in (3).

(3) a. Subject wide scope (**some** > **every**):
       [$_{IP}$ some boy$_j$ [$_{IP}$ t$_j$ [$_{VP}$ every teacher$_i$ [$_{VP}$ admires t$_i$]]]]
    b. Object wide scope (**every** > **some**):
       [$_{IP}$ every teacher$_i$ [$_{IP}$ some boy$_j$ [$_{IP}$ t$_j$ [$_{VP}$ admires t$_i$]]]]

The subject is generated in the specifier of the Inflection Phrase (IP)—or Tense Phrase (TP) under minimalist assumptions—and the object as a complement of the verb within the VP. In the subject wide-scope reading, the subject quantifier raises to a position adjoined to IP and the object adjoins to VP. Therefore, by the Scope Principle, which equates semantic scope with linear c-command at LF, the subject has to take scope over the object. In the object wide-scope reading, the subject adjoins to IP and the object adjoins to a position c-commanding the subject.

Let us now consider the scope disambiguation process involved in (2b). Under May's theory of LF, VP-ellipsis resolution requires copying/

reconstructing the antecedent VP into the elided conjunct. Thus, in the case where the LF corresponding to the antecedent clause is (3a), the constituent that undergoes the copying operation is [$_{VP}$ *every teacher*$_i$ [$_{VP}$ *admires* t$_i$]]. The resulting LF for (2b) is well-formed, as shown in (4):

(4) [$_{IP}$ some boy$_j$ [$_{IP}$ t$_j$ [$_{VP}$ every teacher$_i$ [$_{VP}$ admires t$_i$]]]]
and Mary does [$_{VP}$ every teacher$_i$ [$_{VP}$ admire t$_i$]] too

May (1985) accounted for the asymmetry by claiming that the object wide scope reading of the antecedent would give rise to an illegitimate LF in which the reconstructed VP [$_{VP}$ *admires* t$_i$] has an unbound trace—a copy of the displaced syntactic object—, as in (5). The LF representation is ill-formed because the quantifier *every teacher* does not c-command the trace in the second conjunct, so it cannot bind it.

(5) [$_{IP}$ every teacher$_i$ [$_{IP}$ some boy$_j$ [$_{IP}$ t$_j$ [$_{VP}$ admires t$_i$]]]]
and Mary does [$_{VP}$ admire t$_i$] too

Hirschbühler (1982) showed that this type of approach incorrectly predicts that the quantifier in the object position must always have narrow scope. In the following example, the quantifier *every building* may scope over the subject quantifier yielding the most natural interpretation of the sentence: for every building *x* there is a different Canadian flag *y* in front of it (*every > a*).

(6) A Canadian flag is in front of every building and an American flag is too.

The May-style LF representation for (6) is predicted to be ill-formed, because the trace of *every building* would be ungoverned in the second conjunct after reconstruction. Therefore, May's explanation appears to be too restrictive. Cormack (1984) and Diesing (1992) related the contrasts in (1) to the presence of a proper noun in the second sentence. Diesing observed that the cases in which the object quantifier is forced to a narrow scope interpretation are those in which the overt NP in the correlate clause is "non-quantificational", i.e. a proper noun or a definite, as the examples in (7) illustrate.

(7) a. Some bassoonist played every sonata, but Otto didn't.
b. Every lawyer liked some decisions, but the doctor didn't.

Diesing also argued that when the NP in the second clause is quantificational, the expected scope interactions arise. The object wide scope interpretation of the second conjunct of the sentences in (8) is not blocked.

(8) a. Donkeys kicked every farmer and goats did too.
b. Every donkey kicked three of the farmers and several goats did too.
c. Every frog jumped several fences and most sheep did too.

Summarizing, it seems evident that an account in terms of the classical GB theory of LF does not account for the entire array of attested semantic facts and data. In the next section, Fox's (1995, 2000) syntactic account of the problem is described. This theory is cast within a minimalist framework and has strong theoretical implications with respect to the role of Economy at the syntax/semantics interface and on the determination of scopal relations in a minimalist grammar. After presenting Fox's (1995, 2000) account, I argue that there are important conceptual and empirical inadequacies in his theory, based on the Ellipsis Scope Generalization, and I present an alternative solution which dispenses with the necessity of global Economy in the determination of scopal differences. This solution is consistent with analyses of ellipsis that make use of higher-order unification mechanisms—cf. also Merchant (2001) and van Craenenbroeck (2010) for alternative views where Economy does not play a major role either. Other authors have presented evidence from other constructions in favor of different versions of Economy (Bruening 2001; Sauerland 2000). We will not address these proposals here.

3. Ellipsis and Economy

Fox (1995, 2000) presents a theory of scope interactions in elliptic constructions that attempts to derive their properties from general assumptions of the Minimalist Program (Chomsky 1995). More concretely, the scopal behavior of quantifiers follows from the generalization in (9):

(9) Ellipsis Scope Generalization (ESG): The relative scope of two quantifiers, one of which is in an antecedent VP of an ellipsis construction, may differ from the surface c-command relation only if the parallel difference will have semantic effects in the elided VP.

The generalization is true with respect to the examples that we have considered so far. For instance, in sentence (2b) the scopal order of the quantifiers in the second conjunct, after reconstruction, does not yield a difference in truth conditions. Reconstruction is the process that "reconstructs" or copies back the material elided at Spell Out in the deletion site. The following LFs are truth-conditionally equivalent:

(10) a. Mary$_1$ [every teacher$_2$ [$_{VP}$ t$_1$ admires t$_2$]]
     b. every teacher$_2$ [Mary$_1$ [$_{VP}$ t$_1$ admires t$_2$]]

Fox assumes, contra Cormack and Diesing, that proper names and definites are quantificational and that in the LFs above we have a genuine interaction of two quantifiers. A proper name interacting with any other quantifier will never generate a scope ambiguity, i.e. the interaction has the commutative property (van Benthem 1984). Since the two associated LFs would be equivalent, the ESG predicts that the scopal order of the quantifiers in the source clause or antecedent VP is identical to their surface order, as in (3a). Similarly, in (7b) only the scopal order *every > some* is allowed in the source clause, since the permutation of the scopal order of the definite in the reconstructed clause and any other quantifier yields truth-conditionally equivalent LFs. Hirschbühler's example in (6) and the variant of sentence (2b), where the quantifier expression *some girl* is substituted for *Mary*, are predicted by the ESG to display a scope ambiguity in the source clause by the ESG, as in fact they do. Consider sentence (11a) and its two possible LF representations (11b, 11c):

(11) a. Some boy admires every teacher and some girl does too.
     b. some girl$_1$ [every teacher$_2$ [$_{VP}$ t$_1$ admires t$_2$]]
     c. every teacher$_2$ [some girl$_1$ [$_{VP}$ t$_1$ admires t$_2$]]

In sentence (11a), after VP-reconstruction, the quantifier *some girl* interacts with the quantifier *every teacher* yielding two possible orders, shown in (11b, c). The two LFs above are trivially not equivalent,[1] and according to the ESG the scopal order of the quantifiers in the source clause may be different from the surface order. In other words, the object wide scope configuration is well-formed.

---

1. LF (11b) is true in a model in which every teacher is admired by a different girl, whereas (11a) is false in that model.

(12) every teacher₂ [some boy₁ [_VP_ t₁ admires t₂]] and every teacher₂ [some girl₁ [_VP_ t₁ admires t₂]]

Fox brings in new empirical data from English to support the validity of the ESG. For instance, the combination of two universal quantifiers yields two equivalent LFs:

(13) a. every girl₁ [every teacher₂ [_VP_ t₁ admires t₂]]
      b. every teacher₂ [every girl₁ [_VP_ t₁ admires t₂]]

Consider now the following sentence:

(14) Some boy admires every teacher and every girl does too.

Again, according to the ESG, only the scopal order of the quantifiers in the source clause that is identical to their surface order, i.e. *subject > object*, is allowed, since the *object > subject* order of the quantifiers in the LF corresponding to the reconstructed clause (13b) would not have any semantic effect. It would not be semantically different from the scopal order that preserves the surface c-command order.

Fox claims that the ESG follows from two assumptions which are independently needed: (i) Parallelism, and (ii) Economy. Economy dictates that the object can move by the operation of Quantifier Raising (QR) over the subject only if such movement yields an interpretation which would be unavailable otherwise. Parallelism dictates that an operation applies in one conjunct if and only if a parallel instance of the same operation applies in the other conjunct. In the cases that we have been considering, Economy prevents an application of QR displacing the object quantifier over the subject quantifier and yielding the *object > subject* scopal order at LF if the resulting representation is truth-conditionally equivalent to an LF-representation in which that operation has not applied. When a proper name or a definite-quantifier subject interacts with any other quantifier, an application of QR is semantically inert and violates Economy. This is because "referential" elements are scopeless or free of scope interaction. For example, the interpretation of *John* does not change as a function of whether it is under the scope of a universal term or it has scope over such term. When two universal quantifiers interact, any scope shifting operation is also semantically inert and, as a consequence, uneconomical. Parallelism prevents QR from applying in one conjunct without applying in the other conjunct. Therefore, if QR cannot apply in the reconstructed VP to avoid a violation of Economy it cannot apply in the source clause either to avoid a violation of Parallelism.

4. Global vs. local economy and the ordering asymmetry problem

There are two kinds of objections that can be raised against Fox's theory: theoretical and empirical. From a theoretical point of view, Fox assumes a grammatical architecture which is quite controversial, as pointed out by Tomioka (1995). Fox defends that syntax "must see" the semantic effects of the relative scope of two quantifiers. The Principle of Economy, as formulated by Fox and described in the previous section, rules out as uneconomical LF representations in which a syntactic operation, such as QR, applies without having any interpretive effect—cf. Reinhart (2006). As Fox notes, this principle goes against the Hypothesis of the Autonomy of Syntax or, for that matter, the symmetric hypothesis of the autonomy of semantics. Nevertheless, he considers it "a very local amendment" because "syntax can see the semantic effects of quantifier scope—and perhaps other aspects of compositional semantics which form a natural class with the interpretation of scope—but nothing else" (Fox 1995, 289). Nevertheless, the determination of what constitutes a natural class in this case is too vague, and it seems reasonable to assume that matters of tense, mood and aspect, anaphora and pronoun resolution, etc. will be part of this class, since they interact with the interpretation of quantifiers. Therefore, the most important part, if not all, of what we conceive as compositional semantics will be part of the domain to which syntax has access and the amendment would be far from local. There are two potential solutions to this problem. The first one is to give up the hypothesis of the autonomy of syntax, which has been central to Generative Grammar from the earliest models to the Principles and Parameters (P&P) framework. This possibility was first raised by Marantz (1995) with respect to the Minimalist Program, because the multilevel architecture of P&P is drastically reduced to the interface levels (PF and LF) and the conditions that hold at these levels are of a phonological/semantic nature. This idea is also present in a variety of minimalist approaches (Boeckx 2011).[2]

---

2. In sign-based approaches to grammar, such as European structuralism, categorial grammar and feature-unification formalisms (GPSG, HPSG), syntax has not been essentially conceived as an autonomous component. The Minimalist Program may be viewed as a con-

Still, the problem remains of what concept of Economy is invoked, its generality, and its impact on semantic interpretation. The relevant schema for Economy would be the following one: First, let all derivations that involve the same "numeration" (or collection of lexical items) and terminate in LFs that have the same interpretation be compared; then, choose the derivation involving the least number of steps and whose steps are the shortest. There is no general procedure that I am aware of to decide between derivations having fewer long steps and those having more steps but of a shorter nature. Thus, it is common in the literature on Economy to consider only cases pertaining to one sort of Economy measure at a time (Stabler 1997, 2010). In the cases under scrutiny here, the shorter-steps measure is adopted more frequently. Alternatively, let us assume that the "less number of operations" measure is preferred. In most cases where the issue is whether an object may QR past a subject, this latter measure is probably not the right one. When an object is a generalized quantifier and the verb selecting this term is not intensional, QR will be forced in order to bring the semantic type of the object in line with the one required by the verb. As a consequence, in all of these cases the derivations being compared will involve QR of the object. What is at stake, then, is how far the object moves and, in Fox's account, Economy will prevent it from moving further than it has to, in order for the intended meaning to be achieved.

In sum, the Fox/Reinhart view of Economy has two properties. On the one hand, it is considered a syntactic condition comparing derivations according to a "minimize steps" criterion. On the other, it seems to be a more general evaluation criterion comparing computations according to a mixture of syntactic and semantic criteria, including the semantic nature of quantifiers and equivalence of interpretation. The above properties are characteristic of a global conception of Economy (Chomsky 1998). Complete derivations of syntactic objects are compared according to an evaluation metric and with respect to a global property. This view of Economy was convincingly criticized by Collins (1997), Yang (1997), and Johnson and Lappin (1997, 1999), who defended a local conception of Economy on the basis of empirical issues, mostly the analysis of *there*-insertion constructions—see Collins (2008) for a summary. There are also computational concerns pertaining to the intractability of computations involving global constraints. This latter issue is more controversial, since there have been some results showing that

---

vergence step between generative formalisms and sign-based ones (Morrill 1994; Retoré and Stabler 1999).

global computations are sometimes equivalent to local ones and they can even be more efficient under certain assumptions, as argued by Graf (2010a, 2010b). A discussion of how these issues impact the proper treatment of ellipsis can be found in Kobele (2012).

Even if one leaves these computational concerns aside, there are problems with the specific treatment of ellipsis proposed. If one assumes, following Chomsky (1993, 1995), a "copy theory" of movement and conceives of ellipsis resolution as a copy deletion process, a conflict with Economy arises. Consider (15a) as the expression generated before the copy deletion process that will derive (15b):

(15) a. Some boy admires every teacher and Mary did admire every teacher too.
b. Some boy admires every teacher and Mary did too.

If both conjuncts in (15a) have the same numeration and are convergent or well-formed at LF, as predicted by Parallelism and Economy, then an application of a deletion operation in the second conjunct would be ruled out as uneconomical since it would not have any semantic effect. Even restricting ourselves to Chomsky's notion of Economy, which is independent of semantic considerations, the application of the Deletion operation would be ruled out, given that it is not required by the derivation of the first conjunct. In other words, no notion of Economy based on pure syntactic considerations would justify a transition from (15a) to (15b), because (15b) requires an additional step. Thus, if Economy is conceived along the more/fewer steps dimension it would block deriving (15b) from (15a). One could assume that VP ellipsis is a process deleting VPs in the segment of the derivation between the Spell-Out and PF, and then hypothesize that Economy does not need to consider steps in this portion of the derivation. A simpler hypothesis, which will be defended later in this chapter, is to assume that both conjuncts are never compared in terms of Economy and their respective derivations do not have the same numerations—see also Martins (1994) and Nunes (2004). In section seven, it will be proposed that a sentence such as (15b) is not generated from (15a) by copy deletion, and that ellipsis resolution takes place in the semantic component as an inferential mechanism.

In order to defend an alternative to the Economy hypothesis, it has to be shown that there are empirical reasons to discard the ESG as a valid generalization and, as a consequence, to not viewing the scopal restrictions in VP-ellipsis constructions as a by-product of Economy in the way Fox does. First, there is the problem that the combined action of Parallelism and Economy only holds when the potentially ambiguous clause is the source clause. Consider the following sentence:

(16) Bill praises every teacher and some girl does too.

In this example, an application of QR in the source clause would be semantically uneconomical, since the proper name is scopally independent with respect to the universal quantifier (***Bill* > *every teacher* = *every teacher* > *Bill***). By Parallelism, the ***subject* > *object*** scopal order has to be the only possible one in the second conjunct. But this is not the case. Although the interpretation with parallel ***subject* > *object*** scopal order is the preferred one, the interpretation in which *some girl* has narrow scope with respect to *every teacher* is also possible. If the ESG follows from Parallelism and Economy, then from these two principles it also follows that the ***subject* > *object*** scopal order is the only acceptable one in (16), contrary to fact. Therefore, there is an "ordering asymmetry" problem with the ESG (Tomioka 1995).[3]

It is also the case that some of the judgments presented by Fox are not clear cut, and may simply reflect scope preferences, for example with respect to an example with two universal quantifiers such as (17).

(17) At most ten boys admire every teacher while every girl does.

As Tomioka (1995, 342) points out, "for the interpretation of the first conjunct, the preferred reading is definitely the existential wide-scope reading, but native speakers I consulted think that it is possible to have the universal wide-scope reading". My own fieldwork confirms Tomioka's observation—cf. also Koktova (1999) and Johnson (2008).

5. The ESG and ellipsis in Spanish

In this section, I will consider data from Spanish showing that the ESG is not a valid generalization and needs non-trivial refinements. An additional limitation of Fox's theory is that the interacting operators in most of the examples considered in his data set are QPs headed by *some* and *every*, definite descrip-

---

3. Fox offers a partial account of the contrast between (2b) and (16) that involves a standard belief about how coordinate structures are parsed and the Principle of the Cycle.

tions, negation and intensional verbs. Nevertheless, these operators represent only a small sample of English quantifiers. Additionally, certain characterizing properties of *some* and *every* may be responsible for part of the empirical facts covered by the ESG—see Beghelli (1995), Stowell and Beghelli (1994, 1997), and Liu (1998) for interface analyses of the differential properties of existential and universal quantifiers. If we take into account a wider range of quantifiers, we can test whether the critical relation is surface c-command or if a finer-grained distinction that is sensitive to the semantic properties of the quantifiers is what is needed. The examples analyzed in this chapter involve bare-argument ellipsis, which does not strand a finite auxiliary and is more common in Spanish as an ellipsis strategy. Nevertheless, the differences between these two types of constructions are irrelevant for the purposes of this chapter.[4] First, consider sentence (18):

(18) Dos estudiantes del comité iban visitando a los profesores y María también.
two students of-the committee were visiting to the teachers and María too
'Two students of the committee were visiting the teachers and María did too.'

In this sentence the preferred interpretation is one in which the students do not vary with the teachers. In other words, the same two students visited the teachers. This is the reading corresponding to the ***subject* > *object*** scopal order, which is identical to the surface c-command order. This interpretive fact is predicted by the ESG. Nevertheless, if we substitute another cardinal quantifier for the proper name in the elliptic clause, as in (19), the preferred interpretation is still one in which the involved executives do not vary with the athletes.

(19) Dos dirigentes saludaron a los atletas y dos ayudantes también.
two executives greeted to the athletes and two assistants too
'Two executives greeted the athletes and two assistants did too.'

This contrast may emerge from semantic/pragmatic factors. For example,

---

4. Reinhart (1991) argues that bare argument ellipsis is not ellipsis at all and that it involves LF movement forming a derived conjoined phrase. Under the minimalist view of movement as a combination of copy and merger, the derivational difference between these two constructions becomes irrelevant.

this tends to be the case in the standard situations in which athletes are being greeted, namely during award ceremonies after a competition, etc. Nevertheless, it represents a problem for the ESG as formulated. It could be argued that the scope ambiguity in the first conjunct of these examples is not clearly a scope ambiguity because this type of sentences could be read as having two non-quantificational plural arguments. Under such an interpretation, it should be possible to understand the subject plurality, here *dos dirigentes* 'two executives', as greeting not necessarily the same athletes. In particular, it should be possible to understand this sentence as saying nothing more than that the plurality of directors stands in a greeting relation to the plurality of athletes. A reading in which the directors greet different athletes, therefore, would arise even if *dos dirigentes* does not fall within the scope of *los atletas* 'the athletes'. Nevertheless, this type of counter-argument is radically flawed in that it would imply an important asymmetry between singular and plural DPs. The latter would be always non-quantificational, which is obviously false: They enter into numerous scope relations with other DPs, negation, intensional verbs, etc.

Notice also that the ESG predicts a sharp contrast between (19) and (20).

(20) Dos dirigentes saludaron a los atletas y el presidente del gobierno también.
two directors greeted to the athletes and the president of-the government too
'Two directors greeted the athletes and the president did too.'

The presence of the singular definite quantifier *el presidente* 'the president' in the elliptic clause of (20) makes uneconomical the **object > subject** scopal order in the antecedent clause because the interaction of a definite with any other quantifier will not produce differential interpretations depending on linear scope configurations. In (19), there is not such a restriction, because the scopal orders *dos* 'two' > *los* 'the$_{pl}$' and *los* 'the$_{pl}$' > *dos* 'two' are not equivalent. Nevertheless, it seems that the intended interpretation is the same in both cases: The same two executives greeted the athletes. Consider now (21):

(21) Dos directivos diferentes fueron saludando a los atletas y el presidente del gobierno también
two executives different went greeting to the athletes and the president of-the government too
'Two different directors greeted the athletes and the president too.'

The occurrence of the distributive adjective *diferente* 'different' in (21) makes the **object > subject** reading obligatory—the athletes have to vary with the directors—, independently of the nature of the subject of the elliptic clause and its interaction with the definite plural object *los atletas* 'the athletes'. I am ignoring here the topic-linked reading of *diferente*, i.e. different from a set of individuals mentioned in the previous discourse. According to the ESG, the **subject > object** reading should be obligatory for the source clause in (21), because the subject of the second conjoined clause is a definite quantifier. What we get is exactly the opposite: The **object > subject** reading is the obligatory one. Thus, it has to be concluded that a quantifier phrase modified by *diferente* obligatorily has narrow scope with respect to any other quantifier in the clause.

The scopal behavior of the universal quantifiers *cada* 'each' and *todos* 'all' in VP ellipsis constructions seems to be similar to its behavior in non-elliptical contexts. In the following examples, two sentences with the [+universal] [+distributive] quantifier *cada* and two sentences with the [+universal] [−distributive] quantifier *todos* (cf. Gutiérrez-Rexach 2012) in object position are considered.[5]

(22) a. Un chico alabó a todos los profesores y una chica también.
   a boy praised to all the teachers and a girl too
   'A boy praised all the teachers and a girl did too.'
   b. Un chico leyó todos los libros y María también.
   a boy read all the books and María too
   'A boy read all the books and María did too.'

(23) a. Un chico alabó a cada profesor y una chica también.
   a boy praised to each teacher and a girl too
   'A boy praised each teacher and a girl too.'
   b. Un chico leyó cada libro y María también.
   a boy read each book and María too
   'A boy read each book and María too.'

In the examples in (22), only the **subject > object** reading of the source clause is available, despite the variation in the subject of the elliptic clause. In (22a) and according to the ESG, such variation should allow for the **object > subject** reading, since *una chica* 'a girl' is an indefinite and, when interact-

---

5. See Gutiérrez-Rexach (1996) for a study of the scopal behavior of universal quantifiers in Spanish interrogative sentences, and a description of the relevant features of Spanish universal quantifiers.

ing with a universal quantifier, both readings should be possible in principle (Gutiérrez-Rexach 2003). Nevertheless, the relevant factor seems to be here the feature [-distributive], which prevents the universal quantifier from taking wide scope.

The examples in (23) show a differential scope pattern. In principle, wide scope of the object quantifier should always be available, if distributivity were the only relevant factor. But Parallelism also plays a role in this case. Sentence (23a) is ambiguous. Either the boys vary with the teachers or there is a specific boy who praises all the teachers. What is interesting here is that, when there is variation in the source clause, there is also variation in the elliptic clause, and when *un chico* 'a boy' is non-specific in the source clause it is not specific in the elliptic clause either. This suggests that the role of Parallelism has to be emphasized, since what we are getting is scope Parallelism in both clauses. Again, this undermines the role of Economy in scopal interactions and the validity of the ESG.

Fox discusses examples similar to these in his paper and suggests that what licenses the wide-scope QR of the object in (23a, b) is the presence of an existentially bound event variable. He suggests that, in the case of stage-level predicates, it is possible for an object universal quantifier to be allowed to QR past a name-like subject—in apparent violation of his Economy condition—because doing so licenses a (new) distributive reading over events. A similar process, he argues, is not available to individual-level predicates because of the absence of an event variable in clauses of this sort. The problem that this type of analysis runs into is that it would imply that in the sentences in (22) there would not be quantification over events at all. But this is not the case, since the sentence can be interpreted as 'there is an event such that . . . ' In addition, the predicates in (22) and (23) do not contrast along the stage-level/individual-level dimension (Carlson 1977b; Kratzer 1995).

Finally, pseudo-gapping and anaphora with *hacerlo* 'do-it' (the correlate of *do so* anaphora) provide additional evidence for Parallelism as being the active principle playing a leading role in these cases. Consider the following discourse:

(24) Hoy los EEUU lloran y España ríe. Un norteamericano no ganó la medalla de oro en cada prueba de velocidad, y González lo hizo en ciclismo.
'Today the USA cry and Spain celebrates. An American athlete didn't win the gold medal in every track competition, and González did so in cycling.'

The most natural interpretation of (24) is one in which the American athletes vary with the track competitions, i.e. the distributive determiner *cada* forces wide scope of the quantifier it heads. Again, this goes against the ESG, since the presence of the proper name *González* as the subject of the elliptic clause should precisely block this reading. In sum, the facts considered in this section and the previous one indicate that the ESG is not an accurate generalization and should be dispensed with. In addition, we have sufficient evidence for the claim that Economy, understood in a global sense, does not play a significant role in ellipsis resolution.

6. The extent of Parallelism

Semantic Parallelism goes beyond identity of scopal order. It includes relations such as distributivity/collectivity that have to be identical in the source and in the elliptic clause (Hardt 1993; Asher, Hardt, and Busquets 1998). The following sentence illustrates this point:

(25) Tres chicos comieron una pizza.
three boys ate a pizza
'Three boys ate a pizza.'

Sentence (25) may receive a collective interpretation—one single pizza is eaten by three boys—or a distributive interpretation—each one of the three boys ate his own pizza. On the other hand, sentence (26) has only two possible readings:

(26) Tres chicos comieron una pizza y tres chicas también.
three boys ate a pizza and three girls too
'Three boys ate a pizza and three girls did too.'

In one reading, one single pizza is eaten by three boys and another one by three girls, which amounts to a collective reading of the source clause and a collective reading of the elliptic clause. In the other reading, each one of the six boys and girls ate a pizza, instantiating a different pattern: distributive reading of the source clause and distributive reading of the elliptic clause. There are no mixed readings in which the predicate of one of the clauses is interpreted collectively and the predicate in the other clause is interpreted distributively—collective/distributive or distributive/collective.

The preposition *entre* 'among/between' forces the collective reading of the subject in (27). A distributive reading is not possible:

(27)   Entre tres chicos comieron una pizza.
       among three boys ate a pizza
       'Three boys ate a pizza.'

Parallelism forces the presence of the collective marker in both conjuncts if the collective reading is to be preserved:

(28)   *(Entre) tres chicos comieron una pizza y entre tres chicas también.
       *(among) three boys ate a pizza and among three girls too

Another instance of Parallelism is constituted by indexical identity in pronoun resolution, as shown in (29).

(29)   María lo ama.
       María him loves
       'María loves him.'

The pronominal clitic *lo* refers to a discourse referent introduced in the preceding discourse, available in the common ground and not mentioned in the sentence (Gutiérrez-Rexach 1999b). The preferred interpretation of (30) is one in which both pronouns refer to the same individual, in parallel to (29).

(30)   María lo ama y Rosa también lo ama.
       María him loves and Rosa also him loves
       'María loves him and Rosa loves him too.'

There is a possibility, however, to escape Parallelism here, namely when both pronouns are deictically interpreted. In this case the pronouns may have different referents, for instance, when the utterance is accompanied by different pointing gestures. In (31), there is not such a choice.

(31)   María lo ama y Rosa también.
       María him loves and Rosa too
       'Maria loves him and Rosa does too.'

The interpretation of the pronoun in the elliptic clause is fixed by the interpretation of the pronoun in the antecedent clause. In sentence (32) we have another example of parallel pronoun resolution. Let us compare the interpretation of this sentence with (33), where there is no ellipsis.

(32) María lo ama y cada uno de sus amigos piensa que Rosa también.
Mary him loves and each one of his friends thinks that Rosa too
'Mary loves him and each one of his friends thinks that Rosa does too.'

(33) María lo ama y cada uno de sus amigos piensa que Rosa también lo ama.
Mary him loves and each one of his friends thinks that Rosa too him loves
'Mary loves him and each one of his friends thinks that Rosa loves him too.'

Sentence (33) has two readings: One in which the pronominal clitic *lo* in the second clause is coreferential with the first occurrence of *lo*, and a second one in which *lo* is bound by the universal quantifier in the elliptic clause. In (32), the second reading is not possible. The elided pronoun cannot be interpreted as bound by the universal quantifier. Interpreting the VP anaphor in (32) just as *lo ama* 'loves him' with a free variable (trace) for the pronoun would obviously be wrong. The pronoun would then be able to be bound by the universal quantifier, and two readings should be possible as happens in (33). This contrast would constitute an argument against a copy/deletion theory of ellipsis if a constraint like Parallelism were not assumed, because after copying the VP of the antecedent clause into the elliptic clause, the bound pronoun reading should be possible.

In addition, it has to be noticed that it would be misleading to correlate ellipsis and Parallelism too closely. A similar kind of scope disambiguation (or lack thereof) is observed in phonological deaccenting (or prosodic reduction) as well (Tancredi 1992). Consider the following example:

(34) a. Some girl met every professor, and John *was introduced to every professor* too.
b. Some girl met every professor, and some boy *was introduced to every professor* too.

In these examples, the reduced-italic font indicates prosodic reduction. In sentence (34a), only the first conjunct is unambiguous, whereas in (34b) both conjuncts are ambiguous. These facts show that the Parallelism operation which is responsible for scope (un-)ambiguity in VP ellipsis is a wider mechanism whose field of activity goes beyond ellipsis. In this respect, paying more attention to how Parallelism works in the semantic component allows for a wider generalization.

In the next two sections I will sketch a proposal accounting for the data presented so far, without using the ESG and eliminating the notion of global Economy. The main claim is that the diversity of effects that can be observed is a byproduct of the interaction of various constraints within the process of anaphora resolution. The central elements are: (i) the interpretable semantic features of the quantifiers; and (ii) the effects of Parallelism and focus emerging at the semantic component, i.e. in the process of interface interpretation.

7. Ellipsis resolution and Parallelism

In this section I will explore the role of Parallelism and focus with respect to the scope phenomena previously considered. I take the process of ellipsis resolution to be essentially semantic in nature, along the lines proposed in part by Rooth (1992a), and more generally by Dalrymple (1991), Dalrymple, Shieber, and Pereira (1991), Hardt (1999), and Culicover and Jackendoff (2005). The two coordinates of an elliptic construction are different. Let us assume that the elliptic clause contains a predicate variable in its logical form, whereas the source clause does not. This amounts to the property that the conjuncts do not have the same numeration and, therefore, cannot be compared in terms of global Economy, no matter whether we understand this evaluation metric along the fewer/more steps dimension or along the avoid/apply QR dimension. Consider, for instance, sentence (35a) and its "bare" LF representation in (35b).

(35) a. Juan admira a Pedro y Luis también.
Juan admires Pedro and Luis too
'Juan admires Pedro and Luis does too.'
b. [Juan [Pedro [admira]]] y [Luis [P también]]

It can be immediately seen that the conjuncts in (35b) do not have the same numeration and are not comparable in terms of Economy: The first conjunct has two quantifiers and the second conjunct only one. Ellipsis resolution takes place "after" LF. This means that the representation that feeds the semantic computation is one that contains a variable (a lexical item with semantic features but with no phonological features). The variable *P* stands for a predicate-like element of type <e,t>.[6]

The intended interpretation is obtained by a "matching" process. In more formal terms, from a computational point of view, the matching process can be conceived of either as higher order unification, as in Dalrymple, Shieber, and Pereira (1991), or as generalization, as done by Prüst, Scha, and van der Berg (1994).[7] The matching process merely consists of solving a semantic equation and choosing the solution that satisfies a specific set of constraints. For instance, in sentence (35a) above, the interpretation of the elliptic sentence *Luis también* 'Luis too' is that some property *P* holds of *Luis*, as stated in the corresponding LF representation. Ellipsis resolution determines which property this is. One of the constraints that have to be satisfied is syntactic Parallelism. In sentence (35a), the parallel elements are the subjects *Juan* and *Luis*. Property *P* represents what they have in common, in other words, *P* has to hold of the two parallel elements. When this property is applied to the argument *Juan*, we get the interpretation of the source clause. When it is applied to *Luis*, we get the interpretation of the target clause. In the equation in (36), one side corresponds to the source clause, and the other to the property which applied to the parallel element in the source clause would give as a result the source clause.

(36) P(Juan) = **Admira**(Juan, Pedro)

Applying unification, we arrive at the following solution:

(37) P = λx. **Admira**(x, Pedro)

The interpretation of the target clause is the solution *P* in (37) applied to Luis:

---

6. It might seem that the inclusiveness requirement (Chomsky 1995) is being relaxed, since the presence of a variable *P* in the initial numeration or multiset of lexical items is being postulated. But this is unproblematic, since *P* is assumed to lack Φ-features but is specified as having categorial features, among them its semantic type: <e,t>. An alternative that is also consistent with the principle of inclusiveness would be to claim that the variable *P* is not present in the initial numeration or multiset of lexical resources, and that it is inserted in the semantics by a coercion process (Pustejovsky 1995).

7. Generalization is the dual of the computational operation of unification. They were both proposed by Robinson (1965).

(38) λx. Admira(x, Pedro)(Luis) = Admira(Luis,Pedro)

Ellipsis resolution is a computational process consisting of three steps (Dalrymple, Shieber, and Pereira 1991; Dalrymple 1991): (i) determining the parallel elements in both conjuncts, (ii) solving an equation involving the parallel element in the source clause, as in (36)–(37), and, finally (iii) applying the solution of the equation to the parallel element in the elliptic clause—cf. Asudeh and Crouch (2002) for a slightly different approach. What we are considering here are equations incorporating a higher degree of structure, since our inputs are translations of LF structures encoding scope asymmetries that cannot be directly read off from surface strings. Therefore, the structures to be matched in (35) are as follows: (39) corresponds to the first conjunct in (35) and (40) to the second conjunct.

(39)

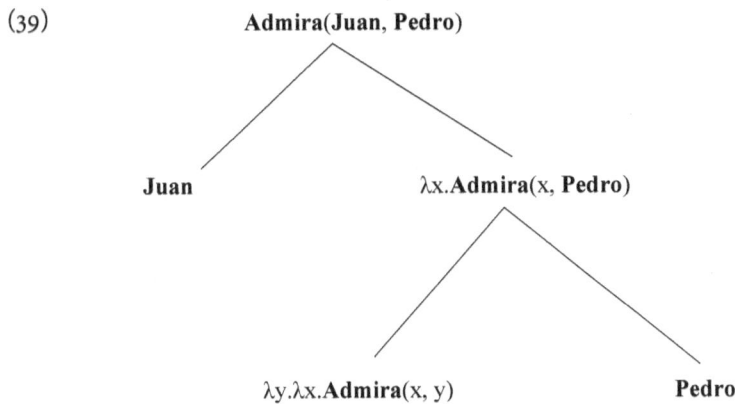

(40)

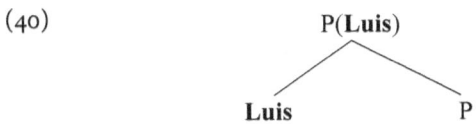

As explained above, the semantic trees in (39) and (40) "match" only if the variable *P* is given the value in (37). Let us now consider cases involving scopal Parallelism. Assuming a theory of the interpretation of scope asymmetries such as the one proposed by Hendricks (1993), one can deal with scope ambiguity by flexible typing the verb of the clause (Szabolcsi 2010). The typings determine the attachment order of the quantifiers to the verb. The choice of the relevant type is triggered by the LF structure working as input to semantic interpretation, so it is sensitive to semantic features of quantifiers such as [+/-distributive] (Stowell and Beghelli 1997), etc. as will be argued in the next section. In a flexible system, every expression is assigned a lexical translation of the lowest type. Translations of higher types are obtained by means of general rules of raising and lowering. Consider sentence (41) and the two potential LFs for the source clause in (42).

(41) Algún estudiante vio a los profesores y alguna secretaria también.
some student saw to the professors and some secretary too
'Some student saw the professors and some secretary did too.'

(42) a. [algún estudiante [los profesores [vio]]
b. [los profesores [algún estudiante [vio]]

According to my intuitions, sentence (41) is two ways ambiguous. The two interpretations are: (i) a specific student saw the professors and a specific secretary saw them too or (ii) all the members of a group of professors were seen by some student—not the same student saw all of the professors necessarily—and the professors were also seen by some secretary. Interpretation (i) corresponds to the scopal order (42a) of the source clause, and interpretation (ii) corresponds to the order in (42b). Interpretation (i) is preferred, but (ii) is not completely unavailable. A sentence such as (43) lacks interpretation (ii), so the only LF input for semantic interpretation is similar to (42a):

(43) Un estudiante vio a los profesores y una secretaria también.
'A student saw the professors and a secretary did too'

Let us see how the two interpretations of (41) are obtained. The basic translations for the constituents are the following ones:

(44) algún estudiante 'some student' $\Rightarrow \lambda P.\exists y[\textbf{Student}(y) \wedge P(y)]$
los profesores 'the professors' $\Rightarrow \lambda P.\textbf{THE}_{pl}x[\textbf{Professor}(x) \rightarrow P(x)]$
ver 'see' $\Rightarrow \lambda x.\lambda y[\textbf{See}(y, x)]$

There are two ways of raising the type of the verb that yield scopally non-equivalent translations:

(45) $\lambda Q_{obj}.\lambda Q_{subj}.Q_{subj}(\lambda y.Q_{obj}(\lambda x.\textbf{See}(y, x)))$

(46) $\lambda Q_{obj}.\lambda Q_{subj}.Q_{obj}(\lambda x.Q_{subj}(\lambda y.\textbf{See}(y, x)))$

In the translations above, Q_{subj} and Q_{obj} are variables that stand for the generalized quantifier denoted by the subject and object noun phrases respectively. The LF in (42a) forces the choice of the type in (45) for the verb, corresponding to the subject wide scope reading, and (42b) forces the choice of (46), corresponding to the object wide scope reading. The semantic tree showing the semantic computation of the subject wide scope reading is as follows:

(47) $\exists y[\textbf{Student}(y) \wedge \textbf{THE}_{pl}\, x[\textbf{Professor}(x) \to \textbf{See}(y, x)]]$

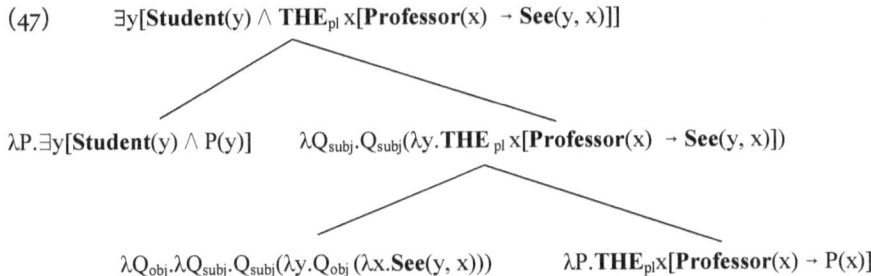

The semantic tree of the object wide-scope reading is (48):

(48) $\textbf{THE}_{pl}\, x[\textbf{Professor}(x) \to \exists y[\textbf{Student}(y) \wedge \textbf{See}(y, x)]]$

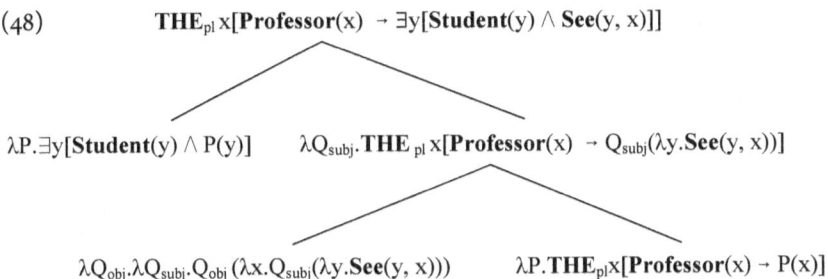

Following our proposal, the semantic tree corresponding to the second conjunct of (41) contains a variable P of type $<<<e,t>,t>,t>$, i.e. a function from generalized quantifiers to truth values:[8]

---

8. Notice that the type of the argument has been raised to the type of a generalized quantifier.

(49)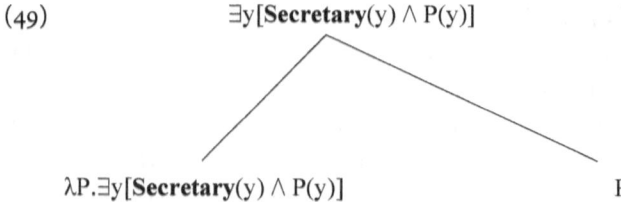

The matching process first establishes that *algún estudiante* 'some student' and *alguna secretaria* 'some secretary' are the parallel elements in the semantic trees. The choice of the relevant semantic equation is a non-deterministic process, because we have two candidate structures for the source clause, namely (47) and (48). If the semantic tree of the **subject > object** reading is selected, the relevant equation is as in (50a) and the solution as in (50b), where Q is obviously a generalized quantifier variable.

(50) a. $P(\lambda P. \exists y[\textbf{Student}(y) \wedge P(y)]) = \exists y[\textbf{Student}(y) \wedge \text{THE}_{pl}x[\textbf{Professor}(x) \rightarrow \text{See}(y, x)]]$
b. $P = \lambda Q.Q(\lambda y.\text{THE}_{pl}x[\textbf{Professor}(x) \rightarrow \text{See}(y, x)])$

Substituting the value of *P* in the semantic tree of the elliptic clause yields the following full semantic tree, where the generalized quantifier denoted by *alguna secretaria* 'some secretary' is construed as having wide scope:

(51)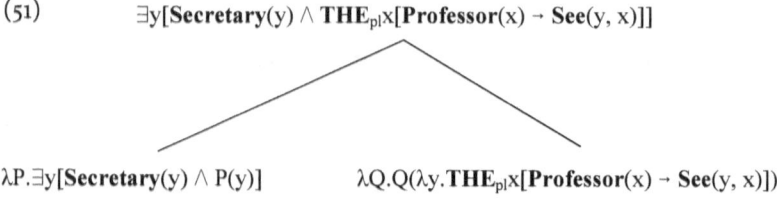

If the semantic tree of the **object > subject** reading is selected, then the relevant equation would be as in (52a) and the solution as in (52b):

(52) a. $P(\lambda P.\exists y[\textbf{Student}(y) \wedge P(y)]) = \text{THE}_{pl}x[\textbf{Professor}(x) \rightarrow \exists y[\textbf{Student}(y) \wedge \text{See}(y, x)]]$
b. $P = \lambda Q.\text{THE}_{pl}x[\textbf{Professor}(x) \rightarrow Q(\lambda y.\text{See}(y, x))]$

When we substitute this solution for the variable in (49), we obtain the object wide scope interpretation of the elliptic clause:

(53)   THE$_{pl}$ x[Professor(x) → ∃y[Secretary(y) ∧ See(y, x)]]

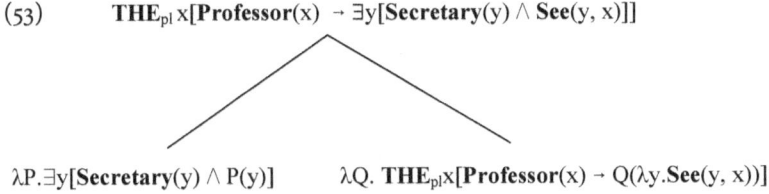

λP.∃y[Secretary(y) ∧ P(y)]   λQ. THE$_{pl}$x[Professor(x) → Q(λy.See(y, x))]

The process of ellipsis resolution derives the two readings of sentence (41) that we described above in a precise fashion. There is a fact missing in this derivation process so far: the fact that the subject wide scope reading is the preferred one. There are two options at this point. One of them is to discard the object wide scope derivation (less economical) and feed the semantic ellipsis resolution process only with the subject wide-scope LF. More or less, this is the essence of Fox' solution. But, as we have argued in previous sections, this hypothesis seems to be too strong and involves the use of global Economy criteria. An alternative solution is to link the choice of one or the other reading to different focus patterns of the source clause, as proposed by Rooth (1992a) and Tomioka (1995, 2008). In other words, it seems that the choice of the relevant structure is conditioned by something which is independent of purely syntactic considerations: it is semantically motivated and syntactically encoded.[9] When the subject of the source clause is focused, the subject wide-scope reading emerges. When the object is focused, the resulting reading is the object wide-scope reading. In elliptic constructions there is a strong tendency to focus the parallel elements of the source and the target clause. In sentence (41), repeated here as (54), this amounts to focus marking of both subjects:

(54)   [Algún estudiante]$_{[+Focus]}$ vio a los profesores y [alguna secretaria]$_{[+Focus]}$ también.
       'Some student$_{[+Focus]}$ saw the professors and some secretary$_{[+Focus]}$ too.'

---

9. It could be argued that sensitivity to a focus feature in the syntax would amount to a violation of the Inclusiveness Principle, since it does not seem reasonable to assume that focus is a feature in the initial feature specification of a lexical item (Zubizarreta 1998). Nevertheless, it would be consistent with a minimalist architecture to assume that lexical items may enter the initial numeration or multiset of resources with such a specification and that convergence would be dictated by checking criteria—whether the feature is checked in the derivational process or not. In the case of wide or constituent focus, the stage of the derivation at which the feature is checked would determine the scope of the focus feature. Alternatively, one may assume that the Inclusiveness Principle prevents the occurrence of empty categories in the initial numerations but features are allowed to be part of that initial multiset.

In Rooth's (1985) theory of focus, a sentence with a focused constituent has two semantic values: an ordinary denotational value and a focus value. The focus value is calculated by substituting the focus element by a variable. In other words, it is the set of alternatives to the ordinary semantic value that we get when we substitute other semantic values for the variable. For any constituent α, we can define the ordinary value $[α]^o$ and the focus value $[α]^f$. Thus, the focus value of the first conjunct of (54) is the set of propositions of the form *y vio a los profesores* '*y* saw the professors' where the value assigned to *y* is a member of the set of contextually determined alternatives to the denotation of *algún estudiante* 'some student'.

(55) ⟦ [Algún estudiante]$_{[+Focus]}$ vio a los profesores ⟧^{f} =
  { p | ∃Q ∈ ALT(λP. ∃y[**Student**(y) ∧ P(y)]) such that
  p = Q (λy. **Saw the professors** (y)) } =
  { p | ∃Q ∈ ALT(λP. ∃y[**Student**(y) ∧ P(y)]) such that
  p = Q (λy. **the professors** (λx.See(y, x)))}

All the propositions *p* in the focus value of the sentence satisfy the **subject > object** scopal order. This squares with the intuition that when the subject of (54) is focused, the inverse scope reading is absent, i.e. we are talking about a specific student. If we add the condition that the result of applying the solution of the ellipsis equation to the designated parallel element in the source clause has to be a member of the focus value of the sentence, it follows that only the semantic equation in (49a) will derive the intended result. In less formal terms, focusing of the subject in (54) introduces a focus-related denotational requirement that can be satisfied only if the ellipsis resolution steps apply to the **subject > object** semantic tree. If the subject is not focused, the requirement disappears. The inverse scope reading becomes available because ellipsis resolution can be applied to the semantic tree corresponding to the **object > subject** scopal order.

8. Ellipsis resolution and distributivity

As it has been observed in previous sections, the scopal requirements of a quantifier may apparently override Parallelism requirements. But this is not problematic if we do not assume that Economy blocks applications of QR that are semantically inert. Consider the following sentence:

(56) Un miembro del comité ejecutivo saludó a cada atleta y el presidente del gobierno también.
'A member of the executive committee greeted each athlete and the nation's president did too.'

The determiner *cada* 'each' in (56) may scope over *un* 'a', yielding the interpretation 'A different member of the executive committee greets each athlete.' A parallel object wide-scope configuration in the elliptic clause is banned as uneconomical by the ESG, since *el N* 'the N' > *cada N* 'each N' = *cada N* 'each N' > *el N* 'the N'. The most salient reading of (56) is not problematic for the theory developed in this chapter because the LF of the elliptic conjunct consists of one quantifier and a variable.

(57)

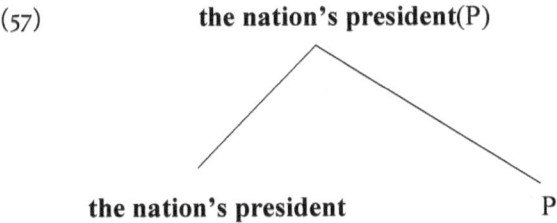

the nation's president(P)

the nation's president   P

Let us assume that *cada N* 'each N' is an intrinsically distributive quantifier, and that the interpretation of the [+distributive] feature obligatorily triggers wide scope of the quantifier it is associated with. This requirement can be properly formulated within Stowell and Beghelli's (1994, 1997) and Beghelli's (1995) theory of quantifier scope. According to these authors, the [+distributive] feature of a quantifier is checked at LF by raising of the quantifier to a designated projection DistP, whereas the quantifier acting as the distributive "share" (Gil 1995) raises to Share P. Thus, a distributive quantifier obligatorily has wide scope over the share quantifier. In this case the LF corresponding to the first conjunct of (56) would be as follows:

(58)

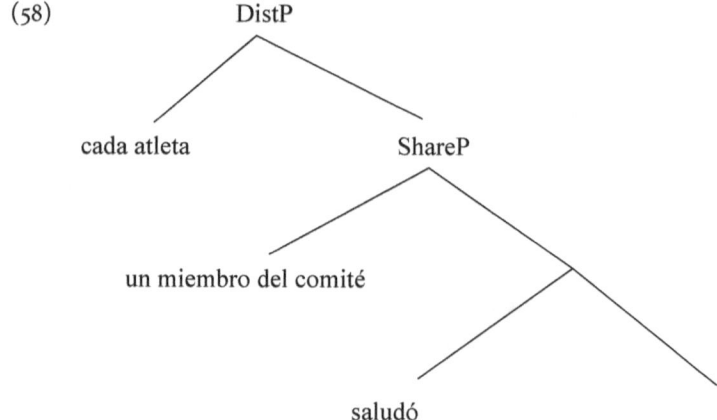

Thus, only one derivation of the first conjunct reaches LF and the application of the ellipsis-resolution steps to the relevant semantic trees yields the intended interpretation, as spelled out in the previous section. On the other hand, modification of a noun by the adjective *diferente* 'different', illustrated in (21) above, triggers movement of the quantifier phrase to ShareP. This would explain why the ***object > subject*** reading was the only one available in this sentence. If the quantifier phrase modified by *diferente* moves to ShareP, then it has narrow scope with respect to the other quantifier phrase in the sentence, which may move either to DistP or to RefP (Stowell and Beghelli 1997).

The facts considered in section five, pertaining to Parallelism effects involving symmetric collective/distributive readings also follow straightforwardly from the theory presented so far, assuming that collective/distributive readings require checking of a relevant feature at LF in the source clause. The Parallelism effect follows in the semantic component when ellipsis resolution takes place. The same can be argued with respect to the identity of pronoun reference in examples (30–33).

In other cases, such as Hirschbühler-type sentences, the role of semantics/pragmatics is more important. The structure of the intended models (situations) filters out the relevant semantic tree. Consider the following contrast:

(59) a. Hay una bandera municipal en el balcón de todas las casas y una bandera regional también.
'There is a city flag in the balcony of every house and a regional flag too.'

b. Hay una bandera municipal en el balcón de todas las casas y una bandera nacional también.
'There is a city flag in the balcony of every house and a state flag too.'

In sentences (59a) and (59b), the only possible reading is one in which every house has a city flag, i.e. the object quantifier obligatorily scopes over the subject, no matter what the nature of the quantifier in the remnant is. The quantifier *todos* 'all' is not obligatorily distributive (Gutiérrez-Rexach 2012), so it is not the case that only one LF feeds the semantic representation. Two LFs may be constructed, and two different semantic trees corresponding to the *subject* > *object* and *object* > *subject* scopal order may be derived. The reason why the *subject* > *object* semantic tree gets eliminated is because the corresponding logical statement will be true only in models in which houses have the same (token) flag. Since this is not possible in the actual world, the only acceptable representation is the one that conforms to a realistic state of affairs.

9. Conclusions

In this chapter, it has been shown that a successful account of scope ambiguities in VP ellipsis and bare argument ellipsis constructions can be built dispensing with the notion of global Economy and generalizations based on it. The proposed explanation relies heavily on mechanisms that operate at the syntax-semantics interface and in the semantic component of the grammar properly. This allows for a simplification of the role of syntactic computation in the determination of scope ambiguities. Thus, it has been argued that an approach based on Fox's (1995, 2000) Ellipsis Scope Generalization faces numerous conceptual and empirical problems. Ellipsis resolution is conceived of as an interface phenomenon with critical resolution elements belonging to semantics properly. It is conditioned by the computation of the semantic features of quantifiers. An approach inspired in higher-order unification theories of ellipsis has been defended. This approach is still compatible with the overall philosophy of minimalist grammar: The process of higher-order unification complies with the principle of inclusiveness (Chomsky 1995) or projection from the lexicon because the relevant semantic equations are set up and resolved at a discourse level, but they are determined by feature-sensitive Logical Forms.

3

Indefinites and Sentential Modality

1. Introduction: Quantificational non-uniformity

One of the cornerstones of grammatical research in the last two decades has been the analysis of certain word classes and their structural and functional properties. Thus, verbs, adjectives, nouns, etc. have been discovered to be non-uniform categories, a hypothesis which can be strongly argued from syntactic and semantic grounds. A relative consensus has also emerged in recent years on the fact that noun phrases do not behave uniformly with respect to their quantificational properties (Szabolcsi 1997, 2010). There are several important consequences of this fact affecting the interface levels: Is this non-uniformity a syntactic property, or is it a matter of lexical specification? How can this uniformity be represented?; Does it trigger differential patterns of interaction with respect to other elements? The last question seems to be extremely important. More concretely, scopal interactions between nominal quantifiers and other quantificational elements (*wh*-expressions, modal operators) have been the focus of numerous studies in the linguistic and philosophical literature. While this is true historically, I believe that recent discoveries on quantificational non-uniformity open important avenues of research for this topic. The issue of how differential properties of different quantifier classes might impact their scopal behavior needs to be examined in detail. In this chapter we look at Spanish indefinites, their particular nature and subclasses, and how these idiosyncrasies affect their scopal interactions.

2. Indefinites and scope: A brief survey

Indefinites are well-known for their exceptional scopal behavior, as initially observed by Fodor and Sag (1982). These authors assume what can be called an "ambiguity hypothesis" for indefinites, and claim that these terms may have either a quantificational or a referential reading. The distinction between these two readings comes from the fact that indefinites do not seem to obey several restrictions satisfied by standard quantifiers. It is a well-attested fact that scopal relations between quantifiers and operators are restricted by syntactic islands (Lakoff 1970; Rodman 1976), since it can be shown that quantifiers are island-bound. This is true in so-called "strong islands," such as complex-NP islands, adjunct islands, or coordinate structures—cf. Bosque and Gutiérrez-Rexach (2009, chap. 7) for a detailed characterization of different island types in Spanish. For example, sentence (1) lacks the interpretation in which the universal quantifier *todo pariente mío residente en Suiza* 'every relative of mine living in Switzerland' scopes over the island domain, as illustrated by the contrasting representations in (2):

(1) Si todo pariente mío residente en Suiza muere, heredaré una fortuna.
if every relative mine residing in Switzerland dies I-will-inherit a fortune
'If every relative of mine living in Switzerland dies, I will inherit a fortune.'

(2) a. [[if every relative of mine living in Switzerland x [x dies]], I will inherit a fortune]
b. *every relative of mine living in Switzerland x [[if x dies], I will inherit a fortune]

The above representations show the available and non-available readings. In other words, (1) only has the reading where if all of the speaker's relatives who live in Switzerland die he will inherit a fortune (2a). Thus, it lacks the reading represented in (2b), namely that with the demise of each one of the relevant relatives he will inherit a different additional fortune. The standard account of this contrast is based on the following well-known structural constraint: syntactic objects cannot be extracted from a strong island, such as the antecedent of a conditional. If we assume that this constraint also operates at the level of Logical Form, we predict that reading (2b) is unavailable because the quantifier is not allowed to "escape" the island and take sentential scope over it. Interestingly, indefinites differ from standard quantificational expressions in that, in addition to having a quantificational (island-bound) reading, they have an island-escaping interpretation. For example, sentence (3a) may be interpreted as (3b):

(3) a. Si un pariente mío residente en Suiza muere, heredaré una fortuna.
if a relative mine residing in Switzerland dies I-will-inherit a fortune
'If a relative of mine living in Switzerland dies, I will inherit a fortune.'
b. There is a relative of mine living in Switzerland x, such that if x dies I will inherit a fortune.

This fact leads Fodor and Sag to conclude that this type of reading is not quantificational. Rather, it has a "referential" nature (sometimes called "specific"; cf. Leonetti 2012). In other words, the involved indefinite refers to a unique individual. The main problem for the referential/quantificational ambiguity hypothesis is the existence of intermediate readings, were an indefinite has wide scope with respect to one quantificational element and narrow scope with respect to another one. Consider the reading of (4a) paraphrased in (4b).

(4) a. Todo el mundo contó varias historias sobre un miembro de la familia.
every the world told several stories about a member of the family
'Everyone told several stories about a member of the family.'
b. Everyone picked a (possibly different) member of the family and told several stories about him.

The reading (4b) corresponds to the scopal order ***todo el mundo*** 'everyone' > ***un*** 'a' > ***varias*** 'several.' In this intermediate reading, the indefinite lacks maximal scope, so it would be predicted to be a quantificational element. Nevertheless, it also occupies a position inside an island at the surface and takes logical scope over it, so it has the behavior of a referential element too. These and related facts have been used as arguments for an alternative approach to the semantics of indefinites, according to which they introduce choice functions in the semantic representation (Reinhart 1997; Winter

1997). There are also more recent technical alternatives to this idea, such as the proposal by Brasoveanu and Farkas (2011), which does not use choice functions and replaces them with the choice of the suitable witness set in an independence-friendly logic. What matters for the purposes of this chapter is that these alternatives are semantically equivalent to the use of choice functions. Thus, this or a related mechanism seems to provide the best solution to the apparent paradox represented by indefinite scope.

There is additional empirical evidence in related directions, supporting the hypothesis that indefinites have to be represented differently in order to capture their non-uniform behavior, and advocating the use of choice functions or similar devices. For reasons of space, we will not consider this extensive literature here—cf. Ruys (1992), Abusch (1994), Kratzer (1998), Matthewson (1999), Gutiérrez-Rexach (2003), and López-Carretero (2011, 2012). Let us consider now the representation of the wide scope (specific/referential) reading of the indefinite in (5a) using choice functions, as shown in (5b).

(5) a. Cada estudiante admira a cierto profesor.
    each student admires ANIM certain professor
    'Each student admires a certain professor.'
  b. $\exists f[CH(f) \wedge \forall x[\textbf{student}(x) \rightarrow \textbf{admires}(x, f(\textbf{professor}))]]$

What (5b) states is that there is a choice function f such that for every student x, x admires $f(professor)$, i.e. the professor selected by the choice function f—technically, the value of the function f applied to the set denoted by *professor*—is the individual selected from that set. The use of choice functions can solve several problems in the semantics of indefinites. Consider now a sentence with a cardinal quantifier expression (*tres tíos míos* 'three uncles of mine') occurring inside a conditional antecedent:

(6) Si tres tíos míos mueren, heredaré una fortuna.
  if three uncles mine die I-will-inherit a fortune
  'If three uncles of mine die, I will inherit a fortune.'

The representation in (7a) would be the LF of the wide scope reading of the plural indefinite in (6), and the corresponding semantic representation is (7b):

(7) a. [three uncles]$_i$[if t$_i$ die, I will inherit a fortune]
  b. $\exists_3 x[\textbf{uncles of I}(x) \wedge \textbf{die}(x) \rightarrow \textbf{I will inherit a fortune}]$

Ruys (1992) observes that this reading is not adequate. It would make the sentence true in situations where, if only one of his three uncles dies, the speaker inherits a fortune. Again, the proper meaning of (6) is that there is a group of three uncles of the speaker such that, if all of them die, he will inherit a fortune. Using choice functions, the proper semantic representation can be derived (Reinhart 1997):

(8) $\exists f[CH(f) \wedge [f(\text{three of my uncles}) \text{ die} \rightarrow \text{I will inherit a fortune}]]$

In the above representation, the choice function f selects a group of three uncles of mine, and then it has to be true that if all of them die the speaker will inherit a fortune. Choice functions also seem to provide a better understanding of the semantics of intermediate readings characterized above. For example, in the intermediate reading of (9), represented in (10), students vary with every professor under consideration.

(9) Cada profesor oyó el rumor de que tres estudiantes (suyos) suspendieron.
 each professor heard the rumor of that three students (of his) failed
 'Each professor overheard the rumor that three of his students failed.'

(10) $\exists f[CH(f) \wedge \forall x[\textbf{professor}(x) \rightarrow \textbf{overheard the rumor}(x, f_x(\textbf{three students}) \textbf{ failed})]]$

The advantage of using choice functions to capture the island-escaping behavior of quantifiers or intermediate scope is that the indefinite expression stays *in situ*, whereas the choice function is introduced at the point where the indefinite element gets scope. This is consistent with a model of grammar in which indefinites are not subject to QR. Following Reinhart (1997), the emergence of wide-scope, narrow scope or intermediate readings is explained by the differential association of the choice function.[1] In Spanish, there are two indefinite determiners: *un* and *algún*. The determiner

---

1. For Reinhart (1997) and Winter (1997) all indefinites introduce choice-function variables, which are existentially closed at different levels, yielding the contrast between "wide" and "narrow" scope interpretations. On the other hand, for Kratzer (1998) and Matthewson (1999), only wide-scope or specific indefinites are associated with choice functions. Following Reinhart and Winter, here I will assume that indefinites systematically introduce choice functions.

algún (and its plural variant *algunos*) is a presuppositional, topic-oriented determiner and tends to have systematic wide scope behavior (cf. Gutiérrez-Rexach 2001b, 2003, 2010; Martí 2007, 2009). Thus, in this chapter we will restrict our observations to the more flexible non-presuppositional indefinites *un/unos*. The former indefinites, of the *alg-* 'some' variety, have also been argued to carry an epistemic modal component (Alonso-Ovalle and Menéndez-Benito 2003, 2010), something which would not be incompatible with the arguments developed in this chapter. Quite the contrary, it would support the claim that the epistemically neutral *un* and *unos* would be the only indefinites capable of receiving variable modal anchoring.

3. Anchoring of modal elements

If we consider the scope of indefinites in modal contexts, not only dependencies with respect to other quantifiers have to be factored in, but also dependencies in-intension with respect to propositional attitude/intensional verbs and modal operators. These dependencies have been considered as evidence in favor of a theory based on evaluation indices (Farkas 1993, 1996, 1997), where scope relations are reducible to dependency relations between indices. In the following structures, constituents are indexed to the world in which they are evaluated: the real world (w_r) or a dream world (w_s). Such indexing is indicated by a subscript on the opening bracket of a given constituent.

(11) [$_{wr}$ [$_{wr}$ Un político] era honrado]
 a man was honest
 'A politician was honest.'

(12) a. [$_{wr}$ Juan soñó [$_{Ws}$ que [$_{wr}$ un político] era honrado]]
 Juan dreamed that a politician was honest
 'Juan dreamed that a politician was honest.'
 b. [$_{wr}$ Juan soñó [$_{Ws}$ que [$_{ws}$ un político] era honrado]]

In (11), the evaluation index of the indefinite and the main predicate is the same. On the other hand, in (12) two different possible worlds have to be considered: the real (actual) world w_r, in which Juan exists, and the dream worlds associated with the verb *soñar* 'dream' (the set W_s). The indefinite *un político* 'a politician' and the predicate *era honrado* 'was honest' can be indexed to the actual world w_r (12a) or to one of the dream worlds w_s (12b).

Beghelli (1998) proposes extending the use of choice functions to include association with possible worlds. Such choice functions would be indexed to a possible-world variable, to indicate that the function selects the relevant individual in a given world. For example $f_w(P)$ indicates that the individual selected by f from the set denoted by predicate P is an individual in the world w. In what follows world-indexed choice functions will be used across the board. Thus, sentence (11) would have the semantic representation (13):

(13) $\exists f[CH(f) \wedge [_{wr}$ was honest (f_{wr}(politician))]]
'There is a choice function f such that the politician selected by f in the real world (w_r) is honest.'

The choice function is indexed to the modal anchor w_r. Thus, the value of the function—the individual chosen from the set denoted by *político* 'politician'—is an individual existing in the real world (w_r), in other words, a real politician. On the other hand, the two readings of (12) are represented in (14):

(14) a. $\exists f[CH(f) \wedge [_{wr}$ Juan dreamed $[_{Ws}$ that was honest (f_{wr}(politician))]]]
b. $\exists f[CH(f) \wedge [_{wr}$ Juan dreamed $[_{Ws}$ that was honest (f_{ws}(politician))]]]

In (14a) *un político* 'a politician' is anchored to the real-world index w_r. In the alternative reading (14b), *un político* depends on or is anchored to the index contributed by the verb *soñar* 'dream' (one member of the set of worlds W_s). Thus, it denotes a man existing in the dream world—technically, with a "counterpart" in the dream world; cf. Lewis (1968). As observed by Farkas (1996, 1997), indefinites contrast with quantificational expressions in that the scope (or modal-anchoring) of the former is unrestricted with respect to modal/intensional verbs or operators. On the other hand, universal quantifiers cannot scope (covertly) over modal verbs. For example, sentence (15) is not ambiguous.

(15) Es posible que todo candidato ganara las elecciones del 2012.
is possible that every candidate won[SUBJ] the elections of-the 2012
'It is possible that every candidate won the 2012 elections.'

The only reading available is the contradictory one in which the universal quantifier has narrow scope, i.e. in an epistemically-accessible world all the candidates won. The reading consistent with the actual world, in which only one candidate won, is expressed by (16).

(16) A todo candidato le fue posible ganar las elecciones del 2012.
to every candidate to-him was possible win the elections of-the 2012
'It was possible for every candidate to win the 2012 election.'

In this sentence, the scopal order of operators matches their overt linear order and, unlike (15), it can be continued with a statement such as ... *pero X acabó imponiéndose.* '... but X won.' Intermediate readings also arise in modal dependency contexts. Consider (17):

(17) Cada profesor soñó que un alumno suyo había ganado el premio Nobel.
each professor dreamed that a student of-his had won the prize Nobel
'Every professor had the dream that a student of his had won the Nobel Prize.'

The above sentence has two readings, represented in (18):

(18) a. $\exists f[CH(f) \land \forall x[_{wr}$ **professor**$(x) \to x$ **dreamed** $[_{Ws} f_{x,wr}($**student of** $x)$ **won Nobel Prize**$]$ $]]$
'There is a choice function f such that each professor x dreamed that a student of x selected by f in w_r (the real/utterance world) had won the Nobel Prize.'
b. $\exists f[CH(f) \land \forall x[_{wr}$ **professor**$(x) \to x$ **dreamed** $[_{Ws} f_{x,ws}$ (**student of** $x)$ **won Nobel Prize**$]]]$
'There is a choice function f such that each professor x dreamed that a student of x selected by f in w_s (a dream world) had won the Nobel prize.'

In (18a), the student in the professor's dream exists in the actual world. Technically, the indefinite is anchored to w_r. In (18b), the student exists only in the professor's dream. In the relevant representation, the indefinite is anchored to a world w_s in the set of worlds associated with the dream W_s. Notice that the choice functions have two variables indexed to them: the world variable (w) and an individual variable (x), in order to indicate the relevant dual dependency.

4. Subjunctive mood and structural restrictions

The relevance of subjunctive mood in the interpretation of indefinites, more concretely in the emergence of non-specific readings, has been highlighted in numerous studies from Rivero (1979) to Quer (1998, 2009). The critical observation is that subjunctive mood triggers referential opacity or, in other terms, the obligatory non-specific reading of the modified indefinite. In the terms that we are using in this chapter, we would claim that certain modal-anchoring effects become blocked in the presence of the subjunctive. There are two structural contexts that will be shown to have an impact on this opacity effect: When indefinites are modified by subjunctive relative clauses, and when they occur inside a subjunctive clause. Let us consider the case of subjunctive modification first, as illustrated in (19):

(19) a. Luisa espera a un reportero que la entrevistará. Su nombre es Juan.
Luisa waits ANIM a reporter that her will-interview[IND] his name is Juan
'Luisa is waiting for a journalist who will interview her. His name is Juan.'
b. Luisa espera a un reportero que la entreviste.??Su nombre es Juan.
Luisa waits ANIM a reporter that her interview[SUBJ] his name is Juan
'Luisa is waiting for a journalist who would interview her.??His name is Juan.'

Indicative clauses, such as (19a), determine the referential or specific interpretation of the indefinite. In this case, the speaker is referring to a unique specific individual in the actual world (the world of the utterance). This amounts to the property of matrix anchoring of the indefinite to the world of evaluation of the matrix clause (the utterance world). The subjunctive clause in (19b) is incompatible with the referential interpretation of the indefinite, invalidating a continuation such as *His name is* . . . , where the specific individual referred to by the indefinite would be identified. Subjunctive mood is also incompatible with adjectives such as *determinado* 'certain,' which also determine or coerce the specific reading of the indefinite (Quer 1998).

(20) *Luisa espera a un determinado reportero que la entreviste.
Luisa waits ANIM a certain reporter that her interview[SUBJ]
"Luisa is waiting for a certain journalist who will interview her."

We can then conclude that the modal nature of the modifying proposition has an effect on the content of the indefinite, blocking or allowing the referential/specific interpretation. Let us now consider indefinites in subjunctive clauses selected as complements of propositional attitude verbs—cf. Quer (2010) for an analysis of broader issues of mood interpretation. In this structural environment, the non-specific reading is not always obligatory. In other words, the fact that an indefinite occurs in a subjunctive clause does not necessarily entail its non-specific interpretation. Nevertheless, this is not a universal generalization. The content of the propositional-attitude verb occurring in the matrix clause matters, as shown by Beghelli (1998). Although most intensional verbs selecting subjunctive proposition also select non-specific indefinites, it is also the case that indefinites selected by mandatory verbs (*ordenar* 'order,' *mandar* 'command,' *imponer* 'impose') and certain volitional verbs (*querer* 'wish,' *esperar* 'hope,' *añorar* 'miss,' etc.) do not block the specific reading of the indefinite. Consider (21):

(21) El coronel ordenó que un cabo sea condecorado, es decir, López.
the colonel ordered that a corporal is[SUBJ] rewarded, is say, López
'The colonel ordered that a corporal be awarded a medal, namely, López.'

In this sentence, the speaker refers to a unique individual who received the medal award. Thus, being in a subjunctive clause does not block a referential interpretation.

5. Islandhood effects and mood

When indefinites are modified by subjunctive relative clauses, this structural domain becomes an island for another indefinite occurring inside it. Consider the following sentences:

(22) a. Luisa quería un libro que perteneciera a un profesor, (??i.e., a Juan).
Luisa wanted a book that belonged[SUBJ] to a professor, (??i.e., to Juan)
'Luisa wanted a book that belonged to a professor, (??i.e., to Juan).'

b. Luisa quería un libro que perteneció a un profesor, i.e., a Juan.
Luisa wanted a book that belonged[IND] to a professor, i.e. to Juan
'Luisa wanted a book that belonged to a professor, (i.e. to Juan).'

In (22a), the embedded indefinite cannot scope over the relative clause, thus satisfying the complex-NP constraint (Ross 1967; Bosque and Gutiérrez-Rexach 2009). This sentence contrasts with (22b), where the modifying relative clause is in the indicative and the embedded indefinite *un profesor* 'a professor' can "escape" the island and receive a specific/wide scope reading.

If the determiner heading the complex DP is a definite, the wide scope (referential/specific) reading of the indefinite embedded in a subjunctive clause is still blocked.[2] Compare (23) and (24) in this respect:

(23) Luisa rechazará el libro que tenga/tenía un párrafo incompleto.
Luisa will-reject the book that has[SUBJ]/[IND] a paragraph incomplete
'Luisa will reject any book with an incomplete paragraph.'

(24) Luisa rechazará el libro que tenga cualquier párrafo incompleto.
Luisa will-reject the book that has[SUBJ] any paragraph incomplete
'Luisa will reject the book with any incomplete paragraph.'

---

2. The same generalization applies to determiners belonging to other semantic classes, such as universal, proportional or partitive determiners. What this seems to indicate is that the scopal behavior of indefinites is not determined by the properties of the c-commanding quantifiers.

The subjunctive variant of (23) is equivalent to (24). The subjunctive and the free-choice determiner *cualquier* 'any' both coerce the non-specific reading of *párrafo* 'paragraph.' In other words, any incomplete paragraph will trigger Luisa's rejection of the book.

When an indefinite occurs inside a subjunctive complement clause, it can escape this clause when the relevant environment is an instance of a complex-NP island configuration. This is the case both with nouns that obligatorily select the subjunctive (*propuesta* 'proposal,' *posibilidad* 'possibility') and those that only do so optionally (*hecho* 'fact'):

(25) El presidente rechazará la propuesta de que un ministro sea
the president will-reject the proposal of that a cabinet-member be
expulsado, (es decir, Juan López).
expelled, (is say, Juan López)
'The president will reject the proposal that a cabinet member be expelled (namely, Juan López).'

Indefinites also escape complex-NP islands headed by world-creating nouns (Farkas 1992), such as *sueño* 'dream,' *ilusión* 'illusion/hope,' *espejismo* 'mirage,' etc. These nouns normally refer to a set of worlds different from the actual world:

(26) Juan se arrepentirá de la fantasía de que cierto/un vecino le agreda.
Juan CL will-regret of the fantasy of that a-certain/a neighbor to-him attack
'Juan will regret the fantasy that a certain/a neighbor attacked him.'

This is also the case when the matrix DP is headed by an indefinite. For example, (27) has an interpretation in which the indefinite has scope over the noun *posibilidad* 'possibility' and its modal index is anchored to the actual world. This is what makes a continuation such as *His name is Luis Sánchez* possible.

(27) Hay una posibilidad de que un interventor sea presidente.
there-is a possibility of that an inspector become[SUBJ] president
'There is a possibility that an inspector be appointed president.'

Considering now the issue of intermediate readings, as was previously described, an indefinite may take intermediate scope with respect to a quantificational matrix element. Subjunctive mood does not block these readings:

(28) Todo profesor sospecha del rumor de que un estudiante haya suspendido.
every professor suspects of-the rumor of that a student has[SUBJ] failed
'Every professor suspects the rumor that a student of his has failed.'

In (28), the intermediate reading is possible, namely the one derived from the scopal order *todo* > *un* > *el*. In this interpretation there is not just one rumor—the scopal order *el* > *un*—, but rather every student is associated with a different one. Note that when world-creating nouns are modified by a relative clause modally specified in the subjunctive, an indefinite is not allowed to scope over the relative clause. Compare (29a), where the indefinite can be anchored to the actual world w_r, with (29b), where *un policía* 'a policeman' is anchored to one of the possible worlds determined by the dream.

(29) a. Juan se tomó a broma el sueño en que un policía lo asesinaba.
Juan REFL took to joke the dream in that a policeman him killed[IND]
'Juan took lightly the dream in which a policeman killed him.'
b. Juan se traumatizaría por el sueño en que un policía lo asesinase.
Juan CL traumatized by the dream in that a policeman him killed[SUBJ]
'Juan would be traumatized by the dream in which a policeman killed him.'

Let us consider now adjunct islands: those sentential environments with a non-argumental function in a sentence (antecedents of a conditional clause, rationale clauses, etc.) Indefinites in adjunct islands can uniformly scope over them, independently of mood choice (indicative, subjunctive), as the semantic paraphrases in (31) of the sentences in (30) show:

(30) a. Si un pariente mío muriera, me alegraría.

if a relative mine die[SUBJ], REFL would-be-happy
'If a relative of mine would die, I would be happy.'

b. Juan ha comprado un juguete para que un hijo suyo se entretenga.
Juan has bought a toy to that a son of-his REFL entertain[SUBJ]
'Juan has bought a toy to entertain a son of his.'

(31) a. There is a relative of mine *x* such that if *x* died I would be happy.
b. There is a son of Juan *x* such that Juan has bought a toy to entertain *x*.

From the empirical evidence that we have just considered, two main issues emerge: (1) Why does subjunctive mood condition scope and modal anchoring possibilities?; and (2) Why are relative clauses different in blocking wide scope (referential) readings and not allowing the island-escaping behavior of indefinites? These issues are somewhat problematic for strictly semantic (non-structural) explanations. For example, for Farkas (1992) intensional verbs would block the anchoring of the indefinite to the actual world. This hypothesis would correctly eliminate (33b) as a potential representation for sentence (32).

(32) La baronesa necesita un sirviente que sea inglés.
the baroness needs a servant that is[SUBJ] English
'The baroness needs a servant who is of English origin.'

(33) a. $\exists f[CH(f) \wedge [_{wr}$ **the baroness needs** $[_{Wn} f_{wn}($**servant who is English**$)]]]$
b. $\exists f[CH(f) \wedge [_{wr}$ **the baroness needs** $[_{Wn} f_{wr}($**servant who is English**$)]]]$

In sentence (32), the speaker is not referring to an actual servant, but to whoever satisfies her needs or requirements. Semantically, the choice function would pick a servant in her needs world. Thus, the representation (33b), where the choice function picks a servant in the world of the utterance, would be inadequate. Nevertheless, a proposal along these lines cannot capture the asymmetries described in this section. Other semantic proposals, such as Giannakidou (1998), claim that mood selection in the modal environment associated with a non-veridical verb or operator determines the frame in which the descriptive content of a relative clause has to be evaluated—cf. also Quer (1998, 2010). This account would also leave the structural facts presented above unexplained.

6. Subjunctive mood and the nature of modal polarity

In order to provide an answer to the empirical problem introduced in the preceding section, we will adopt the proposal by Brugger and D'Angelo (1995) and Beghelli (1998) that subjunctive mood should be treated as a (modal) polarity item—cf. also Bosque (1998a, 2012) on modal polarity in general.[3] Let us consider some evidence in this direction. Kadmon and Ladman (1993) claimed that the difference between the negative polarity and free-choice readings of *any/ningún* 'no' is explained by additional features related to widening and strengthening—cf. Chierchia (2006) for a reconsideration of these properties and their relationship to the computation of conventional implicatures. For example, the presence of *ninguna* 'no-fem.sg,' in *No me gusta ninguna (clase de) patatas* 'I do not like any potatoes' widens and strengthens the statement *No me gustan las patatas* 'I do not like potatoes.' In other words, the statement does not apply to potatoes in general or to a particular instance. Rather it widens its domain of application to any class. Second, negation applies to this entire expanded domain, so the coverage of negation is strengthened. Subjunctive mood exhibits similar properties. With respect to widening, if we compare the sentences in (34), it is apparent that they are similar in meaning.

(34) a. Me gustan los libros de terror.
 REFL like the books of terror
 'I like horror books.'
 b. Me gusta(n) cualquier libro de terror/ los libros que sean de terror.
 REFL like any book of terror/ the books that are[SUBJ] of terror

---

3. In the literature, a distinction is made (Stowell 1993) between intensional subjunctives (triggered by intensional predicates and operators) and polarity subjunctives (triggered by operators such as negation). It is a matter of debate whether the notion of modal polarity could be generalized to the intensional subjunctive (cf. Quer 1998).

'I like any horror book/ the books belonging to the horror genre.'

Sentence (34a) is a generalization on horror books, but not a universal statement. It allows exceptions such as . . . *pero no los escritos por Stephen King* '. . . but not those written by Stephen King.' On the other hand, the first variant of (34b) is a stronger generalization with no exceptions. The quantificational strength of *cualquier* 'any' is universal, not generic. Similarly, the effect of subjunctive mood in the second variant of (34b) is to widen the application domain of the generalization, which now admits no exceptions.[4]

The strengthening effect of the subjunctive, only observed when the subjunctive is under negation, is also apparent in sentences such as (35).

(35) No he visto a un profesor que enseña/enseñe lingüística.
 not have-I seen ANIM a professor that teaches[IND]/teaches[SUBJ] linguistics
 'I have not seen a professor who teaches linguistics.'

In the above example, the indicative counterpart refers to a specific individual teaching linguistics and the subjunctive variant strengthens or extends the scope of the negative statement to any individual who is a linguistics professor. Finally, note that a Negative Polarity Item (NPI) such as postnominal *alguno* 'any' cannot be licensed by non-local (matrix) negation, in an indicative environment, whereas subjunctive mood seems to act as a licenser:

(36) No conozco a persona que *tiene/tenga interés alguno en eso.
 not know ANIM person that has[IND]/[SUBJ] interest any in that
 'I don't know a person who has any interest in that.'

In (36), postnominal *alguno* (*interés alguno*) is an NPI, which can be licensed by negation or the appropriate licensing element (Bosque 1980).

---

4. The widening effect of the subjunctive could be related to the analysis of German *irgendein* and Spanish *alguno* in Kratzer and Shimoyama (2002) and Alonso-Ovalle and Menéndez-Benito (2003, 2010), which explicitly use domain widening to derive their properties. These authors argue that domain widening can be used for effects other than strengthening, such as avoidance of a false exhaustivity inference. The problem is that domain widening will not lead to strengthening in an upward entailing environment such as modal/subjunctive ones. Other accounts of the subjunctive (Villalta 2008) connect this property to its ability to generate contextual alternatives on a scale introduced by a predicate.

Since negation is not local—it occurs in the matrix sentence—we have to conclude that the NPI is licensed by the subjunctive. This raises an important issue, since it is not clear which property of the subjunctive is involved in licensing elements normally licensed by negation. Research on the syntax of polarity items during the nineties hypothesized that polarity relations derive from spec-head agreement relations at LF—cf. Bosque's (1994) treatment of NPI licensing, and Sportiche (1998) and Koopman (2000) for a more general perspective.[5] In this vein, it can be proposed that the subjunctive feature encoded in the verb has to be checked against a modal operator under ModP—a similar hypothesis is proposed by Giorgi and Pianesi (1997) and Manzini (2000).[6] Thus, we can formulate the following Modal Agreement Hypothesis: The modal feature [+subj] in a relative clause is attracted by a modal operator and, in turn, it triggers agreement of the modal index of the indefinite.

Agreement can be understood here as matching or identity in feature valuation, as in recent versions of the Minimalist Program (Chomsky 2001; Lasnik, Uriagereka, and Boeckx 2005; Pesetsky and Torrego 2007; Gutiérrez-Rexach and Sessarego 2011). Certain features of syntactic objects are lexically unvalued (Chomsky 2001), and get valued as a consequence of a syntactic process of agreement with an identical feature of another element (cf. Pesetsky and Torrego 2007). Thus, this recent work on agreement departs from the previous view of this operation as 'feature assignment' mechanism (Chomsky 2000). Rather, this process is viewed as an instance of 'feature sharing' (Frampton and Gutmann 2000; Pesetsky and Torrego 2007).

In the case of modal agreement, the Modal head acting as the "probe" triggers feature sharing with the goal elements within its scope. The relevant configuration at LF is the following one:

(37) $\text{Mod}_\alpha [\ldots \text{V[SUBJ]}_\alpha \ldots \text{INDEF}_\alpha \ldots]$.

Evidence for modal polarity licensing at LF was provided by Uribe-Echebarría (1994), who discussed the English contrast in (38). We will focus

---

5. On the other hand, see Szabolcsi (2004) for a critical analysis of the spec-head agreement position. It runs into problems with the observation that interveners for NPI licensing are also interveners for PPI anti-licensing.

6. The discussion of whether there is only one ModP, several modal projections—as defended by Cinque (1999)—, or if modal features are checked along others under a "syncretic" category—as argued by Giorgi and Pianesi (1997)—goes beyond the scope of this chapter. Similarly, we are neutral with respect to minimalist implementations of spec-head agreement (whether it involves actual feature movement or just the application of the Agree operation).

on the Spanish contrast in (39), in which the presence of the subjunctive brings in similar properties.

(38) a. That anybody would leave the company wasn't mentioned at the meeting.
b. *That anybody will leave the company wasn't mentioned at the meeting.

(39) Que el jefe tuviera/*tendrá que despedir a nadie no fue mencionado.
that the boss had[SUBJ]/will-have-to that fire ANIM nobody not was mentioned
'That the boss had/will have to fire anybody was not mentioned.'

As is well-known, it has been argued that the negative words *anybody* and (object) *nadie* 'nobody' require a c-commanding negation at Spell-Out (Laka 1990), as the ungrammaticality of (40) shows:

(40) *La compañía tuvo que despedir a nadie.
the company had that fire ANIM nobody
'*The company had to fire anybody.'

In this respect, all the sentences in (38) and (39) should be ungrammatical. Nevertheless, the contrasts are due to the nature of the modal auxiliary: *would* vs. *will* (Eng.) and subjunctive vs. indicative (Sp.). Ogihara (1989) claims that *would* has to be in the scope of the [+past] tense specification of the matrix clause at LF whereas *will* has to satisfy the opposite requirement—to be not in the scope of [+past] tense of the matrix clause. The temporal requirement on *will* prevents the reconstruction of the CP as the complement of *(it) wasn't mentioned at the meeting*. Thus, *anybody* is in a position outside the scope of negation and the sentence becomes ungrammatical. In (38b), *would* is not subject to this anti-reconstruction requirement, and the NPI ends up in the scope of matrix negation. Thus, we would have the following contrasting LF-representations, one well formed (41a) and the other ill-formed (41b):

(41) a. t_i wasn't mentioned$_{[past]}$ at the meeting [$_{CP}$ that anybody would$_{[past]}$ leave the company]$_i$
b. *t_i wasn't mentioned$_{[past]}$ at the meeting [$_{CP}$ that anybody will$_{[future]}$ leave the company]$_i$

In Spanish, the presence of the future form *tendrá* 'will have to' prevents the reconstruction of the CP as complement of *fue mencionado* 'was mentioned,' so *nadie* 'nobody' is not in the scope of negation at LF. Following Ogihara's and Uribe-Echebarría's line of reasoning, a subjunctive CP—or, more likely, just its modal feature—has to raise in order to check the modal feature of the verb. Nevertheless, the ulterior reconstruction of this feature/CP to a position where *nadie* 'nobody' is c-commanded by negation is not blocked:

(42) t_i no fue mencionado [$_{CP}$ que el jefe tuviera que despedir a nadie]$_i$

7. The derivation of relative clauses and indexing

Let us go back to our open problem: Why does subjunctive mood block the wide scope/specific reading of indefinites only in relative clauses, given that the modal anchoring of the descriptive content of an indefinite is unrestricted? The proposal that will be defended here is that there are certain derivational conditions on relative clauses blocking modal anchoring.

Within the raising analysis of relative clauses, the head noun originates in a clause-internal position and raises to a higher position in the matrix DP (Vergnaud 1974; Kayne 1994; Bianchi 1999). At the base, the head determiner selects a clause as its complement. The surface order requires raising of the noun to the specifier of CP position. The derivation would be as in (43):

(43) a.   [$_{DP}$ Det [$_{CP}$ ... N ...]]
      b.   [$_{DP}$ Det [$_{CP}$ N$_i$ [C' ... t$_i$ ...]]]

Recall that our proposed treatment of the subjunctive as a modal polarity element requires that it trigger agreement or identity of valuation between the modal indices in its scope. For example, the initial configuration for the spell-out (44a) would be the base representation in (44b).

(44) a.   La baronesa necesita un sirviente que sea inglés.
           the baroness needs a servant that is[SUBJ] English
           'The baroness needs a servant who is of English origin.'
      b.   La baronesa necesita un que sea [$_{SC}$ sirviente inglés]
           the baroness needs a that is[SUBJ] servant English

The arrangement in (44b) conforms to the raising analysis of relative structures. The indefinite determiner heading the DP complement takes a CP as its complement. The nominal restriction *sirviente* 'servant' is the subject of a postcopular adjectival small clause (Moro 1997) in (43b). It is in the scope of the subjunctive, and inherits the same modal index (45a). In order to derive the restrictive-relative clause, and the resulting overt order, the noun has to raise to the specifier position of the CP (45b):

(45) a. [un [$_{CP}$ [$_{C'}$ que Mod$_a$ sea$_a$ sirviente$_a$ inglés]]]
    b. [un [$_{CP}$ sirviente$_{ai}$ [$_{C'}$ que Mod$_a$ sea$_a$ t$_{ai}$ inglés]]]

After reconstruction of the nominal head to its base position, the relevant semantic representation is (46):

(46) $\exists f[CH(f) \wedge$ [$_{wr}$ **the baron. needs** [$_{Wn}$ **a** t$_i$ **that is**[SUBJ] f$_{wn}$(**servant**$_i$ **English**)]]]

Co-valuation or agreement between the modal index of the subjunctive and the indefinite at LF determines that the individual picked by the choice function is in the world w_n, which is a member of the worlds associated with the intensional verb *necesitar* 'need' (the set W_n).

(47) ... **need** ... [$_{Wn}$ V$_{subj=wn}$ ... f$_{wn=subj}$(...) ...] ...

Consequently, a relative clause becomes a "modal island" in the sense that the syntactic derivation must preserve co-valuation between modal indices and the indefinite becomes "trapped" inside the relative construction—cf. Drubig (2001); and von Fintel and Iatridou (2003) for a similar generalization stemming from epistemic modals. Stating it differently, the co-valuation requirement on modal indices would block reconstruction when such co-valuation is not preserved. This seems reasonable, since co-valuation is not the result of non-interpretable agreement in this case so its effects go beyond mere overt agreement (cf. Pesetsky and Torrego 2007). Rather, the co-valued indices will be interpreted semantically as referring to the same possible worlds. Thus, we have an instance of an application of the Agree operation that yields an interpretable result. As such, agreement exponents cannot be deleted and trigger blocking effects with respect to reconstruction. The modal index w_n is determined in (47) by the verb *necesitar* 'need.' On the other hand, transparent or extensional verbs do not impose modal agreement and do not block the modal anchoring of the indefinite, so this term may be anchored to the actual world or to higher indices.

When indefinites occur inside a modifying subjunctive relative clause, the indefinite is obligatorily non-specific, as (48) illustrates:

(48) No hablaré con el hombre que lleve un traje gris.
 not will-talk-I with the man that wears[SUBJ] a suit grey
 'I will not talk to the man wearing a grey suit.'

Modal agreement with the subjunctive determines that the index of the descriptive content of the indefinite's restriction is anchored to the same world as the subjunctive (w_{subj}). In other words, modal subjunctive agreement freezes the restriction of the indefinite in place and forces the index of the corresponding choice function to be identical to the one associated with the subjunctive verb. The Logical Form corresponding to (48) would be (49a), with the relevant co-indexing preserving modal agreement, and the semantic representation is (49b):

(49) a. No hablaré con el hombre [que Mod_a $lleve_a$ un [traje gris] $_a$]
 b. $\exists f[CH(f) \wedge [_{wr}$ **I will not talk to the man wearing** $[_{Wa} f_{wa}$ **(grey suit)**$)]]]$

Going back to example (22a), repeated below as (50), we see that in this case both indefinites (*libro* 'book' and *profesor* 'professor') are interpreted non-specifically:

(50) Luisa quería un libro que perteneciera a un profesor.
 Luisa wanted a book that belonged[SUBJ] to a professor
 'Luisa wanted a book that belonged to a professor.'

The first indefinite (*libro* 'book') is reconstructed inside the subjunctive clause and the second one (*profesor*) is trapped inside the subjunctive relative island, in parallel to the instance in (48).[7] Thus, both indefinites share the modal index of the subjunctive element and are interpreted intensionally in the want-world:

---

7. There are no subject/object or argument/adjunct asymmetries with respect to this property. The non-specific interpretation of the indefinite is obligatory when it occurs inside a relative clause, independently of its syntactic position.

(51) Luisa quería [$_{DP}$ un [$_{CP}$ t$_i$ [que Mod$_a$ perteneciera$_a$ a un profesor$_a$ libro$_{ai}$]]]

8. Not all islands are modal islands

The pattern that we have just seen emerging in relative clauses turns out to be more the exception than the norm, as will be argued in this section. For example, sentential complements of a noun do not act as modal islands. In other words, modal-index assignment to the indefinite is not blocked by the subjunctive environment. Consider (52):

(52) No he oído el rumor de que un trabajador tuyo haya sido despedido.
not have-I heard the rumor of that a worker yours has[SUBJ] been fired
'I have not heard the rumor that a student of yours has been fired.'

The indefinite in (52) may take wide or narrow scope with respect to the verb. It may be anchored to the actual world (w_r) or to the modal index associated to the world-creating predicate, in this case the noun *rumor* "rumor" (w_{rum}). These two options are respectively represented in (53):

(53) a. $\exists f[CH(f) \wedge$ [$_{wr}$ I have not heard the rumor [$_{Wrum}$ that f$_{wr}$ (**worker of yours**) has[SUBJ] been fired]]]
b. $\exists f[CH(f) \wedge$ [$_{wr}$ I have not heard the rumor [$_{Wrum}$ that f$_{wrum}$(**worker of yours**) has[SUBJ] been fired]]]

The modal index of the subjunctive in (53b) is determined by *rumor*, given that the modal feature of the subjunctive has to be checked by a modal operator and this requirement triggers identity of feature valuation. Being more specific, the noun *rumor* imposes a feature-checking (agreement) requirement on the modal head of its complement, a requirement that is satisfied through the Agree operation triggering identity of valuation:

(54) rumor$_a$ [$_{CP}$ Mod$_a$ ...]

Reconstruction is not forced in this case, unlike what happened with relative clauses. Thus, the indefinite *un trabajador tuyo* 'a worker of yours' does not need to stay within the scope of the subjunctive. Its modal index is determined according to Farkas' generalization, and wide, narrow and intermediate scope readings are possible.

When an indefinite occurs inside a strong island—not inside a relative clause—and it is within the surface scope of subjunctive mood, it still preserves its modal-anchoring freedom. Consider (55):

(55) No he oído el rumor de que Juan haya robado un libro tuyo.
not have-I heard the rumor of that Juan has[SUBJ] stolen a book yours
'I have not heard the rumor that Juan has stolen a book of yours.'

If additional structural factors were not into play, the indefinite *un libro tuyo* 'a book of yours' should inherit its modal index from the subjunctive, making the wide-scope reading impossible. In other words, anchoring of the indefinite to the actual world would not be possible. Nevertheless, assuming that modal indexing takes place at LF, the data shows that only the subjunctive operator has to inherit its modal index from *rumor* (a world index in the set W_{rum}). The modal index of the indefinite is determined independently by the modal index w_x of the choice function:

(56) $\exists f[CH(f) \wedge [_{wr}$ I haven't heard the rumor $[_{Wrum}$ that Juan has stolen f_{wx}(book of yours)]]]

Thus, this index can be freely equated to the actual world index or to those associated with *rumor*. The main difference with the representation of subjunctive relative clauses is that, as we argued above, in this latter case the subjunctive determines the index of the descriptive content of the indefinite, no matter whether this element is within its scope originally or after the reconstruction operation has applied. In (56) on the other hand, the index of the descriptive content of the indefinite may differ from the one associated with the subjunctive. Summarizing, there is a significant difference between relative clauses and the rest of the environments that qualify as structural islands but in the end do not behave as modal islands. Only subjunctive relative clauses force the external indefinite head to remain under the scope of the subjunctive after reconstruction and prevent the external anchoring of those indefinites occurring inside it. Clearly, we cannot explain this property by extending the reconstruction hypothesis, since the indefinite in (56) is not in a reconstructed position. The explanation, I claim, has to do with the mechanics of modal agreement.

A modal agreement mechanism has been proposed in this paper, which is in line with general requirements on the Agree operation, as currently understood in recent minimalist proposals. Such agreement operation triggers identity of valuation in the subjunctive index, the indefinites, and the modal operator licensing the subjunctive. The critical question is why other environments do not trigger obligatory modal agreement. Let us continue pursuing the connection between this asymmetry and the specific properties of the raising/reconstruction of the head noun in relative clauses. In Gutiérrez-Rexach (1999e) it is argued that, in certain constructions, raising of the noun is triggered to check agreement features related to degree properties and to activate the wide scope of a degree operator. Recently, Yalcin (2006, 2007) and Papafragou (2006) have proposed analyses of modal operators based on exploiting several denotational properties that are similar to those of degree expressions. If we assume that noun raising and checking of a degree/modal feature trigger obligatory wide scope of the associated operator (and the corresponding index), we can conclude that all other quantificational elements will be in the scopal domain of this operator. If the modal agreement principle has applied, this requirement will force the obligatory non-specific or dependent reading of the indefinites. On the other hand, in sentential complements of nouns and other structures, there is no raising process checking agreement features and activating the wide scope of the modal or degree element. Thus, indefinites within these environments (or modified by them) are free to anchor to other available indices or to the real-world index.

9. Conclusion

In this chapter, new data on the scopal behavior of indefinites in subjunctive environments has been examined. Although there is ample room for further investigation, the evidence seems to point in the direction of a conspiracy of syntactic and semantic factors in the determination of the relevant interpretive patterns. More concretely, the attested scopal freedom of indefinites is constrained by structural factors related to derivational reconstruction and degree agreement in relative clauses. This interplay paves the way for a simpler and more elegant explanation of an apparently unexpected asymmetry.

The old claim that subjunctive mood affects the referential possibilities of Spanish indefinite DPs is reexamined, mostly by considering new data with the goal of framing the issue in the context of current debates on the semantics of these terms. It has also been shown that purely-semantic accounts cannot explain why relative clauses seem to behave as stronger blocking environments than other structurally-similar domains. The proper explanation lies at the syntax/semantics interface and explores how restrictions on the derivation of relative clauses prevent certain indexing possibilities.

4

Existence and Beyond
Varieties of Having

1. Introduction

One of the cornerstones in the semantic analysis of indefinites has been the study of the so-called definiteness or indefiniteness effects and the ensuing distinction among determiner types that has been proposed: weak/strong, indefinite/definite, etc. The most prominent among this constellation of phenomena is probably a contrast that commonly emerges in existential sentences. Indefinite determiners and, by extension, cardinal or weak determiners (Milsark 1977) can occur in existential constructions whereas strong determiners cannot (Milsark 1977; Keenan 1987; de Hoop 1992; McNally 1998; Reuland and ter Meulen, 1987; etc.). The following contrast illustrates this well-established generalization:

(1) a. *There is(are) the/all the/each/every/most student(s) in the garden.
    b. There are some/two/fewer than three/many students in the garden.

"Existential-*have*" environments trigger the same contrast and have been claimed to obey the definiteness restriction too (Keenan 1987). In the following sentences, weak determiners are allowed as complements of the verb *have*, whereas strong ones are not:

(2) a. John has four/fewer than four/many cousins.
    b. *John has most of the/each/every cousin.

Nevertheless, there are several issues that merit further investigation and may lead to a better understanding of the definiteness restriction or of the role that *have*-sentences play in it. First, not all existential-*have* structures are identical, and several different readings can be clearly characterized. In this respect, the issue of their uniformity should also be addressed. This will probably help us in answering the question of whether there is a common core that should be considered the basic content of the verb *have*. Additionally, the distinction between existential/relational readings and non-existential readings will be argued to be a matter of contextual gradience.

A second important issue is related to certain significant evidence coming from cross-linguistic variation in verb choice: the so-called *have/be* alternation or, more properly, the *have/be/∅* alternation. Many languages use *be* instead of *have* to express copular or relational content. For example, Turkish and Latin use *be* systematically and most other languages (including English) do so at least in certain constructions. There are also languages where a copula is not required—some Bantu languages, Malagasy for certain constructions, etc. Morphological weakening or "bleaching" of the copular verb correlates with a language's ability to express certain semantic relations (kin, possession, etc.) through morphological cases. For example, in Turkish the meaning of *have* is expressed by the copula plus a genitive DP (Lees 1972; Kelepir 2007). This option is also possible in English, and other languages for possessive constructions: *This is ours* = *We have this*. In Latin, where the copular verb is *be* (*essere*), possesive meaning is expressed via dative case marking on the postcopular DP (Bauer 1996): *Libri sunt mihi* 'The books are mine.' Finally, in certain Malagasy *have*-constructions there actually is no copula linking the two terms of the *have*-relation (Keenan and Ralalaoherivony 2000; Paul 2006):

(3) Marary znaka Rabe.
    Sick child Rabe
    'Rabe has a sick child.'

(4) Be asa manahirana aho
    big work bother 1SG.NOM.
    'I have a lot of bothersome work.'

Evidence of this sort is the source for the Benveniste/Kayne generalization (Benveniste 1971; Kayne 1993), which amounts to the claim that *have* is the syntactic amalgam of a light or contentless copula and a preposition—cf. also Szabolcsi (1983), Freeze (1992), Uriagereka (1996), and Arregi (2004). If what is argued here is correct, it can be concluded that this analysis is also on the right track from a semantic viewpoint. The Spanish data presented in this chapter seems to be of interest for a general discussion of the issue because Spanish seems to be strongly on the *have* side of the *have/be*-alternation spectrum. In other words, the use of *have* is widespread to express a multitude of relations between the subject and the object. In this chapter, the main properties of the verb *have* and their connection with the (in)definiteness restriction are studied. Several varieties are characterized, in addition to the well-known existential-*have* construction: restricted existence, the locative reading, the essential and accidental readings, idiomatic constructions, etc. It is argued that it is possible to provide a uniform semantics for these constructions, beginning with the idea that *have* denotes a function attributing essential properties. The proposed analysis is implemented in Generalized-Quantifier Theory.

In general, what this chapter shows is that there are subtle interactions between semantics, the lexicon and contextual elements, which have normally been ascribed to pragmatics. Within the interface-centered approach advocated in this book, the evidence and analysis presented here clearly show that a reductionist approach to either the lexicon/semantics or pragmatics components is not desirable or even possible.

2. Existence, proper and restricted

Let us start with a revisitation of Keenan's (1987) generalization: Existential-*have* sentences are like existential-*there* sentences in expressing an assertion of existence—cf. Comorovski and von Heusinger (2007) for a critical study of the structural instantiation of existence. More concretely, one consequence of this generalization is that sentences such as those in (5) are assertions of existence, as the respective paraphrases in (6) show. In this respect, they are equivalent to those in (7):

(5) a. John has a dog.
    b. John has four cousins.

(6) a. A dog (owned by John) exists.
  b. John's four cousins exist.

(7) a. There is a dog owned by John.
  b. There are four cousins of John.

In considering these equivalences, there is an element introducing an apparent asymmetry. In most existential-*there* sentences, an XP modifier restricts the assertion of existence to those individuals in the universe under consideration satisfying the denotation of the XP. The assertion of existence does not normally affect the whole universe but rather a "slice" of it. This property makes contrastive statements such as (8) possible:

(8) There are two students in the garden. There is another student inside the house.

The presence of the restricting modifier is critical. If it is omitted, the discourse becomes odd:

(9) There are two students. ??There is another student inside the house.

The only way of improving (9) is to accommodate a restrictive (locative) relation by a pragmatic/rhetorical operation (Asher and Lascarides 2003). One such relation could be the result of the Contrast operation, accommodating the proposition '*x* not in the house.' Alternatively, the Elaboration operation would yield a similar result. On the other hand, it seems that in existential-*have* environments it is more difficult to accommodate such a restrictive relation. For example, (10) is not felicitous if the chair under discussion has four legs, and the second sentence is not a possible (contrastive or elaborative) continuation:

(10) The chair has three legs. #The chair has another leg too.

Nevertheless, to claim that *have*-sentences are incompatible with an explicit or implicit restriction would be incorrect. A more accurate hypothesis would be that the occurrence of a restriction could be alternatively impossible, possible or even necessary depending on the interpretation of the sentence or, more specifically, on the type of relation expressed by *have*. The modifying adjunct can at times express an explicit spatio-temporal restriction, as in (11):

(11) John has four cousins in the army. Another one is unemployed.

In other instances, the explicit restricting term denotes a property of the object:

(12) The chair has three iron legs. The other one is made of wood.

The restriction delimits the predication relation and, by consequence, the assertion of existence. We can then distinguish two types of assertions of existence: pure or unrestricted, and restricted. In the case of existential-*there* sentences only the restricted-existence reading seems to be possible. This idea would receive support from proposals that consider *there* as an expression of a contextual parameter (Freeze 1992; Hoekstra and Mulder 1990; etc.). The presence of this parameter would make possible the intrusion of a pragmatically-conditioned restriction. In other languages, this adverbial element is optional. Such is the case of weak *ahi* 'there' in Spanish (Gutiérrez-Rexach and Silva-Villar 1998).

(13) Ahi hay dos libros.
    there there-are two books
    'There are two books.'

(14) Hay dos libros.
    there-are two books
    'lit. * are two books'

Nevertheless, as argued by Gutiérrez-Rexach and Silva-Villar (1998) and Gutiérrez-Rexach (1999b, 2001a), both the weak pronominal and its null counterpart—or the incorporated pronoun *y*, if one is assuming a theory without null elements—encode free contextual variables or context sets (Westerståhl 1985). The presence of a context-set parameter activates the possibility of explicit or implicit restrictions. As will be argued below, *have*-sentences also give rise to restricted existence readings, which can be explained as a by-product of the presence of contextual parameters.

3. Existence and location

It has been observed that *there*-constructions have a locative-deictic reading that is quite different from the existential one. Consider the following contrast (Lakoff 1987):

(15) There is a man on the side porch.

(16) There is Harry on the side porch.

What sentence (16) asserts is not an existential statement, but one indicating the spatial location of Harry or is uttered while pointing at Harry. In this respect, the locative-deictic interpretation of *there*-sentences is not merely a variant of the restricted-existence reading that we considered in the previous section. The main contrast of this type of sentences with existential sentences is that the locative-deictic reading does not satisfy the definiteness restriction, as the grammaticality of (16) shows. Any other variant with a definite or strong determiner would also be grammatical: *There are those books on the table,* etc. The postcopular DP is not "discourse new" (Ward and Birner 1995). Additionally, the sentence normally has a characteristic intonational contour, where *there* receives the main pitch/focus accent and loses its clitic-like character, becoming a deictic term. This property is shared by other languages (Kayne 2008). In Spanish, the presence of strong *ahí* 'there' triggers the locative/deictic reading:

(17) Ahí/ahi está Harry en el porche.
 THERE/there is Harry in the porch
 'There is Harry on the side porch.'

This reading is also associated with some additional properties, such as the incompatibility with non-dislocated adjuncts (18b) or with genericity triggers (Gutiérrez-Rexach and Silva-Villar 1998):

(18) a. Ahí está Juan en el parque.
 THERE is Juan in the park
 'There is Juan in the park.' (locative)
 b. *Ahí está Juan, en el parque.
 THERE is Juan, in the park

Have-sentences exhibit the same behavior as *there*-constructions in this respect. A sentence such as (19) is a genuine locative-*have* construction:

(19) There you have the apple.

Sentence (19) is generally uttered to indicate the location of the apple under discussion. This is normally done in a deictic fashion, i.e. accompanying its utterance with a pointing gesture. Locative-*have* sentences do not obey the definiteness restriction either and require the insertion of the prosodically strong counterpart of *there*. In Spanish, only the strong adverbial non-clitic pronoun *ahí* is allowed:

(20) Ahí tienes a dos primos de Juan.
 THERE have-you ANIM two cousins of Juan
 'lit. There you have two of Juan's cousins.'

(21) Dos primos de Juan están ahí.
 two cousins of Juan are THERE
 'Two of Juan's cousins are there.'

There is a wide variety of locative readings, with different implications with respect to predication and event structure, as shown by Moreno Cabrera (2003). Our purpose in this section was to show that locative readings of *have* do not invalidate the existential generalization. They just have to be considered as inducing differential requirements.

4. Essential vs. accidental readings

Hornstein, Rosen, and Uriagereka (2002) claim that the predication relation established between the postcopular DP and the PP coda or adjunct is not semantically uniform. They link the two resulting readings to a contrast between what they call *integral predication* and *standard predication*. Consider (22):

(22) There is a Ford motor in my truck.

The above sentence can be interpreted as either (23) or (24):

(23) My truck runs on a Ford motor.

(24) A Ford motor is loaded in my truck (in the trunk).

The reading in (23) corresponds to the integral-predication relation. Here we will label this reading the *essential interpretation*. The object of the existential predicate in (23) refers to an essential part of the truck, since there is no truck without a motor in it. On the other hand, (24) would be a manifestation of the standard predication relation or what we will be calling the *accidental or contingent interpretation* of (22). In this case, the object is only contingently related to the truck. There could be one object or other loaded on the truck. The associated property is only an accidental property of the truck, subject to contextual variation. This is why we are calling this reading accidental. The predicate in (24) establishes the positional relation of the motor with respect to (inside) the truck. It is important to highlight the fact that we say that the reading is accidental and we are not saying that it emerges "accidentally." We are referring to the philosophical (and semantic) distinction between essential and accidental properties, the latter being those non-essential properties that may be associated with an entity (Carnap 1956; Bennett 1969; Gorman 2005). This distinction overlaps but is not equivalent to the individual-level/stage-level distinction (Carlson 1977b), given that there might be properties that are essential but are instantiated by a stage-level predicate. This characterization appears to be a better fit than the one proposed by Hornstein, Rosen, and Uriagereka (2002), since the relation that is established between subject and object in (23) is essential: One does not exist without the other. Establishing such a relation would be impossible in (25), and the only available reading would be the accidental one:

(25) There are two cans of soda in my truck.

The preference for one reading or the other is also related to contextual factors. Whether I have two cans of soda, a newspaper or a CD in my truck is subject to circumstantial variation. On the other hand, having a motor is an essential property of this truck or of any truck, and actually having one motor brand or other also identifies the model/type or brand of the truck. It is interesting to note that if we express (22) with a *have*-construction, only the essential reading seems to be allowed:

(26) My truck has a Ford motor.

Nevertheless, as it was the case above, this asymmetry between *there*-constructions and *have*-constructions is only apparent. Adding a circumstantial adjunct/secondary predicate dilutes the difference. For example, adding the modifier *in its trunk* forces the accidental reading and adding the modifier *following factory specifications* would trigger the essential reading:

(27) My truck has a Ford motor in its trunk. (accidental)

(28) My truck has a Ford motor installed following factory specifications. (essential)

Thus, it seems that an apparent asymmetry is again the result of the greater ability of *there* to associate with a contextual parameter. There are other factors determining the emergence of one reading or other, such as the nature of the object. For example, (29) only seems to have the accidental reading:

(29) My truck has a dent. (accidental)

This appears to be the case because *dent*, among many other result nouns, describes the object resulting from a previous action or event (Parsons 1990; Rothstein 2004) and, as such, its association with the subject of the have relation is accidental.

5. Varieties of essential *have*

The essential reading is not uniform in nature. There are several well-known varieties, depending on the relation established between the subject and the object:

Possession:

(30) He has a house.

Inalienable possession:

(31) Long John Silver only has one leg.

(32) A donkey's skeleton has 300 bones.

Part-whole:

(33) This house has four windows.

(34) A sonnet has fourteen verses.

Container–containee:

(35) That glass has wine.

When we say that these relations are essential in nature, we are referring to properties that could in principle be essential to the subject, the object or both. Nevertheless, what we will be defending here is that *have*-predication relates the essential attribute directly to the object and only indirectly to the subject. For example, a house and (its) windows are essentially related by the whole-part relation; or a glass and an amount of wine by the container-containee relation. What is not implied, of course, is that it is essential for a house to have four windows or for a glass to have wine, etc. There is an asymmetry in how the predication relation takes place. A given number of windows become an essential part of a house, because houses are customarily associated with having windows. Thus, windows become essentially related to a house. Similarly, wine, or any other liquid, are customarily ingested from a container (glass, cup, etc.), so their association to it becomes essential.

The nature of the relation between subject and object is lexically and contextually determined. Sometimes it is difficult to determine to which subtype an essential relation under consideration belongs, as more than one might be instantiated. Not all relations have existential-*there* equivalents. For example the container-containee relation expressed by (35) has an existential-*there* correlate in (36). The same happens with (37), which expresses the same part-whole relation as (33):

(36) There is wine in that glass.

(37) There are four windows in this house.

On the other hand, inalienable-possession relations are normally not expressed through an existential *there*-sentence:

(38) *There is a leg in Luis.

Furthermore, not all essential relations allow the same type of restriction or certain specific restrictions. For example, the possession relation in (30) can be (spatially) restricted as in (39). This possibility is not available for inalienable-possession and whole-part relations, as shown in (40).

(39) He has a house in New York.

(40) a. *Luis has a leg in ...
     b. *The glass has wine in ...

There are additional semantic constraints that go beyond the definiteness restriction and are a by-product of the nature of the complement. For example, when the relevant essential relation is the container-containee relation, if the containee is expressed by a mass noun, no determiner is allowed (even if it is a weak determiner). Some measure phrases (two tons, etc.) and partitive determiners are allowed:

(41) a. The glass has wine/*a wine.
     b. The boat has wood/two tons of wood.

A similar restriction seems to be satisfied by inalienable-posession relations (Español-Echevarría 1997; Guéron 2003): (42a) is grammatical, in contrast with (42b), because *leg* is a count noun. On the other hand, in the Spanish construction *tener grasa* 'be fatty: lit. have fat' in (43), the complement behaves as in (41):

(42) a. Peter has one/two legs.
     b. *Peter has leg.

(43) Los párpados de Juan tienen grasa/mucha grasa/*una grasa.
     the eyelids of Juan have fat /much fat /*a fat
     'Juan's eyelids are fatty/very fatty.'

6. Idioms in construction with *tener*

The verb *have* is used in many idiomatic constructions (O'Grady 1998; Espinal 2001; Espinal and Mateu 2010), in which the sequence 'verb + NP' behaves as a syntactic and semantic unit. This is why it is normally assumed that the NP incorporates into the noun (Baker 1988). The most interesting feature of these constructions for our purposes is that they share with existential-*have* constructions the property of satisfying the definiteness restriction. The verb *have* combines only with indefinite or weak NPs. There is a wide range of cross-linguistic variation in the use of *have* to express essential relations through an idiom. Among the *have/be*-alternation languages, there are some where *have* is dominant in expressing such relations. Consider the following examples with Spanish *tener* 'have':

(44) tener hambre 'be hungry'
 tener sed 'be thirsty'
 tener cara 'have nerve'
 tener ojo 'be astute'
 tener ideas 'have ideas'
 tener ganas 'be eager'

Idiomatic constructions of this sort have been argued to be the result of pseudo-incorporation operations (Massam 2001). Whereas strict incorporation processes only allow the incorporation of a nominal head into a verb ("V+N" sequences), verb-complement combinations resulting from pseudo-incorporation allow for the presence of full DPs under certain circumstances. First, the definiteness constraint is satisfied. *Tener* only combines with singular/plural bare nouns and weak determiners, as shown by the following examples:

(45) a. tener ganas/muchas ganas/algo de ganas
 have desires/many desires/some of desires
 'be eager/very eager/somewhat eager'
 b. *tener algunas ganas/ tres ganas
 have some desires/three desires
 '*be some-spec. eager/three(times) eagerness'

(46) *tener las/muchas de las/la mayoría de las ganas
 Have the/many of the/the majority of the desires
 'have the/many of the/most of the . . . '

Second, modification of the complement noun is allowed in several restricted cases. The noun can be modified by prenominal adjectives, as shown in (47) and (48). The adjective can be incorporated into the noun, as in (49). Finally, modification by certain PP modifiers is also possible (50).

(47) have a healthy appetite/*have an appetite

(48) a. *tener salud
       have health
       'be healthy'
    b. tener buena/mala salud
       'have good/bad health'

(49) a. tener cara
       have face
       'have nerve'
    b. tener caradura
       have face-hard
       'have a lot of nerve'

(50) a. tener un hambre de mil demonios
       have a hunger of 1000 demons
       'be really hungry'
    b. tener un cuerpo de modelo
       have a body of model
       'have the body of a model'
    c. tener una salud de hierro
       have a health of iron
       'be in perfect health'
    d. tener una borrachera de padre y muy señor mío
       have a drunkeness of father and very lord mine
       'be drunk to the gills'

Syntactically, the strict limitations on adjectival modification—only prenominal or incorporated modifiers are allowed—indicate that "A + N" sequences are not unrestricted. Some authors have actually proposed that prenominal adjectives also occupy head positions, and their surface position is the result of syntactic incorporation mechanisms—cf. Valois (1991); see also Cinque (1994, 2010) for alternative views respectively deriving adjective placement from head (noun) movement or XP movement.

Semantic restrictions on nominal modification are more interesting. We can claim that "N + modifier" combinations satisfy two principles: (i) They identify a class or prototype (Carlson 1977b, 2006; Dayal 2011); (ii) such prototype is familiar in the common ground. For example, in Spanish *tener cara* 'have a nerve' is possible but *tener pie* 'lit. have foot' or *tener espalda* 'have back' are not. Similarly, compare the grammaticality of (50d) above with (51):

(51) ??tener una borrachera nocturna/ilimitada/etc.
      have a drunkenness nightly/unlimited/etc.
      'be unlimitedly drunk/drunk by night'

In (50d) the complement noun is modified by an idiom, but postnominal modification is not productive. In other words, combining adjectives or PP modifiers of a similar content with the noun is not possible. The nature of this restriction is not strictly pragmatic. There is no contextual or real-world incompatibility between being drunk and doing so at night or for an extended period, as expressed in (51). Rather, the idiomatic modifiers in (50) convey protoypes conventionally established in a given language, and related to properties such as 'excess' (Bosque 1995), etc. Finally, note that the the definiteness restriction is also satisfied:

(52) tener una/*la sed enorme
      have a/the thirst enormous
      'be enormously thirsty'

7. *Have* + preposition

Another variety of constructions where the verb *have* exhibits incorporating behavior and is used to express essential properties of the object is the one where *have* and its complement combine through a prepositional element. The role of this preposition is to specialize or fine-grain the meaning of the predicate. Here are some examples:

(53) Have X against: John has something against the Dean
      Have X as: We have an incompetent as director

These combinations are more productive in languages with relational *have*. In Spanish, as in most Romance languages, numerous examples can be found: *tener como* 'consider; lit. have as'; *tener por* 'consider; lit. have for'; *tener contra* 'have against'; *tener para* 'have for'.

(54) a. tener a un idiota como padre
have ANIM a idiot as father
'have an idiot as a father'
b. tener a Pedro por idiota
have ANIM Pedro for idiot
'take Pedro for an idiot'
c. tener al portero de la finca por amigo
have the janitor of the building for friend
'consider the janitor a friend'

The term following the preposition establishes a function or relation of the complement with respect to the subject. In this case, the relation is not objective or extensional. Rather, it is based on a subjective attribution by the individual referred to by the grammatical subject, sometimes with the conversational implicature that such an association is not correct or is misguided (too naive, etc). Discourse continuations expressing a correction, such as the one in (55a), are possible. On the other hand, those expressing agreement are not, as shown by the discourse in (55b), which would become infelicitous after adding the second conjunct.

(55) a. Juan tenía a Pedro por idiota pero no lo era.
Juan had ANIM Pedro for idiot but not it was-he
'Juan considered Pedro an idiot but he was not.'
b. ??Yo tenía al portero de la finca por amigo y fue digno de mi confianza.
I had the janitor of the building for friend and was-he deserved of my trust
'I considered the building's janitor my friend and he was trustworthy indeed.'

The definiteness restriction is satisfied by the term of the preposition:

(56) a. *tener a Pedro por el/ese idiota
take ANIM Pedro for the/that idiot
b. *tener a Pedro como su amigo
have ANIM Peter as his friend

Only elements that may function as predicates and in general identify a class or prototype are allowed as terms of this preposition. Consider the following examples:

(57) a. tener a Pedro y Luis por amigos
 have ANIM Pedro and Luis for friends
 'consider Pedro and Luis friends'
 b. *tener a Pedro y Luis por dos/los amigos
 have ANIM Pedro and Luis for two/the friends
 '*consider Peter and Luis two/the friends'
 c. ??tener a Juan como un amigo
 have ANIM Juan as a friend
 'consider Juan as a friend'
 d. tener a Juan como un amigo de verdad
 have ANIM Juan as a friend of truth
 'consider Juan a true friend'
 e. tener a Pedro por el tonto de Carabaña
 have ANIM Pedro for the idiot of Carabaña
 'consider Pedro the greatest idiot'
 f. tener a sus abuelos por los Reyes Magos
 have ANIM his grandparents for the kings magic
 'consider his grandparents the Three Kings'

In all the sentences above, the adjunct identifies the type of essential relation associating the object and the subject. In general, in the *have somebody P XP* construction the predicate identifies a characterizing property of the object. The object is essentially related to the subject only as much as it becomes an instance of the characterizing property denoted by the XP. Determing which XPs are able to express such a relation is a matter of lexicalization and it also pertains to establishing how constructions become idiomatic in language.

8. Semantic incorporation revisited

Several syntactic and semantic theories have been proposed with the goal of explaining the main structural and semantic data related to *have* and its associated internal argument. A majority of these theories can be described as incorporation theories, although their assumptions and goals are very different. Syntactic incorporation theories are based on the idea that there is an X^0-movement operation incorporating the object noun into the verb. The possibility of having weak DPs as complements is explained by an additional hypothesis on determiner transparency for weak determiners. Weak determiners would not prevent the incorporation of the object into the verb (cf. Baker 1988; Masullo 1992). Other authors defend the hypothesis that bare nominal complements are headed by null determiners (Contreras 1986; Longobardi 1994, 2001), so the asymmetry is related to the requirements associated with a null head (government, etc.)

Semantic incorporation approaches also come in two varieties: (i) type-shifting theories or theories of lexical incorporation (van Geenhoven 1998; Dayal 1999, 2004); and (ii) mode of composition theories (Chung and Ladusaw 2003; Farkas and de Swart 2003). For both types of theories, indefinites have to be treated a properties. In lexical incorporation theories, a type clash is avoided by shifting the type of the incorporating verb:

(58) eat ⇒ $\lambda P \lambda x \exists y[\mathbf{Eat}(x,y)\ \&\ P(y)]$
apples ⇒ $\lambda x[\mathbf{Apples}(x)]$

By function application we obtain:

(59) eat apples ⇒ $\lambda x \exists y[\mathbf{Eat}(x,y)\ \&\ \mathbf{Apples}(y)]$

Thus, an incorporating verb would be one that is specified as combining with properties. In the resulting "V+NP" sequence, the internal argument is bound by an existential quantifier. It follows that the complement's existential force comes from the verb. This idea is not unproblematic. Generic readings of the complements of incorporating verbs would require a different lexical specification for the verb.

Objects in the existential-*have* construction are relational or transitive (Keenan 1987; Partee and Landman 1987; Partee 1999). The noun *friends*—the object of *have* in (60a)—can be considered relational if we assume that it has an implicit of hidden argument that is saturated by the subject, as shown by the following contrast:

(60) a. Juan tiene amigos.
'Juan has friends.'
b. *Juan tiene los amigos de Pedro.
'Juan has Pedro's friends.'

According to van Geenhoven (1998), *have* as an incorporating verb would be different from other incorporating verbs precisely in this requirement. It necessarily combines with a relation R (not with a unary property) and the resulting sequence would also inherit its quantificational force from the verb:

(61) *tener* 'have' ⇒ $\lambda R \lambda x \exists y [R(x,y)]$

The specification of *amigos* 'friends' as a relational noun is as in (62):

(62) *amigos* 'friends' ⇒ $\lambda y \lambda x$ [**Friends**(y) & **HAVE-relational**(x,y)]

The result of semantic incorporation is (63):

(63) *tener amigos* 'have friends' ⇒ $\lambda x \exists y$[**Friends**(y) & **HAVE-relational**(x,y)]

The main problem for this approach is that quantificational force comes from the verb, so we would be forced to postulate different entries for any given incorporating verb, depending on the varying quantificational force of its complement. This problem motivates the alternative theory of semantic incorporation introduced above, which is based on the idea that the verb and its complement would combine by a different mode of composition. For Chung and Ladusaw (2003), this mode of composition is restriction. Under this mode, the internal argument restricts the verb but does not saturate an argument position. For Farkas and de Swart (2003), the verb and the complement combine by the operation of unification.

Theories of semantic incorporation focus on the interaction of the verb and its complement and somewhat downplay the importance of the coda. Contrastingly, in Keenan's (1987) proposal, the role of the coda is critical in determining the truth conditions of existential-*have*:

(64) A VP[*have*] of the form [*have* NP XP] is interpreted as a function mapping an individual *x* to True iff the denotation of the XP is a member of the generalized quantifier denoted by the (transitive) NP applied to *x*.

Let us consider the truth conditions for (65) according to the above definition:

(65) Juan tiene tres amigos en el gobierno.
'Juan has three friends in the government.'

Sentence (65) would be True iff the property denoted by *en el gobienrno* 'in the government' (the set of individuals serving in the government in a particular situation) is a member of the generalized quantifier denoted by *tres amigos* 'three friends (of John).' The main properties of Keenan's account are the following ones: (i) Quantificational force clearly comes from the complement; (ii) the role of the XP coda becomes critical in determining the interpretation of the structure; and, finally, (iii) the semantic content of *tener* 'have' is light (membership). This account also takes care of what Saebo (2009) calls 'the pertinence problem': The subject binds a variable in its complements. For example, in (65a) above the three friends have to be friends of Juan (the subject).

I believe that most of these features are somewhat lost in semantic incorporation accounts. On the one hand, no matter whether we say that quantificational force comes from the verb itself or from an independent mode of composition at the top (discourse/sentence) level, the following insight is lost: For most complements—especially those headed by lexical determiners—, quantificational force seems to be coming from the complement itself. Lexical incorporation (type-shifting) theories cannot explain the interpretation of sentences where the copula is null, given that the pertinent relation between subject and object is established without the participation of a verb. On the other hand, within an account in the spirit of Keenan's original proposal this fact would actually be predicted, since the content of the copula is semantically bleached. It could actually be inferred even if it did not have a lexical expression. In what follows I will develop a more elaborate account of the semantics of *tener* that assumes the main features of Keenan's account. The two arguments of the function denoted by *have* will be treated as generalized quantifiers. The different readings of *tener*-structures will be analyzed as a consequence of the flexibility of *tener* with respect to the property of introducting an array of different relations, from essential to locative. This follows from the idea that *tener* is rather polivalent in nature or, equivalently, it is "bleached" in its core semantic content.

9. *Tener* and the attribution of essential properties

I will assume that the basic semantic content of *tener* 'have' is that of a light or bleached verb (Szabolcsi 1986b; Bosque 2001). It denotes a function relating two generalized quantifiers (sets of properties) (Keenan and Westerståhl 1997; Peters and Westerståhl 2006). This core bleached meaning explains why some languages use a single copula (*be*) for attribution and relational predication and why in some languages no copula is used at all (Doron 1983; González-Rivera 2010). The hypothesis that a zero element is associated with a bleached meaning seems more accurate than assuming that it can typeshift and be the expression of several (contentwise-heavy) semantic relations. The main issue becomes how to characterize the emergence of a relation between subject and object and why this relation is sometimes characterizing or essential, and sometimes it is not. Let us consider the following examples:

(66) Pedro tiene dos primos.
'Pedro has two cousins.'

(67) Pedro tiene jaqueca.
'Pedro has a headache.'

(68) a. *Pedro tiene una lágrima
'Pedro has a tear.'
b. *Pedro tiene una lágrima en el ojo.
'Pedro has a tear in his eye.'

(69) a. ??Pedro tiene una manzana.
'??Pedro has an apple.'
b. Pedro tiene una manzana en el bolsillo.
'Pedro has an apple in his pocket.'

In (66), the relation established between the subject and the object is that of kinship. If somebody is a cousin, he necessarily has to be somebody's cousin. Similarly, in (67) for something to be a headache it has to be a physiological process undergone or experienced by an individual. More concretely, there is no headache if no individual is experiencing it. In (68) and (69) a coda is needed to establish the proper relation. The role of *tener* (or of *be*/∅) is to connect the two terms of a relation, but the nature of such a relation is given by the object. The relationship that associates object and subject has to be one that is essentially/contingently associated with the object. In sum, a sentence of the form [NP$_1$ *tener*$_{ES}$ NP$_2$] establishes an essential relation between the two NPs: kinship, inalienable possession, etc. When the relation is not essential, the context or the XP modifier can supply the relevant relation, as in (69).

We can say that 'to be in a kinship relation with Pedro' is an essential property of *dos primos* 'two cousins' in (66); and 'being experienced by Pedro' is an essential property of *jaqueca* 'headache' in (67). In general, [NP$_1$ tener$_{ES}$ NP$_2$] is true if and only if (iff) one of the essential properties of NP$_2$ is to be in an essential relation R with NP$_1$. Formally:

(70) For arbitrary Q and i, Let Q_{NPi} be the generalized quantifier denoted by NP$_i$, and ES(Q_{NPi}) the set of essential properties of Q_{NPi}. Then, [NP$_1$ tener$_{ES}$ NP$_2$] is True iff $\exists A \in ES(Q_{NP2})$ such that $Q_{NP2}(A) \in Q_{NP1}$.

The issue of what counts as an 'essence' or, putting it differently, of which requirements have to be satisfied by a property in order to count as essential has been the subject of an extensive philosophical debate. Here I will adopt Lebiniz's criterion that there is no essence without existence (Plantinga 1974; Zalta 2000; etc.). A property of an individual can be considered essential for that individual iff that individual cannot exist without this property. If this property were lacking, it would be a different individual. Generalizing, we say that a property *P* is essential for a generalized quantifier *Q* iff it is a requirement for the existence of *Q*. In other words, *P* is an essential property of a generalized quantifier *Q* iff *P* is a member of *Q* iff the property of existence is a member of *Q*. Formally:

(71) Let Q_{NPi} be the generalized quantifier denoted by NP$_i$ and E the property of existence—the denotation of the predicate *exist* (Barwise and Cooper 1981; Keenan 1987). Then, for any property P $\in$ Q_{NPi}, we say that P is an *essential property* of Q_{NPi} (P $\in$ ES(Q_{NPi})) iff P $\in$ Q_{NPi} iff E $\in$ Q_{NPi}.

From this characterization, it would follow that those sentences where the attribution of an essential property takes place satisfy the definiteness restriction and, in the case of *tener*-sentences, Keenan's generalization also holds. Let us see why. Only existential generalized quantifiers (those for which $E \in Q$) occur in existential constructions and that a quantifier be existential would be a requirement for an essential property to be one of its members. If *P* is essential for *Q*, then *Q* has to be a (generalized) existential quantifer. Stating it differently, only generalized existential quantifiers have essential properties as members. The intuition behind this hypothesis seems clear. For example, it would be an essential property of *dos primos* 'two cousins' to be in the kinship relations with somene, as expressed in (66). On the other hand, the same could not be said of *este primo en concreto* 'this particular cousin,' of *todo primo* 'every cousin' etc., since E is not a member of these quantifiers in every model. This is so either because non-existential quantifiers are partial or not defined in some models (such is the case of definites) or because they are vacuously true in empty universes (such is the case with universal quantifiers). From the above discussion, the following semantic characterization of *tener* emerges:

(72) $tener_{ES}$ denotes the function f such that for any generalized quantifiers Q_1, Q_2, $f(Q_2)(Q_1)$ = True iff $\exists P \in ES(Q_2)$ such that $Q_2(P) \in Q_1$.

It follows as a theorem that Q_2 is existential. Let us consider the following sentence:

(73) La casa tiene cinco ventanas.
'The house has four windows.'

This sentence establishes an essential predication relation, that of being in a part-whole relation. It is an essential property of windows to be part of a building, i.e. the range of the whole-part relation (or its "passivization"; Keenan and Faltz 1985):

(74) $RG(\lambda y \lambda x[\textbf{Whole-Part}(x,y)]) = \lambda y \exists x[\textbf{Whole-Part}(x,y)]$

Let Q_1 be the denotation of *la casa* 'the house.' Then, the house has the property 'be in a whole-part relation with five windows,' i.e. the set *five windows*$(\lambda y \exists x[\textbf{Whole-Part}(x,y)])$, that is, $\lambda x \exists_5 y[\textbf{Whole-Part}(x,y) \& \textbf{House}(y)]$ is a member of *the house*. In general:

(75) Let Q_1, Q_2 be generalized quantifiers, R a relation, and for any quantifier Q, ES(Q) the set of essential properties of Q. Then, $tener_{R\text{-}ES}$ (have R essentially) denotes the function f such that $f(R)(Q_2)(Q_1)$ = True iff $RG(R) \in ES(Q_2)$ & $Q_2(R) \in Q_1$.

Consider now the following examples:

(76) a. Pedro tiene una casa.
 'Pedro has a house.'
 b. Pedro tiene una casa en Las Bahamas
 'Pedro has a house in the Bahamas.'

(77) Pedro tiene mi lápiz en el bolsillo
 'Pedro has my pencil in his pocket.'

The essential property P for *una casa* 'a house' in (75a) is 'being owned by somebody', i.e. the range of the possession/ownership relation: $RG(\lambda y\lambda x[Own(x,y)]) = \lambda y\exists x[Own(x,y)]$. Let Q_1 be the denotation of *Pedro*, (the individual generated by Pedro; Keenan 1996). Then, Q_1 has the property 'own a house,' i.e. *a house($\lambda y\lambda x[Own(x,y)]$)* = $\lambda x\exists y[Own(x,y)$ & $House(y)]$. Sentence (75a) is only a statement about home-ownership. On the other hand, (75b) and (76) are slightly different. (75b) is also a statement about home-ownership, but restricted to a particular location. Since the definiteness restriction is satisfied (**Peter has the house in The Bahamas*), we conclude that what is being predicated is an essential (characterizing) property (ownership). Although structurally similar, sentence (76) is very different from a semantic point of view. The speaker only states the location of a particular pencil inside his pocket. As a matter of fact, (76) does not entail or implicate that Peter owns my pencil now, quite the contrary. What we can infer from the above contrasts is that we have to distinguish the notions of essence, restricted essence and location. All of them can be expressed with *have*-sentences, but their semantic ingredients are distinct.

I will propose that the transition from one reading to another is a matter of degree, and that it is a by-product of contextual restriction: restriction to a (context) set. The role of the modifying adjunct is to introduce a context set restricting the predicated property. When the restricted property is still an essential property—the property is still in the set of essential properties (ES)—, then the 'restricted essence' reading arises. When the property is no longer essential (it is not in ES), we get the locative reading.

We will be treating context as a set-theoretical parameter, following Westerståhl (1985) and von Fintel (1994) among others. The notion of restricted essence or of a restricted essential property is defined as follows:

(78) Let Q be a generalized quantifier, E the property of existence and C a context set (usually expressed by the XP adjunct). Then, for any

property $P \in Q$, P is an *essential property* of Q in C ($P \in ES^C(Q_{NPi})$) iff $P \in Q$ iff $(E \cap C) \in Q$ iff $C \in Q$.

When *tener* is the copula used in restricted essential predication, nothing changes in the characterization of *tener*. The only difference is that the relation attributed to the object quantifier is an essential property restricted to a context set. Formally:

(79) Let Q_1, Q_2 be generalized quantifiers, R a relation, and for any quantifier Q, ES(Q) the set of essential properties of Q. Then, $tener_{R-ES-C}$ (have R essentially in C) denotes the function f such that $f(R)(C)(Q_2)(Q_1)$ = True iff $RG(R) \in ES^C(Q_2)$ & $Q_2(R) \in Q_1$.

Let us see how this would work in a concrete example. In sentence (77), a birthmark is in an essential part-whole relation with John.

(80) Pedro tiene una marca de nacimiento en la pierna izquierda.
'Pedro has a birthmark on his left leg.'

The predicative relation expressed here is not merely between Pedro and his birthmark. The adjunct *en la pierna izquierda* 'on his left leg' situates the appropiate whole where the birthmark is. In our terms, the relevant essential relation is 'whole-part' restricted to 'left leg.' The adjunct PP *en la pierna izquierda* determines the relevant context: The property of having a birthmak is an essential property of Pedro's leg (i.e. it is an essential property of Pedro "restricted" to his leg):

(81) Have on his left leg (a birthmark)(Pedro) = True iff RG(Whole-Part) $\in ES^{Left\ Leg}$ (a birthmark) & a birthmark(Whole-Part) $\in$ Pedro

In the locative reading, the relevant relation is not an essential property of the object (neither properly nor in a restricted sense). No restriction is imposed with respect to the relation associating subject and object:

(82) Let Q_1, Q_2 be generalized quantifiers, and R a relation. Then, $tener_{R-LOC}$ denotes the function f such that $f(R)(Q_2)(Q_1)$ = True iff $RG(R) \in Q_2$ & $Q_2(R) \in Q_1$.

10. Essences as modalities

One question that emerges at this point is how different varieties of essence are related to each other. So far, we have talked about properties in the set of essential properties (*ES(Q)*) for a given quantifier Q. An alternative approach would be to treat essence as related to a modal notion—cf. Fine (1994, 1995), Gorman (2005), and Cameron (2010) for alternative views on this issue. Although lack of space prevents a detailed development of this idea, the gist of this treatment would be as follows. First, following Fine's proposal, essences can be claimed to correspond to a special type of modality introduced by the essence operator ($\Box_e$): $\Box_e$ (*F, A*) is True iff it is in virtue of the nature of *F* that *A* iff it is essential for *A* that *F*. A family of operators indicating essence type would have to be introduced to capture the varieties of essential relations associated with the copula. In an existential-*have* construction, the verb *have* denotes a member of this family of essence operators. In (80, 81) we characterize two of these operators as follows:

(83) possession: $\Box_{\text{e-poss}}(Q_1, Q_2)$ = True iff it is essential for Q_2 to be owned by Q_1

(84) whole-part relation: $\Box_{\text{e-whole-part}}(Q_1, Q_2)$ = True iff it is essential for Q_2 to be a part of Q_1

This avenue of inquiry would not be incompatible with what we have established in previous sections. It would further clarify the interplay between the attribution of properties via copular predication and the association of contextual and/or modal parameters.

11. Conclusion

The verb *tener* 'have' is pervasively used in Spanish to express a variety of relations, in addition to possession or ownership. In this chapter we have presented a semantic account of a variety of readings associated to this verb, and we have connected them to its light or bleached nature, which explains its pseudo-incorporating nature. The question still remains as to whether an account of this sort can be extended to other light verbs, or to incorporating/pseudo-incorporating ones (cf. Espinal and McNally 2009, 2011).

5
Free Relatives and Quantificational Variability

1. Introduction

Quantificational force may be associated to expressions that are not considered quantificational in traditional and normative grammars. A paradigmatic instance of this state of affairs is the treatment of *wh*-words and expressions, which are not normally viewed as elements behaving as quantifiers or determiners. Even standard analyses of questions downplay the role of *wh*-elements to a certain extent. Nevertheless, from Higginbotham and May (1981) to Gutiérrez-Rexach (1997), other avenues of research have pursued the option of exploring the quantificational force of *wh*-elements, mostly within generalized-quantifier theory (Keenan and Westerståhl 1997; Peters and Westerståhl 2006). Pursuing this research program one step further, it seems of interest to explore other *wh*-expressions occurring in non-interrogative environments and assess whether their quantificational behavior is similar. The study of the quantificational force of free relatives (FRs) has been the subject of past and recent debates, mostly because some of the English data appears to be non-conclusive. For instance, it has been proposed that FRs are ambiguous between a definite and a universal reading (Tredinnick 1994; Iatridou and Varlokosta 1996). The existence of a universal reading was already noticed by Cooper (1983) who stated that "we shall interpret a headless relative such as 'what Mary says' as if it contains a hidden universal quantifier" (p.96). Consider the example in (1):

(1) What Mary said about John annoyed him.

The above sentence is ambiguous between a universal interpretation, paraphrased as 'everything that Mary said about John annoyed him,' and a definite interpretation, which can be paraphrased as 'the thing that Mary said about John annoyed him.' In the most influential theory on the semantic of FRs, Jacobson (1995) proposed treating FRs as definite-like entities. In ordinary definite DPs, number morphology disambiguates whether quantification is over atoms (absolute uniqueness) or pluralities (quasi-universal force), as the contrast between (2a) and (2b) shows.

(2) a. $\text{the}(\text{Girl}) = \iota x[\text{Girl}(x) \land \forall y[\text{Girl}(y) \to y \leq x]]$
     b. $\text{the}(\text{Girl}_{pl}) = \iota x[\text{Girl}_{pl}(x) \land \forall y[\text{Girl}_{pl}(y) \to y \leq x]]$

Since FRs are not morphologically marked for number, they are ambiguous. The maximality operation is expressed by the Russellian definite-description *iota* operator (ι) (Russell 1905). This operator can take either atoms or pluralities as its argument and selects a unique maximal individual. Thus, a FR denotes the unique maximal individual satisfying the relevant description. This would generate the two different readings characterized above. Jacobson proposes maximality to be encoded in the *wh*-word, implying for *wh*-clauses to always display maximality, regardless of context. Caponigro (2004) argues against this idea, since depending on the context, not all *wh*-questions have to absolutely be answered in a completely exhaustive manner. There seems to be room for the involvement of pragmatic and contextual restrictions on the interpretation of *wh*-clauses. Caponigro attempts to unify the account over both definite and indefinite free relatives (found in Italian) and claims that maximality results directly from the type mismatch itself, between the set denoted by the free relative (type <e,t>) and the fact that the rest of the sentence requires an individual (type *e*). Thus, unlike lexically headed relative clauses, which describe sets of objects, a free relative denotes a maximal plural entity, which explains the maximality presupposition.

More recently, Hinterwimmer (2008) has advocated an approach to free relatives and definite DPs based on the phenomenon of quantificational variability. He assumes that FRs are ambiguous in the following sense: There is always an empty determiner present which takes the overt Complementizer Phrase (CP) (whose specifier contains the *wh*-term) as its complement. This determiner comes in two closely related variants, D_1 and D_2. The first one has the denotation of the definite determiner and it returns an object of type *e*, namely the maximal (sum) individual that satisfies the predicate denoted by the respective CP with respect to either a contextually given situation or the world of evaluation (by default). The second one denotes a kind-forming operator that returns an object of type <s,e>, i.e. a function that for each possible world or situation returns the maximal (sum) individual satisfying the respective predicate in that world—cf. Chierchia (1998) and Dayal (2004). New findings in the area of cross-linguistics analysis, also enforce the idea of a complex picture and a non-uniform mapping between syntax and semantics (Kornfilt 2005; Caponigro and Polinsky 2011; Iatridou 2013).

In this chapter, taking into consideration evidence from Spanish, it will be argued that a uniform account to the problem of the quantificational force of FRs is not desirable or even tenable. The data considered strongly suggest that FRs come in different guises and that they express three different types of quantificational force: indefinite, definite and universal.[1] The quantificational variability of FRs is morpho-syntactically encoded in Spanish in the following fashion: (i) indefinite FRs require the presence of a *qu-* 'wh'-word: *que* 'what' , *quien* 'who', *quienes* 'who-pl.' etc; (ii) definite FRs follow the pattern "Definite Det. + *que*," where *que* 'that' is a complementizer: *el que* 'lit. the that', *la que* 'the-fem. that', *lo que* 'the-neut. that', *ese que* 'that(dem.) that'; and finally (iii) universal FRs are marked by the presence of the verb *-quiera* 'ever (lit.want)', which incorporates into a *qu* 'wh' form: *quienquiera* 'whoever', *cualquiera* 'whichever', *lo que quiera* 'lit. the-neut. that want.'

Several arguments will be presented in this chapter, defending the claim that the morphological classification sketched in the previous paragraph corresponds to or, more precisely, encodes a correlating tripartite distinction in quantificational force. It follows that the phenomenon of quantificational variability and the differences in interpretation that arise are morphologically triggered in a straightforward fashion. In this respect, we are again exploring a genuine interface grammatical property, more specifically, one interfacing morphosyntax and semantics. In the next section, *qu-* FRs will be analyzed. In sections three and four, the contrasting properties of definite

---

1. Wiltschko (1998) defends the hypothesis that FRs have the quantificational force of indefinites. She argues that not only the *wh*-words used in FRs are indefinites but also the universal interpretation should be really considered a generic interpretation. On the other hand, the definite interpretation can be considered a specific interpretation. Cf. Caponigro (2001, 2003) for an alternative approach to indefinite free relatives. This chapter expands and develops the arguments presented in Gutiérrez-Rexach (1999d), where the quantificational-variability hypothesis is also defended.

and universal FRs will be studied. Finally, in section five a semantic explanation of this classification will be proposed.

2. *Qu*-words in free relatives and indefiniteness

The existence of indefinite FRs has been suggested by Wiltschko (1998), Ramos-Santacruz (1994), Gutiérrez-Rexach (1999d), and Caponigro (2001, 2004). There is strong evidence for the claim that Spanish *qu-* 'wh'- FRs are semantically indefinites. First, only *qu*-FRs can occur in existential constructions, as shown in (3):

(3) Hay quien/*el que/*quienquiera que/*cualquiera que llegó tarde.
there-is who /*the that/*whoever that/*whichever that arrived late
'There is somebody who arrived late.'

Apparent exceptions to the above claim are the following examples in which definite FRs and *-quiera* 'want' FRs co-occur with the existential verb *hay* 'there-is':

(4) a. No me gusta lo que hay sobre la mesa.
not me like the-NEUT. that there-is on the table
'I don't like what is on the table.'
b. Pedro escogió uno de los que había para llevarse.
Pedro chose one of the-MASC.PL. that there-was to take
'Pedro chose one that was on the table.'

(5) a. Hablaré con quienquiera que haya en la fiesta.
will-talk-I with whoever that there-is-SUBJ. in the party
'I will talk with whoever is at the party.'
b. Hay cualquier libro *(que busques) sobre la mesa.
there-is whichever book *(that look-for-you-SUBJ.) on the table
'There is any book *(that you are looking for) on the table.'

In the above sentences, the existence of the entities referred to by the FR expression is not asserted. Rather, what is asserted is their location or purpose. In general, instances of locative or purposive *haber* (*haber* + PP) are not incompatible with non-existential determiners (cf. McNally 1998). In these cases, the presence of the PP adjunct is obligatory. In (5b), it is also shown how the addition of a subjunctive clause makes the sentence grammatical, which may lead to the hypothesis that *-quiera* behaves like a modal polarity item, needing a subjunctive modal context to be properly licensed (Bosque 1998a). In this respect, it would behave like other indefinite modal polarity items, such as *alguno* in *trabajo alguno* 'any job.'

A second piece of evidence for the existential force of this class of FRs is that, on a par with indefinite quantifiers, only *qu*-FRs uniformly show quantificational variability effects of the sort discussed by Berman (1991) and Lahiri (1991, 2002), in which the presence of an adverb of quantification alters the quantificational force of the sentence. Apparent universal or generic readings of indefinites are triggered by the presence of overt or covert operators in the clause (Diesing 1992). If we extend the same analysis to FRs, we can conclude that the generic reading of the examples in (6) arises by the presence of a covert generic operator in the clause, whereas in (7) it is contributed by the adverb of quantification *normalmente* 'normally'.

(6) a. Quien bien te quiere te hará llorar.
 who well you loves you make cry
 'Whoever loves you deeply will make you cry.'
 b. Quien ha mentido una vez, mentirá siempre.
 who has lied one time, will-lie always
 'Whoever has lied once, will always lie.'

(7) Normalmente quien estudia aprende.
 normally who studies learns
 'Normally, if someone studies he learns.'

These data have been analyzed in the literature as the result of the unselective binding of an indefinite variable or variables by the operator contributed by the adverb of quantification (Heim 1982; Diesing 1992; Gutiérrez-Rexach 2003). An extension of this analysis to the FRs above would lead to the hypothesis that a generic operator (*Gen*) binds the free variables contributed by the *wh*-words in the FR. Thus, the representation of (6a) would be (8):

(8) Gen x [**Loves you deeply (x)**][Makes you cry(x)]

Of special interest are the contrasts between the situation reading and the part reading of FRs embedded under the adverbial expression *en su mayoría* 'mostly', a phenomenon studied by Lahiri (1991, 2002) in the empirical domain of interrogatives. These readings have not received much attention in recent studies of FRs, but they provide additional important evidence for our claim. Consider the following sentences:

(9) a. Juan en su mayoría adora a quien adoras.
Juan in its majority adores ANIM who adore-you
'Juan mostly adores who you adore.'
b. Juan en su mayoría adora ?al que adoras/ a cualquiera que adores.
Juan in its majority adores ANIM-the that adore-you/ ANIM whichever that adore
'Juan mostly adores the one/whoever you adore.'

The above sentences are potentially ambiguous between two readings characterized respectively by the following property: (i) quantification over events/situations: 'in most occasions, Juan adores who you adore'; and (ii) quantification over individuals (parts/stages of an individual): 'Juan adores most of the traits of whoever you love'. Sentence (9a), the variant with *quien* 'who', can be interpreted as (i) or as (ii). The latter interpretation is absent in the two other variants in (9b), so it can only mean that in most occasions Juan adores who you adore. Thus, only the *qu*-FR exhibits a clear quantificational-variability effect with respect to the nature of the entities quantified over.

There are other factors that complicate the picture with respect to this point. One of them is the nature of the class to which the adverb belongs. For instance, adverbs explicitly introducing quantification over parts tend to trigger reading (ii) above, no matter which relative proform is used, as (10) illustrates.

(10) En su mayor parte, solía coincidir en tu juicio sobre quien/el que/cualquiera que te gustaba.
in its major part, used-to-I agree with your judgment about who/the that/whichever that you like
'I mostly used to agree on your judgment on who you liked.'

The preferred reading of (10) is one of type (ii) above, namely that the speaker agrees on the addressee's judgment with respect to most of the relevant individual's traits. Nevertheless, a reading of type (i) is still possible, depending on the context. Verb meaning may also influence the emergence of the ambiguity or its absence. Some verbs, such as *despreciar* 'despise' in (11), are incompatible with a 'quantification over parts' interpretation. In this sentence, only the reading in which situations are quantified over is allowed.

(11) Juan en general desprecia a quien/al que /a cualquiera que te parece bien.
Juan in general despises ANIM who/ ANIM-the that/ANIM whichever that you seem fine
'Juan in general despises whoever looks fine to you.'

A third piece of evidence of the existential nature of *qu*-FRs is the fact *qu*-FRs, but not those headed by definite determiners, may consistently receive a non-specific or property-like reading (Zimmermann 1993) under the scope of an intensional verb, as the contrast between (12a) and (12b) shows. (12a) is a statement about any person with the needed qualifications whereas (12b) states that Pedro needs a specific person with qualifications.

(12) a. Pedro necesita a quien tiene cualificaciones,
Pedro needs ANIM who has qualifications.
'Pedro is looking for a qualified person.'
b. Pedro necesita a ese que tiene cualificaciones.
Pedro needs ANIM that-(one) that has qualifications
'Pedro is looking for that one who has the right merits.'

All three types of FRs may receive the property-like reading when the embedded verb is in the subjunctive because of the world-creating properties of this mood (Farkas 1985; Quer 1998). This is illustrated in (13):

(13) Pedro necesita a quien/al que/ a cualquiera que tenga cualificaciones.
Pedro needs ANIM who/ ANIM-the that/ANIM whoever that has-SUBJ. qualifications
'Pedro is looking for that one who has the right merits.'

It is also a characteristic property of *wh*-indefinites that they can receive a discourse-dependent or a discourse-independent reading, as a function of whether they are anaphorically linked to an expression in the preceding discourse. *Wh*-expressions modified by *the hell* cannot be linked to a discourse referent already present in discourse—they are aggressively non D-linked in Pesetsky's (1987) terms. In the case of Spanish FRs, only *qu*-FRs can be aggressively non D-linked as a by-product of the attachment of the modifier *demonios* 'the-hell (lit.demons)' as the contrast between the examples in (14) and (15) illustrates.

(14) a. Dónde demonios hayas puesto eso no me importa.
where demons have-you put that not me bothers
'I do not care where the hell you have put that thing.'
b. Desconozco a quién demonios le has dado eso.
not-know-I to who demons him have-you given that
'I do not know to who the hell you have given that thing.'
c. Cómo demonios lo hagas es lo de menos, con tal que lo hagas.
how demons it do-you is it of least with such that it do-you
'As long as you do it, it does not matter how the hell you do it'

(15) a *Desconozo al que demonios le has dado eso.
not-know-I to-the that demons him have-you given that
b. *Desconozco a cualquiera demonios que le has dado eso.
not-know-I to whichever demons that him have-you given that
c. *Este/quien demonios venga da lo mismo.
this/who demons comes gives it same
'It does not matter who comes.'

3. Definite and universal readings of free relatives

Having shown the indefinite nature of *qu*-relatives, in this section a set of differences between "Det+complementizer" FRs and -*quiera*- FRs will be established. The goal will be to set these two relative classes apart from a semantic point of view and support the general claim in this chapter regarding their different quantificational force. Let us first consider differences with respect to the scope of negation. Indefinite FRs and -*quiera*'-ever' FRs exhibit scopal variation with respect to clausal negation. Consider the following sentences:

(16) a. Pedro no se casó con quien le dijeron
Pedro not CL married with who to-him told-they
'Pedro did not married who he was told to'

b. Pedro no se casó con cualquiera que le dijeron
Pedro not CL married with whichever that to-him told-IND—they
'Pedro did not married whoever he was told to'

Sentence (16a) has a reading in which negation scopes over the relative pronoun (*neg > quien*), namely 'Pedro did not marry a person he was told to marry.' The alternative scopal order (*quien > neg*) renders the reading 'there is a person such that Pedro was told to marry her and he did not.' Similarly, (16b) has readings corresponding to the orders *neg > cualquiera* and *cualquiera > neg*. The latter does not represent a commitment on the part of the speaker to knowledge of the identity of the individual referred to,[2] as the paraphrase shows: 'There is a person (whoever she is) such that Pedro was told to marry her and he did not.' On the other hand, definites do not generate a scope ambiguity due to their different quantificational nature (Szabolcsi 1997, 2010). They tend to be scope-independent expressions, especially with respect to extensional quantifiers (over individuals). The only possible interpretation of (17) is: 'There is an individual x such that Pedro did not marry her.'

(17) Pedro no se casó con esa que le dijeron.
Pedro not CL married with that that to-him told-they
'Pedro did not marry the one he was told to.'

It has been argued (Jacobson 1995; Dayal 1997) that English FRs are uniformly definites because they do not exhibit differential results with respect to three standard tests for determining universal force: (i) Only universal quantifiers can be modified by *almost/nearly* (Horn 1972; Carlson 1981) and English FRs cannot:

(18) a. For years, I did almost/nearly everything/anything you told me to do.
b. *For years, I did almost/nearly what/whatever you told me to do.

---

2. See Dayal (1997) for a distinction between the identity and the free choice readings of FRs. Subjunctive mood is incompatible with a wide scope reading of *cualquiera*:

(i) Pedro no se casó con cualquiera que le dijeran
Pedro not CL married with whoever that to-him told-SUBJ—they
'Pedro did not marry whoever he was told to'

(ii) Universal quantifiers license negative polarity items in their restriction (in the first argument of the generalized quantifier function they denote). FRs do not license negative polarity items (Ladusaw 1979; Jacobson 1995; Rullmann 1995b), as shown by the contrast in (19):

(19) a. I can read everything/anything that Bill ever read.
  b. *He got in trouble for what/whatever he did to anyone.

Finally, (iii) FRs support discourse anaphora whereas universal quantifiers do not. In (20a), the pronoun *it* can be resolved by anaphoric linking to the FR whereas this is not possible for its counterpart in (20b).

(20) a. John read whatever Bill assigned—although I don't remember what it was—, but I do know that it was long and boring.
  b. *John read everything/anything Bill assigned—although I don't remember what it was—, but I do know that it was long and boring.

In Spanish, the tests for determining the universal force of FRs are more conclusive and clearly suggest that *-quiera* 'want/ever' FRs are universal quantifiers: (i) The Horn/Carlson test of modification by *almost* is satisfied only by *-quiera* '-ever' FRs. Definite FRs cannot combine with *casi* 'almost' or *aproximadamente* 'approximately' (21), but *-quiera* FRs can (22):

(21) a. *Fui casi con el que me dijiste.
    went-I almost with the that me told-you
    'I went almost with the individual you told me to.'
  b. *Casi esos que llegaron tarde no vieron la película.
    almost those that arrived late not watched the movie
  c. *Aproximadamente esos que comieron pasta enfermaron.
    approximately those that ate pasta became-sick

(22) a. Fui casi con quienquiera que me dijiste.
    went-I almost with whoever that me told-you
    'I went almost with anyone you told me to.'
  b. Casi cualquiera que llegó tarde se quedó sin entrar.
    almost whichever that arrived late CL remained without get-in
    'Almost everyone who was late could not get in.'

c. Aproximadamente cualquiera que comió pasta enfermó.
approximately whichever that ate pasta became-sick
'Almost anyone who ate pasta got sick.'

Additionally, (ii) Only *-quiera* relatives license strong negative polarity items such as *importar un pimiento* 'give a red cent (lit. matter a pepper)' or *mover un dedo* 'lift a finger'(Bosque 1980). Qu- FRs or "Det + complementizer" FRs do not license NPIs in general. The contrast between (23) and (24) illustrates this differential property. Such NPI is licensed in (23) but not in (24).[3]

(23) a. Tu trabajas con quienquiera que le importe un pimiento su vida.
you work with whoever that CL matter a pepper his life
'You work with whoever gives a red cent for his life.'
b. Luis irá dondequiera que mueven un dedo por Africa.
Luis will-go wherever that lift-they a finger for Africa
'Luis will go wherever they lift a finger for Africa.'

(24) a *Tu trabajas con quien le importa un pimiento su vida.
you work with who CL matter a pepper his life
'You work with who gives a red cent for his life.'
b. *Luis irá con el que mueve un dedo por África.
Luis will-go with the that lift-he a finger for Africa
'Luis will go with the person who lifts a finger for Africa.'

Finally, with respect to property (iii), the contrast in (25) shows that *-quiera* FRs do not support discourse anaphora in a consistent manner, whereas "Det + Comp" FRs do so.

(25) a. ??Juan leyó cualquier cosa que el profesor recomendó; aunque no recuerdo lo que era, sí recuerdo que era larga y aburrida.
Juan read whichever thing that the professor recommended, although not remember-I it that was, yes remember-I that was-it long and boring
'??Juan read anything the professor recommended; although I

---

3. Notice that in the examples in (23, 24) it is essential for the emergence of the contrast that the mood is the indicative. Subjunctive mood would license the NPIs independently of the nature of the FR due to its nature as a non-veridical licensor (Giannakidou 1998).

don't remember what it was, I remember that it was long and boring.'

b. Juan leyó lo que el profesor recomendó; aunque no recuerdo lo que era, sí recuerdo que era largo y aburrido.
Juan read it that the professor recommended, although not remember-I it that was, yes remember-I that was-it long and boring
'??Juan read what the professor recommended; although I don't remember what it was, I remember that it was long and boring.'

4. Further evidence on universal free relatives

We can conclude from the data presented in the previous section that -*quiera* FRs have universal force. Furthermore, this hypothesis is confirmed by the behavior of this class of FRs in pseudocleft constructions. Higgins (1973) distinguished between the predicational and the specificational reading of a pseudocleft. Typically, when the expression following the copula is a predicate, the interpretation of the pseudocleft is predicational; when what follows the copula is a referring expression, the interpretation is specificational. Iatridou and Varlokosta (1996) observe that -*ever* FRs are OK in predicational pseudoclefts (26a) but not in specificational pseudoclefts (26b):

(26) a. What(ever) Mary bought was expensive.
 b. What(*ever) Mary bought was *Hamlet*.

To account for the difference between the two types of pseudoclefts, it has been claimed that, in predicational pseudoclefts, the FR is the argument of the expression following the copula. On the other hand, in specificational pseudoclefts the FR behaves as the predicate taking the postcopular expression as its argument (Higgins 1973; Williams 1983; Partee 1986; etc.). The two options are shown in (27):

(27) Predicational: ... $FR_{<e>}$ ...... $XP_{<e,t>}$ ...
 Specificational: ... $FR_{<e,t>}$ ...... $XP_{<e>}$ ...

Thus, only expressions that can type shift between the types <e> and <e,t> are able to participate in both constructions. A definite FR can typeshift between these two types via the *ident* and *iota* operations (Partee 1986) but universal FRs cannot. Thus, a definite FR should be associated with both interpretations, whereas a universal FR should only occur in a predicational construction. This prediction is borne out in Spanish and immediately follows from our hypothesis: "Det+comp" FRs can participate in predicational and specificational pseudoclefts as (28), and *-quiera* FRs behave as expressions of type <<e,t>,t> (universal quantifiers) and are blocked in specificational pseudoclefts, as in (29).[4]

(28) a. Lo que Pedro vio fue increíble.
the that Pedro saw was incredible
'What Pedro saw was incredible.'
b. Lo que Pedro vio fue esa película.
the that Pedro saw was that movie
'What Pedro saw was that movie.'

(29) a. Cualquier cosa que Pedro vio fue increíble.
whatever thing that Pedro saw was incredible
'Anything Pedro saw was incredible.'
b. *Cualquier cosa que Pedro vio fue esa película.
whatever thing that Pedro saw was that movie
'*Anything Pedro saw was that movie.'

The property of uniqueness also sets these two classes of Spanish FRs apart. Definites carry a uniqueness presupposition (Heim 1982; Roberts 2003) and, as expected, "Det + Comp" FRs tend to carry it too (30a), whereas modality-based FRs do not (30b).

(30) a. El/ese que llegó pronto se llevó un premio.
the/that(one) that arrived early CL got a reward
'The one who arrived early got a reward.'

---

4. Alternatively, it could be assumed that what changes is the type of the FR, whereas the type of the postcopular XP remains the same in predicational and specificational pseudoclefts. In "predicational" pseudoclefts, the FR would act as the functor (of type <<e,t>,t>) whereas the XP predicate would be the argument. In specificational pseudoclefts, the FR would have its standard type (<e>) and the XP would act as the functor. A generalized quantifier headed by a definite determiner can be lowered to type <e> (the type of the generator of the generalized quantifier: an individual), but a universal quantifier cannot be lowered to type <e> (they do not have a generator of this type). Thus, assuming with Iatridou and Varlokosta (1996) the identity in type between quantifier expressions and FRs, a definite FR should be associated with both interpretations, whereas a universal FR should only occur in a predicational construction.

b. Cualquiera que llegó pronto se llevó un premio.
whoever that arrived early CL got a reward
'Whoever arrived early got a reward.'

Finally, the incompatibility of *wh* expressions to which the modal element *-quiera* 'want' has incorporated with certain classes of determiners further confirms our point about its incompatibility with definiteness. A relative proform such as *cualquiera* 'whichever' can occur in an adjectival postnominal position within a noun headed NP. In these constructions, the corresponding DP cannot be headed by a definite, proportional or vague determiner. Only genuine existential determiners can co-occur with postnominal *cualquiera*. In (31), only the existential determiners *unos* 'a-pl.' and *tres* 'three' may head the corresponding DP, as shown by (31a). Other combinations with definite determiners (31b), universals (31c), and vague or specific determiners (31d) yield ungrammatical sequences.

(31) a. unos/tres libros cualesquiera
some/tree books whichever
b. *los/esos libros cualesquiera
the/those books whichever
c. *todo libro cualquiera
every book whichever
d. *muchos/algún libro(s) cual(es)quiera
many/some book(s) which(pl.)ever

To finish this section, it is worth mentioning a difference between English and Spanish *-ever* FRs: English *-ever* FRs are incompatible with collective predicates:

(32) a. *Whoever came gathered in the plaza.
b. *To whoever came I gave each an apple.

In Spanish, where there is a morphological contrast in number between the singular form *quien* 'who' and the plural *quienes* 'who-pl.,' the latter form can co-occur with collective predicates as shown by the contrast below:

(33) a. Quienesquiera que vinieron se reunieron en la plaza.
who-PL.-ever that came CL gathered in the plaza
'Whoever/people who came, gather in the plaza.'

b. *Quienquiera que vino se reunió en la plaza.
who-SG.-ever that came CL gathered in the plaza

(34) a. A quienesquiera que entraron les di una entrada a cada uno.
to who-PL.-ever that came CL gave a ticket to each one
'I gave a ticket to whoever came.'
b. *A quienquiera que entró le di una entrada a cada uno
to who-SG.-ever that came CL gave a ticket to each one

5. Free relatives and semantic operations

In the previous sections, it has been argued that Spanish FRs are not uniform in their quantificational force. This was shown by a variety of tests and contrasts which would be almost impossible to explain under the uniformity hypothesis. Instead, they receive a natural explanation under the view that FRs do not have to be associated with a unique quantificational force. We might then ask which element is the uniform or common one in FRs, if there is any. The hypothesis that I want to defend is that the common core of FRs is the representation corresponding to the structural level of a C' layer in a Complementizer Phrase (CP), namely a lambda abstract (see Heim and Kratzer 1998 for details). Thus, the translation associated with the C' expression *que vino* is as specified in (35):

(35) que vino 'that came' ⇒ $\lambda w \lambda x.\text{Came}(x,w)$

The indefinite and definite readings respectively arise from the contribution of operators in the specifier of the Complementizer Phrase (assuming that FRs correspond to a CP structurally). The presence of different operators in the specifier of CP renders the differences in quantificational force that have been shown in the previous sections. In the case of *qu*-FRs, the evidence presented so far suggests that there is an existential operator in the specifier of CP. The insertion of this operator in the process of translation from the syntactic level of LF to a semantic representation language may take place by application of a rule of Existential Closure (Heim 1982), if one assumes that indefinites and *wh*-expressions in general are translated as free variables. Alternatively, it could be claimed that *qu*-proforms are directly translated as existential operators, which would produce an equivalent result. The resulting configuration is the following:

(36)

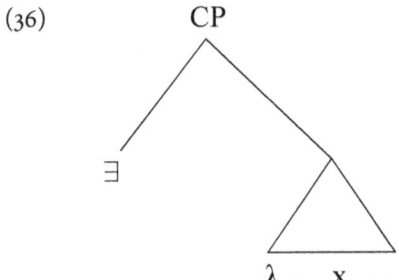

Thus, a FR is structurally a CP of type <<e,t>,t>. The descriptive content of the FR, corresponding to the content of the C', is the restriction of the existential operator, whereas the main predicate of the sentence corresponds to its nuclear scope (Gutiérrez-Rexach 1999a), as illustrated in (37). The existential operator is an expression of type <<e,t>,<<e,t>,t>> -a determiner function (Keenan and Stavi 1986)- and takes two predicates as its arguments: the lambda-abstract representing the descriptive content of the FR, and the lambda-abstract representing the main VP:

(37) [[$_{CP}$ quien [$_{C'}$ vino] ... P ...] ⇒ ∃(λx.Came(x,w))(λx.P(x,w))

Generic readings of *qu*-FRs, such as the one illustrated in (6, 7) in the second section of this chapter, are evidence of a quantificational dependence on adverbs of quantification over situations or parts. If one assumes that existential FRs are not quantificational, then the relevant covert or overt operator would unselectively bind the individual variable contributed by the *wh*-word. In an alternative theoretical scenario where the *wh*-word is translated as an existential determiner, a mechanism of Existential Disclosure (Dekker 1993, 2012; Chierchia 1995) is needed. Then, the existential quantifier is eliminated and the variable is bound by the adverb, yielding an equivalent result.

In the case of "Det + Comp" FRs, a definite description operator contributed by the definite determiner occupies the specifier of CP—see Brucart (1992) for a syntactic analysis along these lines, which would further motivate this proposal. In general, it can be claimed that definite FRs are derived from an LF operation of maximalization (Rullmann 1995a; Jacobson 1995; Grosu and Landman 1998; Gutiérrez-Rexach 1999c, 1999e) of the sort defined in (38) that applies at the CP level.

(38) Max(A) = ιx[A(x) ∧ ∀y[A(y) → y ≤ x]]
    FR (definite): Max(λx.Φ)

Let us now consider the difference between a singular and a plural definite FR. A singular definite FR, illustrated in (39), would receive the compositional translation in (40). Its plural counterpart in (41) is translated as in (42).

(39) el que vino
the that came

(40) **el (que vino)** = Max(λx.Came$_{sg}$(x)) =
ɿx[Came$_{sg}$(x) ∧ ∀y[Came$_{sg}$(y) → y ≤ x]]

(41) los que vinieron
the-pl. that came-pl.

(42) **los (que vinieron)** = Max(λx.Came$_{pl}$(x)) =
ɿx[Came$_{pl}$(x) ∧ ∀y[Came$_{pl}$(y) → y ≤ x]]

Thus, the only difference between them is a contrast in number that parallels the difference between singular and plural noun phrases. The maximality operator in (40) ranges over singular individuals and the one in (42) quantifies over plural individuals. The resulting structural configuration is in both cases as depicted in (43):

(43)

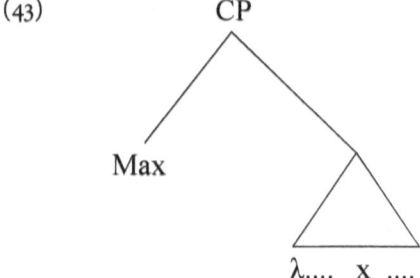

Generic readings also emerge in definite FRs in the presence of overt adverbs of quantification or habitual contexts:

(44) El que resiste vence.
the that resists wins
'the one/whoever resists wins.'

In this case, a dependence is established between the situation variable bound by the adverb of quantification or generic operator and the maximality operator on individuals. The sentence above means that in most situations under consideration the individual who resists ends up winning, as the English corresponding sentence states:

(45) Normally, the person who resists wins.

Let us now consider the semantics of *-quiera* FRs. Following Dayal (1997) and Kratzer's (1981, 2012) semantics for modality, it can be claimed that *-quiera* contributes a universal quantifier over possible worlds to the semantic representation. Rivero (2011) presents a more detailed analysis of the contribution of this element in postnominal contexts, such as (46):

(46) Deme dos libros cualesquiera.
 give-me two books whichever
 'Give me two books whatsoever.'

She takes as point of departure proposals on prenominal *cualquiera* (Arregui 2006; Menéndez-Benito 2010) instantiated in examples such as (47):

(47) Déme cualquier libro de estos.
 Give-me whichever book of these
 'Give me any of those books.'

Rivero argues that the postnominal version of *cualquiera* is a free choice item without inherent quantificational force. This item inherits a numerical value from a pronominal cardinal. It is a compound formed by the quantificational item *cual-* 'which' and the modal item–*quiera* 'ever; lit.-want'. This compound acts as an operator that induces modality.

The FR headed by an element based on–*quiera* is interpreted with respect to a set of alternatives to the world of evaluation and these worlds differ from the actual world only in the denotation of the FR. In (48), the translations corresponding to sentences with three different types of universal FRs is considered:

(48) a. Cualquier(w) 'which-want' ... P. ... Q ⇒
 $\forall w'[w'Rw \wedge \exists!(\lambda x.P(x,w'))(\lambda x.Q(x,w'))\,]$,
 where R is a contextually determined relation that defines for every

world w, the relevant alternative worlds w' in the knowledge/belief base of the speaker.
b. Quienesquiera (w) 'who-pl.-want' ... P. ... Q ⇒
 ∀w'[w'Rw ∧ ∃$_{\geq 2}$(λx.P(x, w'))(λx.Q(x, w'))]
c. Lo que quiera (w) 'the-neut. that want' ... P. ... Q ⇒
 ∀w'[w'Rw ∧ ι(λx.P(x,w'))(λx.Q(x,w'))]

As the translations above show, the content of the morphologically-complex universal relative proforms is factored in two different ingredients: (i) universal quantification over worlds and reference to a contextually determined relation between worlds that will determine for each world w, the set of alternative worlds that has to be considered; (ii) the *wh* or determiner element. This latter element determines the content of the second conjunct in the translations in a straightforward fashion. For example, if the *wh*-element is *cual* 'which,' there will be existential quantification over individuals in the alternative worlds w', with an additional uniqueness assertion/presupposition, as shown in (48a). If the *wh*-element is *quienes* 'who-pl.', the existential operator will carry a cardinality restriction (greater or equal to 2), as in (48b). Finally, in (48c), where the modal element syntactically incorporates into the sequence *lo que* 'the-neut that', the corresponding operator is a maximality operator. From this semantic configuration, it follows that there is a difference between English and Spanish universal FRs. Dayal argues that -*ever* FRs are underlyingly definite descriptions. As we have seen, this is not always the case in Spanish. It depends on the morphology of the element into which the modal verb incorporates. Our approach shares some similarities with Tredinnick's (2005) proposal, who argues that not all–*ever* FRs display universal behavior. She correlates this ability to the projection behavior of their presuppositions.

6
Correlatives and Degrees

1. Patterns of correlativization cross-linguistically

The study of quantification in relative clauses has taken a somewhat secondary role in current syntactic research on relative constructions of different varieties. It has normally been associated with island-like effects, as the ones described in chapter three of this book and many other ones. Nevertheless, this aspect does not tell us the whole story. A more intriguing step in the right direction would be to consider whether varieties of relative clauses not frequently considered either in contemporary formal grammar or in traditional and descriptive approaches encode or make possible subtle quantificational patterns. I believe this to be the case, and the purpose of this chapter is to explore one instance of such an approach: correlative structures.

There has been a surge in interest in the study of correlativization in the last decade, given its numerous ramifications at the syntactic and semantic levels. Nevertheless, a generalization that has remained unchallenged until recently is that correlativization is a strategy mostly limited to Indo-Aryan languages, possibly related to head-finality (Keenan 1985; Srivastav 1991; Bhatt 2003). Consider the Hindi example of a correlativization structure in (1):

(1)　Jo CD sale-par hai, Maya us CD-ko khari:d-egi.
　　　rel CD sale-on be-PRES, Maya DEM CD buy-FUT

'Maya will buy the CD that is on sale.'
lit. 'Which CD is on sale , Maya will buy that CD.'

This sentence exemplifies the correlativization process, where the relativized constituent has as its correlate not an empty element but rather an overt constituent, the demonstrative phrase *that CD,* instantiating the schema in (2):

(2) [[. . . Rel-XP$_i$ . . .] . . . Dem-XP$_i$ . . .]

In this chapter, I will argue that Romance languages, more concretely Spanish, also have correlative structures. Furthermore, correlativization is semantically restricted to relativization on degrees, as illustrated in (3):

(3) a. Cuanto más lo miro, (tanto) más me gusta.
         how-much more it look-I, (so-much) more me like-I
         'The more I look at it, the more I like it.'
     b. Cuanto menos bebo, (tanto) menos me enfado.
         how-much less drink-I, (so-much) less me get-angry-I
         'The less I drink, the less angry I get.'

As the above examples show, the overt presence of the correlate *tanto* 'so-much' is optional. The sentences in (3) and others of a similar nature instantiate the following pattern:

(4) [[. . . Rel-XP/deg$_i$ . . .] . . . DemPron-XP/deg$_i$ . . .]

As will be explained later, there are also other sentential variants of the degree correlativization schema, such as (5):

(5) A menos bulto, más claridad.
     to less clutter, more clarity
     'The less cluttered things are, the more clarity there is.'

This would show that correlativization is quite productive in Spanish—cf. also Sánchez López (2009) for a synchronic perspective and Elvira (1986) for diachronic evidence. These instances of correlativization should not be confused with other cases in which correlativization is only apparent:

(6) Quien mal anda, mal acaba.
who bad walks, bad ends
'Whoever misbehaves (to degree d), fails (to degree d).'

Here a parallel is established between degrees but, as will be argued below, correlative structures satisfy more stringent syntactic and semantic requirements. In what follows, I will be detailing the criteria that will eventually help us elucidate why (3) and (5) are correlative structures but (6) fails to meet the relevant conditions. In (6) we do not have a correlation between a constituent and a pronominal degree demonstrative, which is essential for the emergence of the 'dependent' correlative reading of (3). The repetition of the manner adverb *mal* 'bad' in (6) is optional, and any other word can be substituted for it, as in (7a). The dependence between degrees is also optional. For example, in (7b) there is no dependence or correlation between degrees.

(7) a. Quien come demasiado, acaba mal.
who eats too-much ends bad
'Whoever eats too much, ends up in trouble.'
b. Quien come demasiado, se acaba indisponiendo.
who eats too much, REFL ends getting-sick
'Whoever eats too much, gets sick.'

On the other hand, the correlation between degree terms established in sentences (3, 5) and others similar to them is stricter and has several systematic properties. Thus, it is not an instance of accidental or optional correlation. This chapter develops an analysis of the syntactic and semantic properties of Spanish degree-correlative constructions. A movement analysis for the construction is defended, along the lines of recent proposals on correlatives cross-linguistically. At the semantic level, the *wh*-form is claimed to behave as an unselective operator heading a tripartite quantificational structure on degrees. Several empirical properties are claimed to follow from this characterization. Culicover (1999) and Culicover and Jackendoff (1999) have studied this construction in English and defended their sui-generis status, in which idiosyncratic syntactic properties cannot be associated in a compositional/derivational fashion with semantic features. Culicover (1999) concludes that its special status as a 'syntactic nut' defies a compositional non-constructional treatment. Den Dikken (2005), taking cross-linguistic evidence into account, argues for a syntactic representation of comparative correlatives as genuine correlative constructions, the first clause being a relative clause adjoined to the second clause.

This chapter will be structured as follows: First, the fundamental structural properties of Spanish degree correlatives will be laid out; a syntactic analysis based on movement of the degree terms involved will be defended; and finally, the semantic properties of these constructions and others related to them will be analyzed. Overall, additional goals are to highlight the importance of syntactic edges in the computation of semantic properties at the syntax/semantics interface and to show how degree-related features are associated with quantificational structures instantiating well-known patterns in other domains.

2. A review of the fundamental structural facts

The degree correlative construction can take several shapes. Generally, a strict repetition of the comparative degree proform occurs (*más . . . más* 'more . . . more'; *menos . . . menos* 'less . . . less'):

(8) a. Cuanto más hablas, más te equivocas.
         how-much more talk-you more you are-wrong
         'The more you talk, the more mistakes you make.'
     b. Cuanto menos gano, menos quiero trabajar.
         how-much less earn-I less want-I work
         'The less money I make, the less I want to work.'

A cross-polar correlation of degree terms is possible too. In other words, the correlated terms can denote degrees or extents situated at opposite points of the relevant degree scale (*más . . . menos; menos . . . más*):

(9) Cuanto más comía, menos hablaba.
     how-much more ate-he less talked-he
     'The more he ate, the less he was able to talk.'

As shown by Kennedy (1997), cross-polar elements denote degrees in scales of opposite directions. A correlation is established between two opposite scales: a positive or increasing scale and a negative or decreasing scale. In essence, the critical point is to have a correlation between extents or degrees and also between degree shifts or changes. The fact that such degrees or degree changes instantiate contrasting monotonicity directions does not seem to be relevant in blocking or not the emergence of the correlation. What becomes critical in sentences such as (9) is that an increase associated with the event described in the first clause (eating to degree d) is correlated with an equivalent or parallel decrease in the degree associated with the event in the second clause (talking to degree d'). Thus, what is being correlated in (9) is not a particular degree but a degree increase and the corresponding decrease.

Finally, the correlate in the main clause may be a synthetic comparative (*mejor* 'better,' *peor* 'worse'). In (10), we have an instance of a cross-polar correlation with synthetic comparatives:

(10) Cuanto menos trabajo, peor me siento.
how-much less work-I worse me feel
'The less I work, the worse I feel.'

There is ample evidence showing that this structure is an instance of (single headed) correlativization and that it is related to matching or identity of degrees or degree changes. First, if the degree proform is absent either in the relative clause or in the main clause, the sentence becomes ungrammatical:

(11) a. *Cuanto lo miro, más me gusta.
 how-much it look-I, more me like-I
 '*The I look at it, I like it more.'
 b. *Cuanto menos corro, ando.
 how-much less run-I walk-I
 '*The less I work, I walk.'

The omission of *más* in the relative clause in (11a) or of *menos* in the matrix clause of (11b) renders the sentences ungrammatical. The degree demonstrative *tanto* 'such' is allowed as a modifier restricting the proform, whereas other degree quantifiers are blocked. For example, *tres veces* 'three times' is not allowed in (12a), and the elative *muchísimo* 'a lot-ELAT' is not possible in (12b). Scalar modifiers are also excluded, as (12c) shows.

(12) a. *Cuanto más lo miro, tres veces más me gusta.
 how-much more it look-I three times more me like
 '*The more I look at it, three times more I like it.'

b. *Cuanto menos trabajo, muchísimo más me canso.
how-much less work-I much-ELAT more me get-tired-I
'*The less I work, I get tired a lot more.'

c. *Cuanto mucho peor te portes, menos regalos te daré.
how-much a-lot worse you behave, fewer presents you will-give-I
'*The much worse you behave, I will give you fewer presents.'

Full comparatives are excluded, as in (13). Amount quantifiers, such as *pocos libros* 'few books' in (14), are not allowed in the correlative clause either.

(13) *Cuanto peor te portes, menos regalos te daré que ayer.
how-much worse you behave, fewer presents you will-give-I than yesterday
'*The much worse you behave, I will give you fewer presents than yesterday.'

(14) *Cuantos pocos libros más lees, menos te educas.
how-many few books more read-you less you become-educated
'The fewer additional books you read, the less educated you become.'

This is a specific characterizing property of the correlative construction. Relative clauses in general, or any other construction with inter-clausal dependents, do not trigger this specific restriction. In other words, open ended, free and unrestricted semantic comparison or correlation with degree quantifiers is possible and common in other structures, such as the coordinate structure in (15a) or the embedded clauses of a rationale/concessive kind in (15b, c):

(15) a. Lo miré mucho y me gustó tres veces más que antes.
it looked lot and me like three times more that before
'I took a hard look at it, and I liked it three times more.'

b. Parece que porque trabajo menos me canso muchísimo más.
seems that because work-I less me get-tired much-ELAT more
'It looks like, since I work less, I get a lot more tired.'

c. Cuantos más libros lees, aunque sean pocos, más te educas.
how-many more books read-you although are-they few more you educate

'The fewer additional books you read, the less educated you become.'

It may be concluded from this asymmetry that there has to be a 'matching' correlation between degrees in correlative constructions, a property that we will be characterizing later in more detail, since it appears obvious that this match is of a very specific kind, with a set of associated requirements. This matching requirement can arguably be related to a claim originally made by Srivastav's (1991), namely that the *wh*-degree term is coindexed with a pronoun. If this proposal is correct and a certain sort of coindexation is present, this would explain why open-ended, free or imprecise comparison or correlations are not possible. Finally, notice that there are no 'multiple-headed' degree correlatives in Spanish:

(16) *Cuantos más libros ... más ... más ...
how-many more books ... more ... more ...

This scenario contrasts with the situation in other languages, where multiple-headed correlatives are allowed. One possible explanation for this property is the fact that correlativization is restricted to degree elements in Spanish and, as we will be arguing later, the corresponding degree quantifier only binds one degree variable. In this respect, it should be noticed that constructions such as the one in (17) are instances of a coordinated structure, not multiple-headed correlatives, and as such they do not count as exceptions to this generalization:

(17) Cuanto mejor te comportes y más deberes cumplas, más te recompensarán.
how-much better you behave and more duties fulfill-you more you will-reward-they
'The better you behave and fulfill your duties, the more rewards you will receive.'

From the evidence considered so far, it seems that we can conclude that the correlative construction also exists in Spanish, even if it has not received much attention to date. It can also be concluded that this Spanish construction has several properties in common with correlativization in other languages, but it also has several idiosyncratic characteristics. Thus, a more detailed analysis seems to be of potential significance, not only for attaining a deeper knowledge of the map of relativization in Spanish and the syntax and semantics of correlativization in general, but also for exploring how degree restrictions on quantification operate at the interfaces.

3. Arguments for a movement analysis

There are two main competing analyses of correlative structures: (i) a base-generated adjunction analysis, defended by Srivastav (1991); and (ii) a movement analysis, argued for in Mahajan (2000), Bhatt (2003), and Pancheva and Bhatt (2004). For a theory of type (i), the relative CP is base-generated as an adjunct to the matrix TP—an IP in pre-minimalist terms. Thus, we would have an analysis such as (18):

(18)　[$_{TP}$ [$_{CP}$ cuanto DegP$_i$ ...] [$_{TP}$ pronoun$_i$]]

The CP has been argued to denote a generalized quantifier over degrees and bind a variable within the TP(IP) domain it is adjoined to. The 'matching' property is thus reduced to the quantifier-pronominal variable relation. On the other hand, those defending theories of type (ii), i.e. a movement analysis, propose the base structural analysis schematized in (19a):

(19)　a.　[$_{TP}$ [$_{DemP}$ [$_{CP}$ cuant- DegP] [$_{DemP}$ ...]]]
　　　b.　[$_{TP}$ [$_{CP}$ cuant- DegP ...]$_i$ [$_{TP}$ [$_{DemP}$ t$_i$ [$_{DemP}$ ...]]]]

The configuration in (19b) would be the structure derived after movement of the relative CP. Thus, for type-(ii) theories the relative CP is generated as an adjunct to the Demonstrative Phrase (DemP) in the matrix clause, and subsequently moves to an A-bar position, namely as an adjunct to TP. The matching property can be related to the binder-trace(copy) relation.

In general, the relevant issue at stake here is how to elucidate which one of these two analyses is the correct one, as applied to Spanish degree correlatives. In what follows, I will present several arguments showing that an analysis of type (ii) is to be preferred and that there is syntactic movement involved in the derivation of degree correlatives in Spanish. Evidence for the raising analysis comes from positional data and also from island-violation data. With respect to constituent positional data, it can be easily observed that degree elements have to occur in preverbal position. This generalization applies both to the degree pronoun in the matrix clause and to the degree pronoun in the relative CP. Consider the following contrast:

(20) a. Cuanto más leo, más aprendo.
   how-much more read-I more learn-I
   'The more I read, the more I learn.'
   b. *Cuanto más leo, aprendo más.
   how-much more read-I learn-I more
   c. *Cuanto leo más, más aprendo.
   how-much read-I more, more learn-I

Sentence (20a) becomes ungrammatical in (20b): *aprendo* 'I learn' precedes *más* 'more' in the matrix clause. Sentence (20c) is ungrammatical because *leo* 'I read' precedes *más* 'more' in the correlative clause. A similar reasoning can be applied to the patterns in (21).

(21) a. Cuantos más libros leo, más cosas interesantes aprendo.
   how-many more books read-I, more things interesting learn-I
   'The more books I read, the more interesting things I learn.'
   b. *Cuantos leo más libros, más cosas interesantes aprendo.
   how-many read-I more books, more things interesting learn-I
   c. *Cuantos más leo libros, más cosas interesantes aprendo.
   how-many more read-I books, more things interesting learn-I
   d. *Cuantos más libros leo, más aprendo cosas interesantes.
   how-many more books red-I, more learn-I things interesting
   e. *Cuantos más libros leo, aprendo más cosas interesantes.
   how-many more books read-I, learn-I more things interesting

Sentence (21a) shows the standard grammatical linearization. The NP *más libros* 'more books' cannot be split from the degree *wh*-word *cuantos* 'how much,' as shown in (21b, c). In a parallel fashion, the Degree Phrase *más cosas interesantes* 'more interesting things' has to be displaced to a peripheral position. It is not possible to leave the NP *cosas interesantes* 'interesting things' *in situ*—as in (21d)—or the whole DegP—as in (21e). Finally, movement of the DegP to the preverbal field is associated with subject inversion:

(22) a. Cuanto más lee, más aprende Pedro.
   how-much more read-he, more learns Pedro
   'The more Pedro reads, the more he learns.'

b. *Cuanto más lee, más Pedro aprende.
how-much more read-he, more Pedro learns

The preverbal placement of a displaced constituent and subject-verb inversion generally indicate movement to a left-peripheral position (Torrego 1984; Suñer 1984; Rizzi 1997; Gutiérrez-Rexach 1999e; Bosque and Gutiérrez-Rexach 2009). This data naturally leads to the hypothesis that the relative constituent [*cuant- más/más* XP] is a displaced constituent in Spec CP. The correlate *más* is also in a displaced position in Degree Phrase (DegP), as a 'matching' degree copy/variable. Thus, we would have the structure in (23):[1]

(23) [$_{TP}$ [$_{CP}$ cuanto más ...]$_i$ [$_{TP}$ [$_{DegP}$ t$_i$ más$_j$ [$_{TP}$ ... t$_j$ ...]]]]

Both the degree CP, which we can assume to denote a generalized quantifier as stated above, and the degree pronoun occupy specifiers of the same degree phrase at one point in the derivation. This would be possible if we assume a multiple-specifiers configuration, as we will be arguing here. In other words, syntactic projections are not limited to a single specifier layer (Koizumi 1995). The degree generalized quantifier moves one step further to check a feature related to sentential scope, given that degree quantifiers obligatorily take sentential scope (Heim 1996; Bhatt 2003). Further evidence of movement of the 'lower' degree pronoun/XP—the one in the matrix TP—is provided by island-violation data. The displacement of the degree element cannot escape strong islands. For example, sentence (24a) is fine but the structure in (24b) instantiates a violation of the complex-NP island constraint; and a sentential adjunct island is crossed in (24c):

(24) a. Cuanto más tiempo tengo, más libros creo que leo.
how-much more time have-I more books believe-I that read-I
'The more time I have, the more books I believe I read.'
b. *Cuanto más tiempo tengo, más libros reconozco el hecho de que leo.

---

1. For expository purposes, we use structural analyses with constituent labels and explicitly marking the points in the derivation where the copy is visible. Nevertheless, what we are saying could be easily implemented in a framework in which categorial labels where not used and derivations are driven by probe/goal requirements. Similarly, the movement operations advocated here (for consistency with the literature on the topic), can be more properly viewed as instances of internal merge along minimalist lines. This chapter develops some of the ideas presented in Gutiérrez-Rexach (2009).

how-much more time have-I more books see-I the fact of that read-I
'*The more time I have, the more books I see the fact that I read.'

c. *Cuanto más tiempo tengo, más libros me alegro si leo.
how-much more time have-I more books me be-happy if read-I
'*The more time I have, the more books I am happy if I read.'

The displacement of the DegP in the correlative clause is also constrained in strong-island environments, as the ungrammaticality of the examples in (25) illustrates. Movement of the degree relative *wh*-phrase also triggers weak-island violations, especially negation, as shown in (26).

(25) a. *Cuantos más libros es evidente la posibilidad de que lea, más voy a aprender.
how-many more books is evident the possibility of that read-I more going-I to learn
'*The more books it is clear the possibility that I read, the more I am going to learn.'

b. *Cuantos más libros me alegro si leo, más aprendo.
how-many more books me be-happy if read-I more learn-I
'*The more books I am happy if I read, the more I learn.'

(26) *Cuanto más no pidas, más te daré.
how-much more not ask-you, more you will-give-I
'*The more you don't ask for, the more I'll give you.'

This property is expected when movement of a degree quantifier is involved, as observed by Rizzi (1990), Szabolcsi and Zwarts (1993), and Bosque (1998b), among several authors. The explanation of what triggers sensitivity to weak islands developed by Szabolcsi and Zwarts (1993) is that there is an incompatibility between the denotational domain associated with degrees (a linear order) and the meaning corresponding to negation (the operation of complementation). Degrees have a scalar structure, so they denote a linear order. On the other hand, the negation operator denotes a function performing a complementation operation over a given domain. Thus, negation and degree quantification are incompatible. There is no element that can be identified as the complement of other in a linear order. Syntactically, movement of the degree term leaves associated degree copies (traces) behind. Thus, the matching requirement between degree elements that has been observed in the literature and that we also attested in section two has to be a match of all the relevant copies. There are two degree elements, one in the lower clause and another one in the preposed relative clause, as we mentioned above. These two terms have to be under the same projection at a certain point in the derivation (Koopman 2000; Kayne 2005). Actually the derivation advocated here bears a certain resemblance to the one proposed by Sportiche (1998) for clitic constructions.

We will assume that the degree proform moves to a Degree Phrase (DegP) projection to check its degree feature (Corver 1997; Neeleman, van de Koot, and Doetjesl 2004). Thus, the matching requirement between degree elements is syntactically expressed, as it is also the case with free relatives (Groos and van Riemsdijk 1981; Harbert 1983; Suñer 1984; etc). We postulate that the relevant semantic matching of degree terms takes place in a multiple-specifier configuration in DegP—cf. Koizumi (1995) for multiple specifiers in general; Matushansky (2002) for justification of the idea of movement of degree terms; and Gutiérrez-Rexach (1999e) for its application in other constructions. The proposed structure is represented in (27):

(27) $[_{DegP} [_{CP} DegQP] DegP_i [_{TP} \ldots t_i \ldots]]$

We now have all the ingredients needed in order to characterize the derivation of a degree correlative construction such as (28). The derivational steps are given in (29).

(28) Cuanto más leo, más aprendo.
How-much more read-I more learn-I
'The more I read, the more I learn.'

(29) a. $[_{TP}$ aprendo más $[_{CP}$ cuanto más leo$]]$
b. $[_{DegP} [_{CP}$ cuanto más leo$]_i$ más$_j [_{TP} \ldots t_j \ldots t_i \ldots]]$
c. $[_{TP} [_{CP}$ cuanto más $\ldots]_i [_{TP} [_{DegP} t_i$ más$_j [_{TP} \ldots t_j \ldots t_i \ldots]]]]$

The first step, sketched in (29b), would be movement of the degree relative CP and the degree pronoun to the specifier positions of the left peripheral DegP, deriving the matching requirement. A subsequent movement operation is shown in (29c). The relative clause would target the adjunct position of the matrix TP, in consonance with the raising analysis of correlatives advocated here. This would derive the expected Spell-Out order. The ungrammaticality of (12c) and (14) above suggests that the *wh*-word and the scalar modifier compete for the same structural position, namely the specifier of the projection headed by *más/menos* at some point of the derivation—cf. Brucart (2004) for the position of scalar modifiers with comparative operators. Den Dikken (2005) presents an alternative account, based on cross-linguistic evidence but ignoring several critical semantic facts.

We noted at the beginning of the chapter that correlativization is restricted to degree terms and that there are no nominal correlative structures. Nevertheless, there are a few constructions that might appear to be possible candidates. Sentences such as the one in (30), which are very common in sayings or 'refranes,' appear to be nominal correlatives. The same would apply to (31)):

(30) Dime con quién andas y te dire quién eres.
    tell-me with who go-you and you will-tell-I who are-you
    'Tell me who you hang around with, and I'll tell you who you really are.'

(31) Dime de qué presumes y te diré de lo que careces.
    tell-me of what brag-about-you and you will-tell-I of the that lack-you
    'Tell me what you brag about, and I'll tell you what you are lacking.'

Nevertheless, this idea can be easily dismissed once one realizes that the relationship between the two *wh*-terms in (30), and *quien* 'who' and *lo (que)* 'the (that)' in (31), is not one of correlativization. First, the two sentential fragments are connected by coordination, and there is no adjunction of one clause to the other one. Additionally, correlation or matching between the two *wh*-terms is not required. As a matter of fact, probably these terms could even be of different types. Although the *refranes* correlate terms of the same type in general, changing one of them to include expressions categorically different or denoting different entities is still unproblematic. Finally, the positional and movement-related restrictions attested in degree correlatives are not observed in this case. The presence of the second *wh*-term is not obligatory either. For example, sentence (32) is grammatical, and there is no correlating *wh*-element:

(32) Dime de qué presumes y te diré que careces de muchas cosas.
 tell-me of what brag-about-you and you will-tell-I that lack-you of many things
 'Tell me what you brag about, and I will tell you that you lack many things.'

4. The semantics of degree correlatives

In what follows, it will be claimed that the interpretation of degree correlatives is very similar to that of comparative conditionals (McCawley 1988; Beck 1997). Consider sentence (33):

(33) The more you read the more you learn.

The comparative conditional in (33) is interpreted as 'There is a degree/quantity d such that if there is an increase in the number d of books that you read, there is a corresponding increase d in what you learn.' Formally, we can treat *the* as denoting a determiner function on degrees. As such, it takes a degree argument to form a generalized quantifier on degrees (Heim 2006). This generalized quantifier combines with a second degree property (the main TP property) to yield a truth value.

(34) **the**$_d$ [you read d-more][you learn d-more]

The meaning of *the* can be taken to be the standard one associated with definite descriptions, namely the Russellian *iota* operator conveying uniqueness, existence and salience. We can treat these properties as presupposed content, as done in standard treatments by Heim (1982), and Roberts (2003) among others (this position is nevertheless subject to debate).

(35) ι_d [you read d-more][you learn d-more]

Thus, the operator corresponding to the determiner combines with two degree properties and binds two occurrences of the degree variable d. These occurrences are associated to the copies of the displaced degree terms in overt syntax. Let us now consider how this preliminary treatment of comparative conditionals can be applied to Spanish degree correlatives. In this case, we do not have an overt definite determiner. Rather, the correlative clause is headed by the *wh*-word *cuanto*. We have two options at this point. One possibility is to say that *wh*-elements do not have quantificational force of their own (Berman 1991). According to this hypothesis, *wh*-words would behave like indefinites in contributing free variables to the logical form of a sentence. These variables would be bound by an adverb of quantification or by a covert operator present in the surrounding context, hierarchically c-commanding the relevant variables. A prediction of this account is that quantificational variability effects are to be expected. In other words, since the *wh*-word does not have quantificational force of its own, the force of the sentence is to be determined by a covert/overt operator. Let us check whether this is the case for degree correlatives. Consider sentence (36):

(36) Generalmente, cuantos más libros leo, menos películas veo.
generally how-many more books read-I fewer movies watch-I
'Generally, the more books I read, the fewer movies I watch.'

Here the presence of *generalmente* 'generally' should be associated with the proportional ('most'-like) reading of the *wh*-variable. If *generalmente* 'generally' were an unselective binder in this example, i.e. an adverb of quantification binding more than one variable, the associated logical form would be as in (37), where the generic operator (*Gen*) binds both the individual variables x,y associated with *libros* 'books'/*películas* 'movies' and the degree variable d:

(37) $\text{Gen}_{x, y, d}$ [I read books(x) d-more][I watch movies(y) d-fewer]

Nevertheless, if we consider the actual reading of (36), it is clear that it would not be the one corresponding to (37). Rather, the correct logical form for the intended reading of (36) is (38):

(38) $\text{Gen}_e \, \iota_d \, \exists_{x, y}$ [I read(e) books(x) d-more][I watch(e) movies(y) d-fewer]

The formula in (38) can be paraphrased as 'In general, there is a number (degree) d such that if I read more books to that number (d-more books), I watch fewer movies in that amount (*d-fewer movies*).' The generic quantifier (*Gen*) associated with *generally* is a selective binder quantifying over events. The force of the quantifier associated with the individual variable restricted by the bare plurals is existential. Finally, the degree variable is bound by a definite determiner: In (36) we are referring to a unique degree (number or number interval). Thus, we have to conclude that a proposal that would leave the degree variable free (subject to external binding) would not make the correct empirical predictions with respect to the semantics of (36).

In general, definites do not give rise to pure unselective readings. Compare (39a) and (39b). Sentence (39b) lacks a reading with a generic/universal interpretation of the definite determiners, whereas (39a) is the paradigmatic example showing that indefinites do have generic/universal interpretations.

(39) a. If a farmer owns a donkey he beats it.
b. If the farmer owns the donkey, he beats it.

The variant with a definite determiner only has the felicitous reading in which the uniqueness and familiarity presuppositions of the definites are satisfied. We are talking about a particular (unique and familiar) farmer who beats the donkey he owns. In this respect, we have an almost complete parallelism with the comparative correlative construction from a semantic point of view. *Cuantos* 'how many' is not associated with a free variable lacking quantificational force. Rather, in (38) there is a iota operator (corresponding to a definite determiner) on degrees, as in (35). This property would also make degree correlatives similar in quantificational force to most free relatives, as defended by Jacobson (1995) among others—see also Caponigro (2004) on this issue, and chapter five on how some variation may arise. For example, the free relative in (40) has the quantificational force of a definite:

(40) Lo que leas es tu problema.
the that read-you is your problem
'What (i.e. the things) you read is your problem.'

Amount relatives (Carlson 1977a) are headed by the *wh*-word *cuanto(s)* 'how much/many' and also behave like definite descriptions quantificationally. In (41) we are saying that 'The amount of books you read is your problem,' where *cuantos* again has the force of a definite.

(41) Cuantos libros leas es tu problema.

How-many books read-you is your problem
'The number of books you read is your problem.'

The hypothesis that seems to be more natural and consistent with the empirical evidence seen so far is that the degree correlative is part of a tripartite quantificational structure headed by a degree definite determiner. The degree correlative thus denotes a generalized quantifier on degrees. The semantic representation of sentence (42) would be (43):

(42) Cuanto más lees, más aprendes.
      how-much more read-you more learn-you
      'The more your read, the more you learn.'

(43) Cuanto$_d$ [lees d-más][aprendes d-más]

As, can be inferred from (43), the *wh*-determiner simultaneously binds the degree variable in the free relative and the variable corresponding to the degree proform in the main clause. Binding of both occurrences of the degree variable forces the interpretive 'correlation' or match between the two degree terms. Intuitively, (42) means that, if you increase your reading by a certain amount, what you learn will also increase accordingly. In other words, there is a match or correlation between what you read and what you learn. Let us explain why this is so. It has been proposed (Kennedy 1997; Schwarzschild and Wilkinson 2002) that degree variables do not necessarily range over points but rather over intervals. In this respect, the ontological structure of degrees is similar to the structure of times, where the denotation of a variable t is a time interval not a moment. What this means is that the denotation assigned to a variable d would be a degree interval. Then—assuming that our proposal on the quantificational nature of *cuantos* is correct—the definite determiner would bind both degree variables in (43), and, as a consequence, d in (43) would be referring to a (unique and salient) degree interval d such that if your read d-more, you learn d-more. This is exactly the intended reading of (43).

There are a number of additional predictions that follow from this hypothesis. First, if the degree variables in (43) are bound by the determiner associated with *cuanto*, it is expected that no other degree quantifiers can occur in this sentence, given that they would lack a variable to bind. This would explain why a sentence such as (12a), repeated here as (44), is ungrammatical:

(44) *Cuanto más lo miro, tres veces más me gusta.
how much more it look-at-I, three times more me like
'*The more I look at it, three times more I like it.'

In this case, *tres veces* 'three times' would bind the occurrence of *d* in its most immediate scope and, as a consequence, *cuanto* 'how much' would fail to bind a variable in its nuclear scope, violating the principle against vacuous quantification. This principle (Kratzer 1995) states that quantifiers must bind a variable in their restriction and nuclear scope. The corresponding logical form would be ill-formed as shown in (45):

(45) *Cuanto$_d$ [I look x d-more][three times$_d$ [I like x d-more]]

Notice that it is not possible for one of the occurrences of the degree variable to be bound by a comparative operator either, as shown in (46):

(46) *Cuanto más cansado está que Pedro, más grita.
how-much more tired is-he than Pedro, more shouts-he
'*The more tired he is than Pedro, the more he shouts.'

This would follow from the commonly accepted idea that comparative operators bind degree variables—cf. Moltmann 1992 among many others. In (46), the comparative operator corresponding to *más ... que* 'more ... than' would bind the degree variable, preventing *cuantos* from doing so. Nevertheless, there are a few apparent exceptions to the generalization that we have just stated about the incompatibility of degree correlatives and other quantificational elements on degrees. For some speakers, sentences such as the ones in (47) improve if the complement of the two quantifiers is made explicit:

(47) a. Cuanto más cansado está que Pedro, más grita que Ana.
how-much more tired is-he than Pedro, more shouts-he than Ana
'lit. The more tired he is than Pedro, the louder he shouts than Ana.'
b. Cuanto peor te portes que tu hermano, menos regalos te daré que a tu hermana.
how-much worse CL behave-you than your brother fewer presents you will-give-I than ANIM your sister

'lit. The worse you behave than your brother, I'll give you fewer presents than your sister.'

These sentences are not grammatical in my own dialect, and in those of a majority of speakers I have asked. A more interesting case is represented by sentences such as (48):

(48) Cuanto peor te portas, aún más te odio.
how-much worse you behave, even more you hate-I
'The worse you behave, even more I hate you.'

It would seem that (48) contradicts what we have said with respect to (46) and (47). Nevertheless, this is only apparent, since in this case *aún* is a modifier, not a genuine quantifier. *Aún* does not bind the degree variable of *te odio* 'I hate you.' Its only role is to restrict the range of this variable to a contextually determined subdomain. It is not coincidental that *aun* also works as a focus particle, more or less equivalent to *even*. For example, in (49)

(49) Aun Pedro lo sabe.
even Pedro it knows
'Even Pedro knows it.'

Without getting into this connection in detail,—there are several prosodic, syntactic and semantic differences between the focal adverb *aun* and the modifying *aún*—, the role of modifying *aún* seems to also be related to evoking a set of degree alternatives (Rooth 1992b) and choosing one of them, leading to the relevant restriction. This is not the only particle with a similar function. In a related fashion, notice that the role of *más* 'more' and *menos* 'less' in (36) or *más* 'more' and *más* 'more' in (42), and so on, is precisely to restrict the range of the degree variable. This role is not incompatible with the quantificational requirements imposed by *cuanto*. Hence, the variable can be restricted by opposite degree modifiers, and we still get the required matching configuration. For example, the simplified logical form of (50) would look like (51):

(50) Cuanto más comas, menos vivirás.
how-much more eat-you less will-live-you
'The more you eat now, the less you will live.'

(51) Cuanto$_d$ [comas d-más][vivirás d-menos]

The modifiers *más/menos* 'more/less' restrict the range of the variable and indicate the relevant direction within the denotational domain of degrees (a linear order, cf. Szabolcsi and Zwarts 1993).

An interesting issue that will not be pursued here in detail for reasons of space is whether in some instances there is only indirect or functional dependence between the variables, in other words, whether there is an intermediate functional variable bound by an existential quantifier taking the second occurrence of the degree variable as its argument. This would allow for more flexible forms of correlation so that *d*-increments or changes in the restriction and the nuclear scope would not necessarily be identical. Recall that we made ample use of such functional variables in chapter three, when analyzing the scope of indefinites in relative clauses. The logical form of (50) would be (52):

(52) Cuanto$_d$ [comas d-más] ∃f [vivirás f(d)-menos]

5. Correlation and dependence

Since our main hypothesis is that the force of *cuanto* is that of a definite determiner, it would be interesting to check whether a true definite determiner would be able to substitute for this *wh*-word in a correlative construction. There is one clear candidate in this respect, namely the neuter determiner *lo*, which participates in a majority of degree relatives (Gutiérrez-Rexach 1999e):

(53) No sé lo alto que es.
    not know the tall that is-he
    'I don't know how tall he is.'

Interestingly, correlativization is not possible when a degree correlative clause is headed by *lo*, as shown in (54):

(54) *Lo más que compras, más quieres.
    the-neut more that buy-you, more want-you
    'The more you buy, the more you want.'

This incompatibility can be related to the different semantic content of *cuanto* 'how much' and *lo* 'the-neut.' It is true that they both function as definite determiners, i.e. they have uniqueness, familiarity, and salience preconditions (presuppositions) associated to them. Nevertheless, there is an important difference. The degree determiner *lo* imposes an additional condition of epistemic acquaintance. This condition can be formalized as a presupposition of specificity. Notice that the form *lo* is commonly used in exclamative constructions (Gutiérrez-Rexach 2001c), which normally require this presupposition:

(55) ¡Lo alto que es!
the-neut tall that is-he
'How tall he is!'

An utterance of (55) by a speaker would be felicitous only if he has a specific degree interval (height) in mind and he expresses surprise, amazement or some other emotional attitude towards that degree. Normally, what (55) expresses is that the person in question not only is very tall but also exceeds the speaker's expectations with respect to his height. On the other hand, *cuanto más* 'the more' tends to lack a specificity presupposition and behaves like a weak definite (Carlson 2001). The main characteristic of weak definites is that they normally support dependent readings. For example, the reference of the *bride* in (56) is not fixed to a 'specific' individual. Rather, it varies with the different situations (weddings) under consideration:

(56) Whenever I go to a wedding, I kiss the bride.

In Spanish, free-relative constructions with *wh*-terms tend to be associated with dependent readings—cf. chapter five, and Caponigro (2003). In the case of correlatives, the dependent reading is forced, since a correlation is established between two terms. There is another construction in which the dependent nature of *cuanto* is highlighted. It involves instances where a semantic correlation is established between two degree *wh*-terms (*cuanto . . . cuanto*). Here we talk only about semantic correlation because—as we mentioned before—these constructions do not meet the syntactic requirements needed to qualify as degree correlatives of the sort studied in this chapter. Here is an example:

(57) Tanto en cuanto me pides tanto en cuanto te presto.
so-much in how-much me ask-you so-much in how-much you lend-I
'I will lend you as much as you ask me.'

In this case, we have a correlation or dependency between what is being asked for and what is lent. Nevertheless, the syntactic derivation previously described does not apply here. There are no movement restrictions. The presence of the second correlative term is also optional, as shown in (58):

(58) Te prestaré dinero, tanto en cuanto me sea de utilidad.
 you lend-I money, so-much in how-much me is of utility
 'I will lend you as much money as I find it useful to me.'

In (58), the correlation or dependence of *cuanto* is with respect to a hidden modal/temporal operator. What (58) asserts is that in future situations the speaker will lend the addressee as much money as he sees fit. Thus, this type of dependent degree relatives does not appear to need a correlative term in order to trigger the required quantificational association. Another difference is that degree directional modifiers are not allowed in this case:

(59) *Tanto en cuanto más me pidas . . .
 so-much in how-much more me ask-you

Nevertheless, the main semantic difference with the standard correlative construction seems to be that in this type of sentences there is no quantification over interval/amount increases, but rather over fixed amounts/degrees. The logical form of (57) would be (60):

(60) **Cuanto$_d$** [you ask me for d][I'll give you d]

We have just examined a case of correlation that does not follow the pattern examined in this chapter. Nevertheless, it seems legitimate to inquire whether there are other constructions where the combination of syntactic and semantic properties that we have spelled out so far is also observed. Interestingly enough, there is one. Consider the sentence in (61):[2]

(61) A más guerra, más dolor.
 to more war, more pain
 'The more war there is, the more pain there is.'

---

2. There are also additional dialectal variants: *entre más. ., más; contra más . . . más . . .*

In (61), the same type of correlation or dependence between degree properties is satisfied, and the quantificational force of the sentence is that of a definite determiner. The most interesting property of (61) is that there is no overt *wh*-term. The correlate degree pronoun is required, and its absence triggers ungrammaticality:

(62) *A más guerra, dolor.
 to more war, pain

The most natural explanation for this asymmetry is that in (61) there is a hidden degree quantifier. As a matter of fact, the presence of *a* in the correlative clause seems to indicate this property. Recall that it has been claimed that *a* is in Romance a prepositional complementizer, with evidence coming from different constructions (Kayne 1994; Rivero 1994). For example, Rivero (1994) claims that Spanish infinitival imperatives—such as (63)—are complementizers headed by *a*, with an empty illocutionary force operator (64):

(63) ¡A correr!
 to run
 'Run!'

(64) [$_{CP}$ Op [a PRO correr]]

We can extend this proposal to (61), claiming that [*a más* ...] is a correlative CP. In this case, the null or covert operator would be one equivalent to *cuanto*, namely a definite description (ι) operator. This property would result in the identity in meaning with respect to standard degree correlatives.

6. Conclusion

In this chapter, it has been shown that Spanish has a productive correlativization construction: the degree correlative. This construction has very particular syntactic and semantic properties which have not been studied so far in detail—for a survey of the properties of this construction in English, see Smith (2010), and for several associated issues in Spanish see Sánchez López (2009). A movement analysis for the construction is argued for, relying on movement of two degree operators. Semantically, the *wh*-form is claimed to head a tripartite quantificational structure on degrees. Several properties have been shown to follow from this characterization. From a cross-linguistic viewpoint, the study of this type of correlatives also bears some interest, since it may show that correlativization involves more strategies than previously thought. This hypothesis would crucially depend on the nature of the entities quantified over, which will give raise to different matching effects—cf. Bhatt 2006 for a comparison of Hindi and Hungarian on this point. Ultimately, correlation of degrees, as a quantificational strategy required for the emergence of correlativization, entails a complex web of requirements at the syntax-semantics interface.

7

Concessive Conditionals and Scalarity

1. Prepositional conditionals

The analysis of conditional structures and their interpretation has taken numerous directions in the last decades: from the consideration of their status within different logical systems to the precise typology of structures instantiating conditional meaning. A very important ingredient which is still missing is to determine how to characterize the precise content of constructions having a conditional meaning at its core but also conveying other notions such as concession, opposition, etc. Finding the proper answer to these questions is important not only for the study of conditionals in natural language but also for a broader inquiry concerning the various relationships between grammatical structure and the semantic and pragmatic components, and the precise status of such interfaces.

In this chapter, a class of subordinate CPs introduced by the prepositions *por/con* 'by/with' will be studied. This construction can be described in strictly linear terms as follows: the prepositions *por* 'by' or *con* 'with' introduce the embedded or "subordinate" clause (EC). A quantificational term (a QP) or an adjectival phrase or term (an AP) follows the preposition and precedes the complementizer *que* 'that.' The remaining part of the embedded clause (EC) and the main clause (MC) follow. Schematically, the linearization arrangement in as in (1):

(1) Por/con + QP/AP + que + ... EC ..., ... MC ...

The main clause may also be linearized preceding the subordinate clause. The effects of this differential arrangement of clauses will be ignored here and only surface linearizations of the type described above will be analyzed. In other words, we will not consider in this chapter arrangements where the subordinate clause follows the root structure. The associated effects are mostly of a pragmatic nature (Bosque and Gutiérrez-Rexach 2009) and do not affect the issues addressed here.

The following sentences instantiate the construction type described above:

(2) Por más que estudies, no aprobarás.
by more that study-you not will-pass-you
'No matter how hard you study, you won't pass.'

(3) Por mucho dinero que tenga Pedro, seguirá sin ser feliz.
by much money that has Pedro, continue without being happy
'No matter how much money Pedro has, he will still remain unhappy.'

(4) Por poco que estudies, aprobarás.
by little that studies, will-pass-you
'If you study a little, you will pass.'

(5) Con algo que entretengas al niño, estará contento.
with something that entertain-you to-the child, will-be happy
'If you entertain the baby a bit, he will be happy.'

This construction has not received systematic attention in the Spanish tradition of grammatical studies. When it has been considered, it has normally been treated as a variety of the class of concessive constructions. A representative of this idea is Alarcos (1994, 375), who groups these types of examples as concessives. In his own words: "*Sinónimas son ciertas construcciones degradadas por 'que' contiguas a un adjetivo o a un adverbio precedidos por la preposición 'por'*" ('Several constructions degraded by *que* and attached to an adjective or an adverb preceded by the preposition *por* are equivalent'). Alarcos' intuition about the structural similarity of these sentences seems to be correct and, in section four, some arguments will be provided pertaining not only to surface similarity but also to uniformity of derivation and semantic composition.

At the same time, however, there are two main amendments that have to be made with respect to a proper semantic/pragmatic characterization. First, all these examples are "degree constructions" (Gutiérrez-Rexach 1999e), i.e. constructions where reference to degrees and degree properties is made. Additionally, despite the fact that these constructions share a structural similarity or core, it can be shown that they may be split in two clear different groups from a semantic/pragmatic point of view: concessive conditionals and material conditionals.

Sentences (2, 3) are concessive constructions. In RAE (1972), it is stated that "*en el periodo concesivo, la subordinada expresa una objeción o dificultad para el cumplimiento de lo que se dice en la oración principal; pero este obstáculo no impide su realización*" ('in a concessive sentence, the subordinate clause expresses an objection or difficulty to the fulfillment of what is stated in the main clause. Nevertheless, this difficulty does not prevent its realization') (p. 557). Other constructions expressing concessive content, although not identical to (2, 3), are the following ones—see RAE (1972, 558); Alarcos (1994); Koenig (1992); Koenig and van der Auwera (1988); Koenig and Siemund (2000); Crevels (2000); Flamenco García (1999); RAE (2009, §47); etc. for description and analysis of concessive constructions:

—*Disjunctive concessives:*

(6) Estudies o no estudies, no aprobarás.
study-you or not study-you, not will-pass-you
'Whether you study or not, you will not pass.'

(7) Vayamos al cine o no, la tarde va a ser aburrida.
go-SUBJ.we to-the cinema or not, the afternoon goes to be boring
'Whether we go to the movies or not, the afternoon is going to be boring.'

—*Free choice concessives:*

(8) Estudies lo que estudies, no aprobarás.
study-you the-NEUT. that study-you, not will-pass-you
'Whatever you study, you will not pass.'

(9) No importa cuanto estudies, no aprobarás.
    not matter how-much study-you, not will-pass-you
    'No matter how much you study, you will not pass.'

—*Focus concessives, namely, sentences introduced by a focus particle* (incluso/hasta *'even,'* etc.):

(10) Incluso si estudias mucho, no aprobarás.
     even if study-you much, not will-pass
     'Even if you study a lot, you will not pass.'

(11) Hasta cuando lleva maquillaje, la presentadora resulta fea.
     even when has make-up, the anchor-woman looks ugly
     'Even when she is in full makeup, the anchor woman still looks ugly.'

On the other hand, sentences (4, 5) are material conditionals semantically. The subordinate clause is the protasis or antecedent of the conditional construction, and the main clause is the apodosis or consequent. As is well known, the protasis states a sufficient condition for the truth of the apodosis. Sentences (12) and (13) are equivalent to (4, 5). It is also obvious that they do not express a concessive relation between the antecedent and the consequent proposition.

(12) Si entretienes al niño algo, estará contento.
     if amuse-you to-the child something, will-be happy
     'If you entertain the baby a bit, he will be happy.'

(13) Como estudies un poco, aprobarás.
     if study-you a little, will-pass
     'If you study a little, you will pass.'

The mismatch between apparent surface syntactic identity and semantic interpretation calls for an explanation not offered in traditional grammars. In this chapter, it will be claimed that concessive structures such as the ones illustrated above should be treated as concessive conditionals. These conditionals have several contrasting properties with respect to material conditionals. After examining these properties in sections two and three, and giving the semantic characterization of the relevant constructions in section three, the representation of concessive and material conditionals will be explored in section four. It will be derived from uniform procedures and conditions. Thus, it can be concluded that these concessive constructions are built using compositional operations and are not constructional entities of a fixed nature. What is also of interest for the general purposes of this monograph is that such operations incorporate constraints of a semantic and pragmatic nature and are shown to be relevant at the interface levels.

2. Concessive structures as conditionals

Following Koenig (1986, 1992), the concessive structures in (2, 3) can be treated as concessive conditionals. In general, concessive-conditional structures differ from standard material conditionals with respect to a host of important properties. First, it is a general property of concessive conditionals that they entail their consequent or apodosis (Bennett 1982; Iatridou 1991). We say that a proposition p entails a proposition q if and only if p is true in a situation/world s, then q is also true in s. Sentence (14) entails (15) and (16) entails (17). In other words, all situations s in which (14) or (16) are true are situations in which (15) are (17) are respectively true.

(14) Por mucho que Juan llegue temprano, no le dejarán entrar.
by much that Juan arrives early not to-him will-let come-in
'No matter how early he arrives, they still will not let him in.'

(15) No le dejarán entrar (a Juan).
not to-him will-let come-in (to Juan)
'They will not let Juan in.'

(16) Aunque Pedro se entrenó, siguió sin ganar.
although Pedro CL trained continued without winning
'Although Pedro trained hard, he still did not win.'

(17) Pedro siguió sin ganar.
Pedro continued without winning
'Pedro still did not win.'

This property is also shown by the fact that the conjunction of a concessive conditional sentence and the negation of its consequent is a contradiction.[1]

(18) #Aunque Pedro se entrenó, siguió sin ganar y al final ganó.
although Pedro CL trained continue without winning and at-the end won
'Although Pedro trained, he still did not win, but in the end he won.'

The proposition in the consequent is entailed in a certain situation not only by the proposition literally expressed in the antecedent but also by any extension of the situation or by any alternative to it. This extension or alternative situation may be even one in which propositions that are opposite in content to the antecedent proposition hold. In this respect, the consequent holds (is entailed) "no matter what". If (19a) is true in a situation s, then there is no extension/alternative situation s', such that the antecedent proposition is false in s' (the addressee does not study at all) or modified in one direction or other (the addressee studies more or less) and the consequent proposition is true in s'.

(19) a. #Por más que estudies, no aprobarás. De lo contrario, aprobarás.
by more that study-you not will-pass of the contrary, will-pass
'No matter how hard you study, you won't pass. Otherwise, you will pass.'
b. #Por mucho que entretengas al niño, llorará. Si no, no llorará.
by much that entertain to-the child will-cry. if not, not will-cry
'No matter how much you entertain the baby, he will cry. If you don't he will not cry.'

Nevertheless, consequent entailment may be contextually restricted to the speaker's and/or addressee's expectations. In other words, there might be a propositional element that matters and blocks consequent entailment. In this respect, the nature of the quantificational element following the preposition seems to be relevant. Consider the following discourse sequences:

---

1. In general, assume $p \rightarrow q \models q$. Then, $(p \rightarrow q) \wedge \neg q$ is a contradiction since it would be the case that $q \wedge \neg q$.

(20) a. Por mucho que entretengas al niño, llorará. Claro que si te vistes de payaso, no llorará.
by much that entertain to-the child will-cry. clear that if CL dress of clown not will-cry
'Even if you entertain the baby a lot, he will cry. Of course, if you dress as a clown, he will not.'

b. #Por más que entretengas al niño, llorará. Claro que si te vistes de payaso, no llorará
by more that entertain to-the child will-cry. clear that if CL dress of clown not will-cry

In (20a), the context can be expanded with the introduction of a proposition expressing a circumstance which normally does not hold. The inclusion of that proposition—in (20a) the proposition that the addressee dresses as a clown—cancels the entailment of the consequent proposition. On the other hand, in (20b) the addition of this "out of the ordinary" proposition does not make a difference with respect to consequent entailment, and the discourse becomes contradictory. The difference obviously relates to the specific nature of the quantificational elements *mucho* 'much' and *más* 'more'. It could be related to a contrast in the scalar properties of these quantifiers or, alternatively, related to the aspect or part of the situation that is being considered. In (20a), the alternative propositions that may modify the context are different ways of entertaining the baby in question, so there could always be one which, given its unexpected nature, succeeds in achieving that goal. On the other hand, in (20b) alternatives with respect to the degree of entertainment are considered and, given that *más* 'more' denotes the highest point in a contextually determined scale, there is no alternative proposition in which a higher degree can be attained.

The conditional in (21) is a standard material conditional:

(21) Con poco que entrenara iba a ganar, pero al final no ganó.
with little that trained-SUBJ-he was-he-going to win, but at-the end not won
'With a little bit of training, he was going to win. In the end, he did not win.'

Being a material conditional, it does not entail its consequent. Thus, adding the second sentence introduced by *pero* 'but,' and thus cancelling what is asserted in the preceding statement does not make the discourse contradictory. What this means is that this sentence does not hold "no matter what" either. Similarly, the sentences in (22) do not hold "no matter what." The negation of the antecedent proposition is compatible with the negation of the consequent, as is always the case with standard material conditionals.[2] The following discourses are felicitous:

(22) a. Por/con poco que estudies, aprobarás. De lo contrario, no aprobarás.
by/with little that study-you will-pass of the contrary, not will-pass
'If you study a little, you will pass. Otherwise, you will not pass.'
b. Con poco que entretengas al niño, no llorará. Si no, llorará.
with little that entertain to-the child not will-cry. If not, will-cry
'If you entertain the baby a bit, he won't cry. Otherwise, he will cry.'

3. Standing and introduced concession as opposition

Concessive conditionals do not always entail their consequent. Bennett (1982) distinguishes between "standing" conditionals and "introduced" conditionals. Both have the form of concessive conditionals (*even if* conditionals in English) but only introduced conditionals entail their consequent. The same distinction arises in the case of Spanish prepositional concessive conditionals. They can be either standing or introduced conditionals. Interestingly, only concessive conditionals built with the focus particle *incluso* 'even' exhibit this particular ambiguity. Scalar prepositional concessive conditionals do not. Consider the sentences in (23):

(23) a. Incluso si le compras regalos, Luisa estará enfadada.
even if to-her buy presents Luisa will-be upset
'Even if you buy her presents, Luisa will be upset.'

---

2. If $p \rightarrow q$ holds in the preceding discourse, adding $\neg p \rightarrow \neg q$ would be compatible with the semantics of the material conditional, but not with a consequent entailing conditional.

b. Por más que le compres regalos, Luisa estará enfadada.
by more that to-him buy presents Luisa will-be upset
'No matter how many presents you buy her, Luisa will be upset.'

The above examples assert that Luisa will be upset no matter what. Both of them entail their consequent and constitute "introduced" conditionals in Bennett's (1982) terminology. Standing conditionals are those where there are other conditional propositions in the context (von Fintel 1994). The antecedent contributes another condition for the consequent to hold, but the consequent does not hold "no matter what". *Incluso si* 'even if' concessive conditionals may act as standing conditionals, as the following example illustrates:

(24) En esta empresa hay que tener cuidado. Que no se te ocurra fumar o beber. Incluso si llegas tarde un día, perderás tu puesto.
in this company have that have care that not CL you occur smoke or drink even if arrive-you late a day will-lose your job
'In this company, you have to be careful. Do not think about smoking or drinking. Even if you are late a single day, you will lose your job.'

The proposition in which the addressee loses his job does not hold "no matter what". The antecedent adds another sufficient condition for the consequent to hold. In this respect, the conditional does not express a concessive meaning anymore. On the other hand, prepositional concessive conditionals lack the "standing" interpretation. The correlate of the discourse in (24), in which *por más que* 'lit. by more that' is substituted for *incluso si* 'even if', is anomalous since the antecedent is an introduced conditional element.

(25) Que no se te ocurra fumar o beber. #Por más que llegues tarde un día, perderás tu puesto.
that not REFL to-you occur smoke or drink by more that arrive-you late a day will-lose your job
'Do not think about smoking or drinking. No matter how late you arrive one day, you will lose your job.'

As observed by Alarcos (1994, 376), there is a "semantic contraposition" between the protasis and the apodosis of a concessive conditional. Typically, this contraposition is instantiated as a polar opposition: one term is positive and the other one is negative:

(26) Por mucho que corras, no llegarás a batir el récord del mundo.
by much that run-you not will-get to break the record of-the world
'No matter how fast you run, you will never break the world record.'

(27) Por más que no molestes, te sigue odiando.
by more that not disturb-you CL continues hating
'No matter if you do no bother him, he still hates you.'

In other occasions, the polar opposition is brought about simply by a downward entailing term such as a PP headed by *sin* 'without'—see Sánchez-Valencia (1991) and Dowty (1994) for the downward entailingness of these PPs, and Oltra-Massuet and Pérez-Jiménez (2011) for other general properties—or the negative adverb *nunca* 'never'. This is shown in (28):

(28) Por mucho que te esfuerces, seguirás sin ganar la carrera.
by more that you make-an-effort will-continue-you without winning the race
'No matter how much of an effort you make, you still will not win the race.'

(29) Por más que Pedro intentó mejorar, nunca rompió el récord del mundo.
by more that Pedro tried improve never broke the record of-the world
'No matter how much Pedro tried to improve, he never broke the world record.'

Nevertheless, a simple contrast between two properties suffices in most occasions, a contrast that might be contextually determined. Two positive terms in (30) and two negative terms in (31) are conceived as opposed and this opposition suffices for the concessive meaning to emerge.

(30) Por más aspirinas que tomé, me seguía doliendo la rodilla.
by more aspirins that took me continued hurting the knee
'No matter how many aspirins I took, my knee still hurt.'

(31) Por más que no te drogues, no vas a ser feliz de repente.
by more that not you get-drugged not go to be happy of sudden
'Even if you stop doing drugs, you are not going to be happy instantly.'

Here is how the concessive meaning emerges. For example, taking an aspirin or aspirins is normally associated with the cessation of pain and the property of taking an aspirin is contrasted with the property of the continuation of knee pain in (30). Similarly, not taking drugs or stopping the intake of drugs is normally associated with an increase in the overall happiness of the individual and the two clauses in (31) are opposed in this fashion.

This contrastive opposition between terms is not necessary in the case of regular *si*-headed or prepositional material conditionals, as illustrated by (32):

(32) Por poco que le ayudes, te estará siempre agradecido.
by little that him help-you to-you he-will-be always thankful
'If you help him a little, he will always be thankful.'

In the above sentence, the action of helping at least a little is not opposed to being thankful on the part of the helped person. Rather, being thankful is viewed as a consequence of being helped.

4. Conditional perfection and emphasis

Material conditionals trigger an invited inference or implicature of "conditional perfection" (Geis and Zwicky 1971) of the form *if not p, not q*. The truth conditions of a sentence of the form *if p, then q* are associated to a peculiarity when translated into the material conditional of first order logic (using the conditional connective). When the antecedent is false, the conditional is true, independently of the truth value of the consequent. This is a property of the conditional connective that does not square well with natural language intuitions. Geis and Zwicky's solution restores the desired fit. The inference of "conditional perfection" is an implicature of material conditionals which is triggered in a majority of contexts. As such, in the case of (32) above, there is the implicature that the consequent does not hold if there is no help at all. The implicature of conditional perfection can be derived from Grice's Maxim of Quantity (Grice 1989). If a speaker utters (32) or (33), the addressee will infer, following the maxim of quantity, that if the addressee does not help the individual referred to, he will not be thankful.

(33) Si le ayudas, te estará siempre agradecido.
    if to-him help-you to-you he-will-be always thankful
    'If you help him, he will be always thankful.'

Concessive conditionals do not trigger an inference of conditional perfection. Rather, there is the opposite assertion: No matter how or how much the antecedent proposition is strengthened, the consequent proposition does not hold. Consider (34):

(34) Por más que le ayudes, no te estará agradecido.
    by more that to-him help-you not to-you he-will-be thankful
    'No matter how much you help him, he will not be thankful.'

An inference of conditional perfection for (34) does not arise, independently of the scope of negation. If the antecedent is negated, it is obvious that the negation of the consequent does not hold either. In (34), if the addressee does not help, the proposition that the third party referred to will be thankful is still false. It cannot be simply just the negation of the degree term either, since the following sentence paraphrasing the inference would be false: 'If you do not help him (more/a lot), he will be thankful to you.' Not even an implicature in which, if the antecedent is strengthened sufficiently, the consequent will not hold is triggered. As discussed before, (34) does not implicate that if the addressee helps more (than expected) he will be thanked for his action. This inference is out of the ordinary and may be triggered only by a change in the context or in the relevant expectations.

Concessive conditionals are also ambiguous between a true strong concessive meaning (consequent entailing) and an emphatic meaning (Koenig 1986, 1992). In the emphatic reading, "no generalization is expressed, but the question raised in the antecedent is pushed aside in order to assert the consequence with more emphasis" (Koenig 1992). Sentence (35) is a concessive conditional of the first sort, whereas (36) is an emphatic concessive and does not involve a generalization stating that for every way in which the situation may evolve, the consequent will be true.

(35) Incluso si le das más tiempo, no terminará el examen.
even if him give-you more time not will-finish the exam
'Even if you give him more time, he won't finish the exam.'

(36) Pese a parecer un poco lento, de hecho es muy inteligente.
despite to seem a little slow of fact is very smart
'Despite looking a little bit slow, in fact he is very smart.'

The same ambiguity appears in the case of prepositional concessive conditionals. All the examples considered so far are strong concessives, whereas (37) is an emphatic concessive.

(37) Por más que parezca un poco lento, de hecho es muy inteligente.
by more that seem a little slow of fact is very smart
'No matter whether he looks a bit slow, in fact he is very smart.'

In sum, there is enough evidence to conclude that Spanish concessive structures, such as the ones illustrated in (2)–(5) at the beginning of the chapter, are not uniform from a semantic/pragmatic point of view. Furthermore, the differential behavior can be successfully related to the semantic contrast between concessive conditionals and material conditionals.

5. Conditionals and scalarity

In this section, I will explore the conditional semantics of these constructions in more detail. To do so, we will assume a widely accepted view on the semantic structure of conditionals. Kratzer (1986, 2012), following Lewis (1975), presents an analysis of conditionals in which the meaning associated with these constructions is not merely the one associated to the binary material implication operator. Rather, the protasis or antecedent of the conditional restricts an overt or covert modal operator or an adverb of quantification. Adopting this view will allow us to provide a systematic analysis of the differences between the conditionals studied and also of their similarities.[3]

In concessive conditionals, and probably also in prepositional material conditionals of the sort analyzed here, the operator restricts the relevant situations to those satisfying a property of degrees, as in (38):

(38) Op [λs[Qd[P(s, d)]]] [λs[Q(s)]]

Thus, the operator in (38) takes two sets of worlds/situations as its arguments. Actually, the first argument is a relation between situations s and degrees d. Therefore, there has to be quantification over degrees in the antecedent clause. In this type of tripartite quantificational structures, the quantificational force of the operator is contextually determined and this property gives rise to so-called "quantificational variability effects." In neutral contexts, there is a default universal interpretation: In all situations in which the antecedent holds, the consequent holds. The presence of an overt adverb of quantification changes the quantificational force of the sentence. For example, in (39) the quantifier *normalmente* 'usually' introduces a majority (proportional) quantifier over situations identical in quantificational force to the quantifier *most* in the domain of quantification over individuals. In (40), *a veces* 'sometimes' acts as an existential quantifier over situations.

(39) Normalmente por más que lleves dinero no puedes comprar lo que quieres.
normally by more that have-you money not can buy the that want
'Normally, no matter how much money you have with you, you still cannot buy what you want.'

(40) A veces con poco que hagas apruebas el examen.
some times with little that do-you will-pass the exam
'Sometimes, you pass the exam just making a little effort.'

Spatio-temporal restrictions also have an effect on the domain of quantification, restricting it to a concrete spatial or temporal region. In (41), the

---

3. It might be claimed that there might be an incompatibility between the Lewis-Kratzer analysis of conditionals and the treatment of the material conditional in the previous section. However, this is not always true. If one assumes default universal force, the semantics of the material conditional under the standard analysis is equivalent to the operator restriction analysis. The conditional connective represents the inclusion relation between the sets of worlds denoted by the propositional expressions.

universal quantifier over situations is restricted to a deictically determined country. In (42), the situations under consideration are temporally restricted:

(41) En este país con poco que uno haga se hace millonario.
in this country with little that one does CL becomes millionaire
'In this country, one becomes a millionaire just doing a little.'

(42) Por las mañanas, por mucho que uno lo intente no se hace nada
by the morning by much that one it tries not CL does anything
'In the early morning, no matter how hard you try, you do not get anything done.'

There is also a c-command condition on the adverb of quantification. Descriptively, the adverb of quantification cannot be "inside" the restrictor in order to obtain the desired interpretation, as the examples in (43, 44) illustrate.

(43) Por más que lleves dinero normalmente, no puedes comprar lo que quieres.
by more that have money normally not can buy the-NEUT. that want
'No matter how much money you normally have with you, you still cannot buy what you want.'

(44) a. Por más que lleves dinero, normalmente no puedes comprar lo que quieres.
by more that have money normally not can buy the-NEUT. that want
'No matter how much money you have with you, normally you cannot buy what you want.'
b. Normalmente, por más que lleves dinero, no puedes comprar lo que quieres.
normally by more that have money not can buy the-NEUT. that want
'Normally, no matter how much money you have with you, you still cannot buy what you want.'

Let us now consider the scalar nature of the quantificational element following the preposition. Firstly, concessive *por* 'by'-conditionals only allow intensive quantifiers in the specifier of the restrictor CP (*muy* 'very', *mucho* 'much', *más* 'more') and not quantifiers such as *algo* 'something', *un poco* 'a little', etc. as the contrast between (45) and (46) shows.

(45) Por mucho/más/más horas que estudies, no aprobarás.
by much/more/more hours that study-you, not will-pass-you
'Even if you study a lot/more/more hours, you will not pass.'

(46) #Por algo/un poco/poco que estudies, no aprobarás.
by some/a little/little that study-you, not will-pass-you
'#Even if you study something/a little/little, you will not pass.'

The quantifiers in (45) are expressions denoting high points in a contextually determined scale. On the other hand, those in (46) denote low points on such a scale. This sort of evidence shows that the interpretation of the quantificational operator is scalarly determined, along the lines initially proposed by Horn (1972), Fauconnier (1979), etc. The use of the quantifier is associated with a scale of expectations. More specifically, the quantifier associates with the highest point on such a scale—see also Schwenter (1999) for an analysis of conditionals and scalarity. There is a scalar presupposition associated with concessive conditionals or, more specifically, with the degree operator following the preposition. Informally, if the degree property *P* holds for a degree *d*, then *d* is maximal with respect to *P*. Formally:

(47) Let $D = <D, \leq >$ be an ordered set of degrees. Let $Op[\varphi][\psi]$ and $\varphi = \lambda s[Qd[P(s, d)]]$, for $d \in D$. Then, for all other $d' \in D$: if $P(d')$ then $d' \leq d$.

Let us explore further consequences of (47). First, cardinal quantifiers are not generally admitted in concessive conditionals. Consider (48):

(48) #Por dos meses que estudies, no aprobarás.
by two months that study-you not will-pass-you
'Even if you study two months, you will not pass.'

The scalar presupposition is violated in the above sentence. The cardinal quantifier *dos meses* 'two months' does not ordinarily denote a high point in a scale of periods of study. Nevertheless, it can be contextually coerced to do so, as shown by the contrast in (49):

(49) a. Por dos meses que te tires estudiando, no vas a aprobar.
by two months that CL stay studying not go-you to pass
'Even if you keep on studying two months, you will not pass.'
b. Por treinta y siete meses que estudies, no vas a aprobar.
by thirty and seven months that study-you not go-you to pass
'Even if you study thirty seven months, you will not pass.'

In (49a), the expression *tirarse estudiando* 'keep on studying' indicates that the speaker considers that the corresponding period of time exceeds a subjective normality criterion. In (49b), the presence of a cardinal quantifier denoting a quantity which obviously exceeds normal measures for study periods renders the conditional felicitous. Thus, even if the relevant quantifier or measure phrase does not denote a high point on a scale, by virtue of participating in this construction it does so. In other words, the relevant event measured by the quantifier phrase is perceived as exceeding a norm or standard. If the quantifier is not in the specifier of CP—linearly, preceding the complementizer *que*—there is not such a restriction. For example, *dos meses* 'two months' in (50) occurs in the standard object position—not in a displaced position—and is not associated with a high point on a scale.

(50) Por más que estudies dos meses, no aprobarás.
by more that study-you two months not will-pass-you

Cardinal quantifiers are admitted in prepositional material conditionals without restrictions:

(51) Con dos copas que te tomes das positivo en el control de alcoholemia.
with two glasses that CL drink give positive in the control of alcohol
'Just taking two glasses of wine, you will test positive in a traffic control.'

Material conditionals do not have the scalar presupposition in (47). Rather, they have the opposite implicature: The degree of the property in the antecedent proposition is minimal. Stating this differently, for any other contextually-available degree, the degree of the property is less than or equal to that degree. Formally:

(52) Let **D** = <D, ≤ > be an ordered set of degrees. Let Op[φ][ψ] and φ = λs[Qd[P(s, d)]], for d ∈ D. Then, for all other d' ∈ D: if P(d') then d ≤ d'.

Another property that can be related to the scalar characterization of concessive prepositional conditionals is that quantifiers of excess, including *demasiado* 'too much' or *más de lo normal* 'more than average' (Bosque 1995) are also anomalous in concessive prepositional conditionals as shown in (53, 54).

(53) #Por demasiado que entreno, sigo sin batir el record.
by too-much that train-I, continue-I without break the record
'Even if I train too much, I still do not break the record.

(54) #Por más de lo normal que bebas, no se te quita la sed.
by more of the normal that drink-you not CL you go the thirst
'Even if you drink more than the average, you will still be thirsty.'

This property can be related to the fact that quantifiers of excess denote out of scale points. As stated in (47), the scalar presupposition of concessive conditionals dictates that the degree of the property has to be maximal within a (contextually determined) scale/ordering of degrees. Thus, a quantifier of excess would violate this presupposition.[4]

When a gradable adjective, such as *alto* 'tall' and *tonto* 'stupid' in (55, 56) follows the preposition in its surface raised or displaced position, the sentence is only compatible with a top of scale interpretation of the degree property denoted by the adjective. Sentences (55) and (56) are respectively equivalent to (57) and (58).

(55) Por alto que escale, seguirá sin ser reconocido como campeón.
by high that climbs, will-continue without being recognized as champion
'No matter how high he climbs, he still will not be recognized as the champion.'

---

4. One could assume a wider pragmatic scale, one reaching the level of "too much" or "more than average," as provided by the context. Then, the scalar presupposition could be satisfied within that scale. I think that the semantic content of quantifiers of excess is what prevents this undesired consequence. A quantifier of excess cannot shift the context to a scale of excess. Rather, it situates the relevant degree out of the contextually available scale.

(56) Por tonto que seas, esto es fácil de entender.
by stupid that are-you, this is easy of understand
'No matter how slow you are, this is still easy to understand.'

(57) Por muy alto que escale, seguirá sin ser reconocido como campeón.
by very high that climbs, continue without being recognized as champion
'Even if he climbs very high, he will not be recognized as the champion.'

(58) Por muy tonto que seas, esto es fácil de entender.
by very stupid that are-you, this is easy of understand
'Even if you are very slow, this is still easy to understand.'

What this shows is that the high-degree interpretation of the conditional does not require an overt high-degree element to be activated. A potential problem for the previous hypothesis is that other properties that are not of a gradable nature can also occur in the restrictor. For example, *saber francés* 'know French' in (59) and *estar muerto* 'be dead' in (60) denote properties that are apparently not gradable.

(59) Por mucho que sepas francés, tu acento es bastante malo.
by much that know-you French your accent is rather bad
'Even if you know French, your accent is pretty bad.'

(60) Por más que esté muerto, sigue siendo una amenaza.
by much that is dead, continues to-be a menace
'Even if he is dead, he is still a menace.'

The solution to this problem comes from the hypothesis that the operator makes any property (or its effects) gradable. In general, inertia situations have to be considered in the determination of gradability (Dowty 1979). Inertia situations are those related to the situation by an accessibility relation. In (59), the situations to be considered are those in which the addressee is proficient in French and has most of the contextually relevant traits related to this proficiency in a high grade. In (60), it can be understood that the individual referred to has several prominent surviving features that still make him a menace.

The interpretation of material prepositional conditionals is also scalarly regulated, but in the opposite direction, as stated above. Only quantifiers that can be associated with the lowest point of a contextually determined scale, such as *poco* 'little', *un poco* 'a little', *algo* 'something', or *una migaja* 'a bit', are allowed.

(61) Con una migaja/poco/un poco que le des como limosna, estará contento.
with a bit/ little/a little that CL give-you as charity will-be-he happy
'If you give him just a bit/ a little as a charity gift, he will be happy.'

Quantifiers such as *mucho* 'much' and *más* 'more' cannot denote the lowest point of a scale and are infelicitous, as shown in (62–64):

(62) #Con mucho/más que le des como limosna, estará contento.
with much/more that to-him give as charity will-be-he happy
'If you give him a lot as a charity gift, he will be happy.'

(63) #Con mucho que te esfuerces, podrías aprobar.
by much that you make-efforts, could-you pass
'If you study a lot, you could pass.'

(64) #Con más que le hubieras regalado a Luis, te lo habría agradecido.
with more that CL had given to Luis, to-you it had appreciated
'If you had given Luis more presents, he would have appreciated it.'

To conclude this section, an explicit characterization of the semantics of other concessive conditionals (cf. 6–11) will be given. In this case, the modal/quantificational operator is assumed to have universal force. To begin with, disjunctive conditionals can be claimed to have the following semantics:

(65) $(s: s \in [p \cup \neg p]) \subseteq (s': s' \in q)$.

What (65) states is that a disjunctive conditional simply states that the situations in the disjunctive proposition antecedent ($p \cup \neg p$) are a subset of the situations making the consequent q true. The translation of the concessive structure in (66) would be as shown in (67):

(66) Vengas o no, quedarás mal.
   come-you or not will-look-you bad
   'Whether you come or not, you will look bad.'

(67) $\lambda s[\textbf{Come}(s) \vee \neg \textbf{Come}(s)] \subseteq \lambda s'[\textbf{Look\_bad}(s')]$

Free-choice concessives have the content in (68), where for a context C, ALT_C is the set of alternatives contextually determined in C:

(68) $(s: s \in [\{p\} \cup ALT_C(p)]) \subseteq (s': s' \in q)$

Following (68), what a free concessive expresses is that the situations making a given antecedent proposition and its contextually relevant alternatives true, also make the consequent true. In this case, there is an additional implicature:

(69) $\exists p' \circ [\{p\} \cup ALT_C(p)]$ [$\textbf{Likelihood}(s)(p'(s) \rightarrow q(s')) \geq \kappa$]

The implicature is that there is a contextually-determined likelihood that $(p'(s) \rightarrow q(s'))$ holds. Sentence (70) belongs to this class:

(70) Coma lo que coma, Pedro nunca engorda.
   eat the that eat Pedro never gets-fatter
   'No matter what he eats, Pedro never gets fatter.'

Sentence (70) is a standard free concessive. What it states is that for any proposition we might consider in which Pedro eats a given amount, or its contextually relevant alternatives in which he eats different amounts, he will never get fatter. The implicature is that we are referring to a certain threshold for his eating.

Focus concessives are a different subclass of concessive structures. They have the following content:

(71) $(s: s \in p) \subseteq (s': s' \in q)$

The associated implicature is (72):

(72) **Likelihood**(s)(p) ≤ **Likelihood**(s)(p': p' ∈ ALT$_C$(p))

In (73) and (74), it can be seen how the scope of focus affects the interpretation of the concessive sentence because it changes the composition of the set of alternatives to be considered.

(73) Incluso si baila [$_F$ todos los días] Pedro no adelgaza.
 even if dance-he all the days Pedro not gets-thinner
 'Even if he dances every day, Pedro does not get thinner.'

(74) Incluso si [$_F$baila todos los días] Pedro no adelgaza.
 even if dance-he all the days Pedro not gets-thinner

What (73) states is that whether Pedro dances every day or fewer days in a given period, he will not lose weight. The implicature here is that the least likely scenario is precisely that he dances every day. Thus, even if he does that, the consequent still holds. The importance of focus for the interpretation of this type of constructions is that, depending on which element is under the scope of the focus operator *incluso*, the alternatives to be considered change. In (73), the relevant alternatives involve situations in which there is dancing fewer or more days. In (74), the relevant alternatives are related to situations in which there is dancing every day or performing any other activity.

6. Matters of Logical Form

The Logical Form that I will be proposing for the two types of prepositional conditionals analyzed in this chapter is similar to the one proposed by Chierchia (1995) for *if/when*-conditionals: The protasis/restrictor reconstructs into the adjunct position of the intermediate level at the Temporal Projection (TP) of the apodosis/nuclear scope. The required configuration at the level of Logical Form (LF) is the following one:

(75)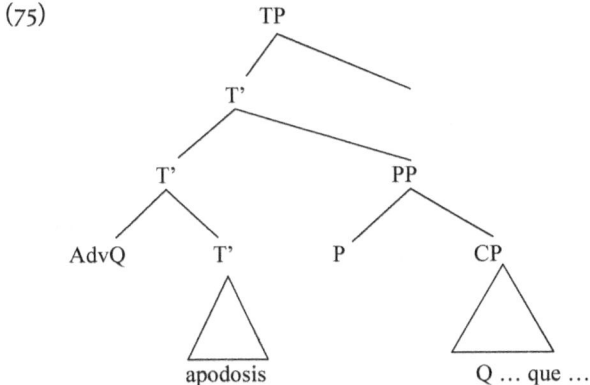

There is evidence confirming that the protasis of both types of prepositional conditionals requires reconstruction. Firstly, in (76, 77) a violation of Principle-C of the Binding Theory does not arise because the pronoun acts as a bound variable after reconstruction—only overt subject pronouns are taken into consideration here for simplicity purposes. When the relevant pronouns are null or clitic non-subject pronouns, the contrast tends to disappear:

(76) Por más que él$_i$ se esfuerce, Pedro$_i$ nunca acabará la carrera.
 by more that he$_i$ CL make-effort, Pedro$_i$ never will-finish the degree
 'Even if Pedro makes a lot of effort, he will never finish his degree.'

(77) Por poco que él$_i$ se esforzara, Pedro$_i$ no dejaría la carrera.
 by little that he$_i$ CL make-effort, Pedro$_i$ not would-leave the degree
 'If Pedro tried a little bit harder, he would not have to quit his studies.'

Sentences (78, 79) violate Principle-C because the proper noun is coindexed with the pronoun at LF. In other words, it is not free.

(78) *Por más que Pedro$_i$ se esfuerce, él$_i$ nunca acabará la carrera.
 *by more that Pedro$_i$ CL make-efforts, he$_i$ never will-finish the degree
 'Even if Pedro makes a lot of effort, he will never finish his degree.'

(79) *Por poco que Pedro$_i$ se esforzara, él$_i$ no dejaría la carrera.
 *by little that Pedro$_i$ CL make-effort, he$_i$ not would-leave the degree
 'If Pedro tried a little bit harder, he would not have to quit his studies.'

Secondly, the CP constituent may serve as the surface antecedent of a neuter proform, as illustrated in (80):

(80) a. Por [mucho que llores]$_i$, ello$_i$ /pro$_i$ no te va hacer sentir mejor.
 by much that cry-you it not you going make feel better
 'Even if you cry a lot, this will not make you feel better.'
 b. Con [poco que le hubieras regalado a Luis]$_i$, te lo$_i$ habría agradecido.
 with little that to-him had given to Luis you it would-have thanked
 'Even if you had given him little as a present, he would have been thankful.'

Finally, in (81, 82) assuming that Negative Polarity Items (NPIs) have to be c-commanded by negation at LF (Uribe-Echebarría 1994), the clauses containing the NPIs *oportunidad alguna* 'any chance', *error alguno* 'any mistake' have to reconstruct in order for the NPIs to be licensed:[5]

(81) Por mucho que le dieras oportunidad alguna, no mejoraría su conducta.
 by much that CL gave chance any, not would-improve his behavior
 'Even if you give him a chance, he will not improve his behavior.'

(82) Por poco que cometas error alguno, no te dejarán en el equipo.
 by little that make-you mistake any, not you will-leave on the team
 'If you make a single mistake, they will not let you on the team.'

The specifier of CP position is occupied by an operator on degrees, as defended in Gutiérrez-Rexach (1999e) for neuter degree constructions

---

5. As is well-known, an alternative semantic hypothesis is that NPIs are licensed in the protasis of conditional sentences because these are decreasing environments.

specifically and degree constructions in general. The resulting LF structure would be as depicted in (83):

(83)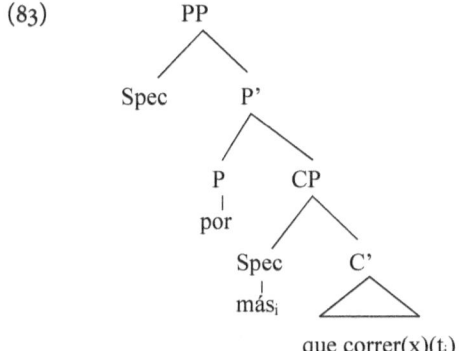

There is evidence that the degree operator moves from a position internal to the C' constituent. The examples in (84) exhibit standard subjacency violations (Bosque and Gutiérrez-Rexach 2009, chap. 6), whereas (85) shows how successive cyclic movement is still possible:

(84) a. *Por más que te preguntes quién corre, no ganará.
    by more that CL wonder who runs, not will-win
    'Even if you wonder who will run, he will not win.'
  b. *Por más que sepas el hecho de que corre, no ganará.
    by more that know-you the fact of that runs-he not will-win
    'Even if you know the fact that he runs, he will not win.'

(85) Por más rápido que le digas que corra, no ganará
   by more fast that CL say-you that run not will-win
   'Even if you tell him to run faster, he will not win'

There is a contrasting difference between concessive and material prepositional conditionals with respect to the possibility of *in situ* interpretation. In concessive conditionals, the quantificational element cannot remain in its initial position within the sentence (Temporal Phrase or TP), as shown in (86). On the other hand, in material conditionals, the quantificational element can remain *in situ*. The QP *un poco* 'a little' in (87) appears in its original position and the interpretation is not altered.

(86) *Por que corras más, no vas a ganar.
by that run-you more not go to win
'Even if you run faster, you will not win.'

(87) Con que corras un poco, vas a ganar.
with that run a little go to win
'As long as you run a little, you will win.'

We can thus conclude that the degree quantifier/operator has to be attracted to the CP position before Spell-Out in concessive prepositional conditionals. However, this is not necessarily the case for material conditionals. It is also a property of certain CPs with exclamatory or quasi-exclamatory force—and an associated scalar presupposition or implicature—that the triggering syntactic feature related to illocutionary force has to be checked by movement or attraction of a [+degree] lexical element. See Zanuttini and Portner (1998) for Italian exclamatives and Gutiérrez-Rexach (2001c) for certain Spanish exclamatory constructions. In the Spanish exclamatory construction illustrated in (88), the adjective is attracted to the [+focus] specifier of CP:

(88) ¡Vaya tonto que estás!
go-subj. silly that are-you
'How silly you are!'

Finally, more evidence of a generalized raising pattern comes from the syntactic origin of the concessive complementizer *aunque*, a particle which has undergone an incorporation process of the raised degree adverb *aun* 'even' into the complementizer *que* 'that'. When the element occurring in the specifier of CP (Spec,CP) is a full DP, the concessive/material interpretation is absent. Only a causal interpretation is possible (Alarcos 1994, 376).

(89) Por lo mucho que estudió lo aprobaron.
by the much that studied him passed
'He passed because he studied a lot.'

(90) Por lo poco que estudió lo suspendieron.
by the little that studied him failed
'He failed because he studied little.'

7. Conclusion

In this chapter, it has been claimed that, although prepositional conditionals do not exhibit structural differences at LF, there are strong arguments to divide this construction type in two classes: concessive and material conditionals. These arguments are principally related to the semantic/pragmatic component of the grammar. Thus, an interesting bifurcation takes place at the juncture between grammar and meaning in this case, where properties belonging to the semantics/pragmatics interface seem to be critical in creating the intended contrast. This chapter also contributes to the scarce literature on the cross-linguistic study of conditional varieties and to the study of the influence of pragmatic scales in the semantics of conditionals.

8

Superlatives, Degrees, and Focus

1. An ambiguity of superlative expressions

In a groundbreaking paper, Szabolcsi (1986a) observes that superlatives are not unambiguous expressions. Rather, they tend to have two readings. This ambiguity is not accidental and can be attested cross-linguistically, in languages as diverse as Hungarian, German, English, or Romance languages in general. Several theories have been developed to account for the properties related to this ambiguity. Some of them actually stress the connection between these readings and focus, as Szabolcsi originally did, for example, Heim (1996), Farkas and Kiss (2000), Sharvit and Stateva (2002) and Gutiérrez-Rexach (2006b, 2011) among others. There are certain similarities and differences among these analyses. For example, Sharvit and Stateva propose treating the definite as a covert indefinite and also postulate the presence of an identity operator or possible worlds. Farkas and Kiss's account does not rely on syntactic movement operations, such as Quantifier Raising. On the other hand, Gutiérrez-Rexach (2006b, 2011) is an interface-based approach where syntactic and semantic operations play an important role. Reasons of space prevent me from undertaking a more detailed comparison of these approaches. In general, I stay here closer to the spirit of my own treatment in the aforementioned articles.

In Spanish, the superlative description (superlative DP) *la novela más larga* 'the longest novel' in (1) may have two interpretations.

(1) Pepa leyó la novela más larga.
 Pepa read the novel more long
 'Pepa read the longest novel.'

The first reading is the ABSOLUTE READING, corresponding to an interpretation of (1) as 'Pepa read a novel longer than any other novel,' for example if Pepa read *War and Peace*. The second reading is the COMPARATIVE READING, corresponding to the interpretation 'Pepa read a novel longer than the novels anybody else read.' This would be true, for example, in a situation in which Pepa read *Don Quijote,* María *La Celestina* and Luisa *El Lazarillo*. Szabolcsi (1986a) also observes that the emergence of the comparative reading is related to the presence of contrastive focus. Consider (2):

(2) Luis le compró a Pepa la novela más larga.
 Luis CL bought to Pepa the novel more long
 'Luis bought Pepa the longest novel.'

The sentence above has one absolute reading, namely 'Luis bought Pepa a novel longer than any other novel' and two comparative readings, depending on whether *Luis* or *Pepa* are focused as follows. Using [. . .]$_F$ to indicate that the constituent in brackets is focused, *Luis* would be the focused constituent in (3) and *Pepa* would be in focus in (4):

(3) [Luis]$_F$ le compró a Pepa la novela más larga.
 Luis CL bought to Pepa the novel more long
 'Luis bought Pepa the longest novel.'
(4) Luis le compró a [Pepa]$_F$ la novela más larga.
 Luis CL bought to Pepa the novel more long
 'Luis bought Pepa the longest novel.'

The interpretations associated with (3) and (4) would respectively be: 'Luis bought Pepa a novel longer than the novels that anybody else bought her' and 'Luis bought Pepa a novel longer than the novels that he bought anybody else'. Thus, focus prominence has an obvious impact and clear systematic correlate with a semantic property: the emergence of two readings. In this chapter, this critical empirical fact will be taken as a point of departure to argue that there is no ambiguity in the interpretation of Spanish superlatives, in line with the general hypothesis advocated in Gutiérrez-Rexach (2006b, 2011). The two readings that have been described here are a byproduct of the context-dependent nature of superlative definite descriptions. The chapter is structured as follows: In section two, a general semantics of superlatives is developed, treating them as a subclass of definite DPs; in section three, contextual factors affecting the interpretation of superlatives are explored; after establishing a distinction between the context set of a definite and the frame of comparison (section four), a theory of how focus determines the comparative readings is presented in section five. Finally, in sections six and seven, further evidence from interrogatives and existential constructions is laid out.

2. Superlative descriptions and their definite-like nature

The most natural starting point to determine the semantic content of a superlative description of the form *el X más Y* ('lit. the X more Y = the Y-est X') is to decompose it in two separate elements: the definite determiner (*el*) and a superlative operator (*más*). I will assume a relatively standard or uncontroversial semantics of definites, as proposed in Generalized Quantifier Theory (Keenan and Westerståhl 1997; Peters and Westerståhl 2006). Definite determiners, like demonstrative and interrogative determiners, denote inherently restricted functions. Consider the following sentences:

(5) a. Two students are waiting in the hallway. The tall student is from Germany.
 b. Two students are waiting in the hallway. This one is from Germany.
 c. Two students are waiting in the hallway. Which one is from Germany?

In (5a), the interpretation of *the* is restricted to a two-membered set of men students waiting in the hallway. Similarly, in (5b, c) the preceding discourse determines the set restricting the interpretation of the demonstrative quantifier and the interrogative quantifier. In general, we assume that certain determiners are restricted to CONTEXT SETS, as proposed by Westerståhl (1985, 1989). See also von Fintel (1994) for a more general application of this notion. In Gutiérrez-Rexach (1997) the property of being discourse-linked, characteristic of certain *wh*-phrases, is also related to the presence of context sets.

For E a universe of individuals, D a determiner function over E, and A, B, $C \subseteq E$, we say that D^C is the restriction of D to C iff $D^C(A)(B)$ iff $D(A \cap C)(B)$. The variable C represents the context set of the determiner function and restricts the first argument of a determiner function. The function denoted by the determiner *the* is defined in (6):

(6) $\text{the}_{sg}{}^C(A)(B)$ = True iff $(C \cap A) \subseteq B$ and $\text{Card}(C \cap A) = 1$.

The definite determiner is thus a restricted inclusion determiner. Establishing the content of the set C is critical for assigning an actual value to the determiner function. In less formal terms, we can only ascertain whether a statement with a definite determiner is true or false if we know the composition of the contextual restriction of such determiner. Let us now analyze the contribution of the superlative operator. The syntactic analysis of superlative descriptions that we propose follows current syntactic assumptions in the sense that determiners head an independent DP projection, adjectives are generated in the specifier of a Number Phrase, and nouns raise to NumP to check their number features—cf. Giorgi and Longobardi (1991), Cinque (1994, 2010), and Bosque and Gutiérrez-Rexach (2009) for other options on adjective ordering; and Gutiérrez-Rexach and Sessarego (2011) for the status of gender and number in current theories. The superlative operator occupies the specifier of an intermediate functional projection between DP and NumP, presumably a Degree Phrase (Gutiérrez-Rexach 1999e). The adjective raises and incorporates into the superlative morpheme -*est* (7a). In Spanish, adjective raising and incorporation into the superlative operator (*más* 'more') takes place at LF (7b, c).

(7) a. [$_{DP}$ the [$_{DegP}$ bright$_i$ -est [$_{NumP}$ t$_i$ man$_j$ [$_{NP}$ t$_j$]]]]
   b. [$_{DP}$ el [$_{DegP}$ más [$_{NumP}$ alto [$_{NP}$]]]]
   c. LF: [$_{DP}$ el [$_{DegP}$ alto$_i$ más [$_{NumP}$ t$_i$ [$_{NP}$]]]]

Following Heim (1985, 1996), it can be proposed that English -*est* and Spanish *más* combine with a gradable property (a relation between individuals and degrees) and yield a property of individuals (a set). The restricted determiner *the* takes this property as its first argument. The resulting semantics of *más* is as in (8):

(8) $\text{más}(R)(x) = 1$ iff $\exists d\ [R(x, d)\ \&\ \forall y \neq x\ [\neg R(y, d)]]$

The operator *más* is then a binary function that is true of a gradable property (R) and an individual (x) if and only if there is a degree d such that x has the property R to d and no other individual has property R to that degree. For example *más(alto)(Juan)* will be true if it is the case that there is a degree (height) such that Juan is tall to that degree and no other individual is tall to that degree.

3. The dynamics of context

In this section the conditions under which discourse dynamics determines the composition of a context set restricting the definite determiner. Consider the following sentence:

(9) Juan fue al centro comercial. Le compró a su mujer el regalo más caro.
Juan went to-the mall. CL bought-he to his wife the present most expensive
'Juan went to the mall. He bought his wife the most expensive present.'

The above example has two readings—excluding those readings in which *su mujer* 'his wife' is in focus. The first reading of this sentence can be paraphrased as 'Juan bought his wife a present more expensive than any other present in the mall'. The second reading would be 'Juan bought his wife a present more expensive than any other present he had bought her'. The second reading can be considered a special type of focus-dependent interpretation. It is one in which the tense morpheme is focused and where the past time referred to is contrasted with previous past times in which Juan bought presents for his wife. What is of importance here is that both readings entail (presuppose) that Juan bought that present in the mall. Therefore, it seems that in the simplest cases the discourse preceding the occurrence of the superlative description determines the composition of the context set. In the following examples, the superlative description occurs in the nuclear scope of an adverb of quantification. This adverb is instantiated as either an overt or a covert element respectively related to the connectives *dondequiera* 'wherever' and *cuando* 'when.'

(10) a. Dondequiera que Juan pasa sus vacaciones, escala la montaña más alta.

wherever that Juan spends his holidays climb-he the mountain more high
'Wherever Juan goes on vacation, he climbs the highest mountain.'

b. Cuando Juan tiene tiempo en sus vacaciones, escala la montaña más alta.
when Juan has time in his holidays climb-he the mountain more high
'Whenever Juan has time during his vacation, he climbs the highest mountain.'

Sentence (10a) has the reading that in every place Juan spends his vacation, he climbs a mountain higher than any other mountain in that particular location. Similarly, (10b) means that during his vacation time Juan climbs a mountain higher than any other mountain in the location where he spends that concrete vacation. A second 'absolute' reading of each sentence of (10), in which Juan climbs the same mountain every time he has a chance during his vacation, seems much less preferred or even impossible. This fact suggests that the restriction determines the class of objects belonging to the context set in tripartite quantificational structures. Sentence (11) confirms this idea:

(11) Cuando Juan va de viaje, le compra a su mujer el regalo más caro.
when Juan goes of travel CL buys to his wife the present more expensive
'When Juan goes on a trip he buys his wife the most expensive present.'

The above sentence states that every time Juan goes on a business trip, he buys his wife a present more expensive than any other present available for purchase during that trip. The absolute reading does not seem to be possible. In other words, (11) cannot be interpreted as stating that every time Juan goes on a business trip, he buys his wife a present more expensive than any other present that he could possibly purchase during the time spent on that trip.

Given that the availability of comparative/absolute readings is certainly influenced by discourse-related factors such as focus or the quantificational partition of a clause, it seems reasonable to defend an account of the semantics of superlatives which is dynamic in nature. Most theories of dynamic semantics defend a move from the study of truth conditions to the study of context change potentials as the basic task of semantic analysis—cf.

Chierchia (1995); Groenedijk, Stokhof, and Veltman (1995, 1996); Dekker (2012). The dynamic content of a proposition *p* in a discourse state *s*, is the state *s'* resulting from updating *s* with *p*. Models are tuples $M = \langle D, W, I \rangle$, where *D* is the domain of discourse entities, *W* is the set of worlds and *I* is the set of possibilities. A possibility *i* in *I* is a pair $\langle w, r \rangle$, where *w* is a member of *W* (a world) and *r* is a sequence of discourse entities (a member of D^N). A state *s* is a subset of *I*, in other words, a state is a set of possibilities: the set of world-discourse referent pairs compatible with the information available at that stage.

Building the context set for a determiner requires identifying the relevant set of discourse entities restricting the determiner function. Going back to the discourse in (9), the first sentence makes the discourse referent *m* (the mall) available. Thus, it corresponds to a location in *D*. How do we get to the proper context set for *el* in *el regalo más caro*? The context set cannot be a set of locations *m* satisfying the condition *mall(m)*, but rather an appropriate set of objects in that location. Following Cresswell (1996), Gutiérrez-Rexach (2006b, 2011) introduces an accommodation function f_x mapping a world *w* and an object *x* to the set of objects *y* that stand in a contextually relevant relation *R* with *x* in *w*:

(12) $f_x(w)(x)(R) = \lambda y[R(w)(x)(y)]$

For instance, a potential accommodation function that can be inferred from the first sentence of the discourse in (9) would be $f_m(w)(m)(\mathbf{In})$ (= $\lambda y[\mathbf{In}(w)(m)(y)]$), namely the set of objects y in the mall in *w*–the set of objects standing in the ***In*** relation with the mall in *w*. Another potential accommodation function would be $f_m(w)(m)(\mathbf{Purchasable})$ (= $\lambda y[\mathbf{Purchasable}(w)(m)(y)]$), i.e. the set of objects that can be purchased in the mall, etc. This function could be accessed once the verb in the second sentence is processed. In (9a) a place variable *p* would be quantified over. The relevant accommodation function is $f_p(w)(p)(R)$, where *R* is in this case the spatial part-whole relation. This function is accommodated in the nuclear scope and the relevant set of entities *y* becomes accessible as the context set for the definite determiner.

Context sets are assumed to be dynamically created "on the fly", so there is no fixed context set for a given expression. Calculating the context set would depend on the situation, the discourse referents activated at that situation and text-specific factors, such as if and how these referents are available in a given discourse. Thus, blocking effects are expected. These effects emerge when a certain connective blocks the availability or accessibility of a discourse referent previously introduced in discourse. In this respect, connectives can have a "dynamizing" or "stratifying" effect. Calculating the dynamic effect of a given connective is thus relevant.

The simple concatenation of sentences in a discourse semantically amounts to the dynamic conjunction of the sentences in that discourse. When sentences are connected by connectives that are not dynamic, such as disjunction (*o* ... *o* ...) (Kamp and Reyle 1993), a potential context set created by an accommodation function in the first disjunct is not accessible to a superlative description in the second disjunct. This is exactly what happens in the following examples, where the context set for *el* in *el regalo más caro* 'the most expensive present' (13a) cannot be the set of objects that (can be) purchased at that particular mall. Similarly, the set of mountains that function as a context set for the definite determiner in (13b) is not associated to the location of Juan's vacation.

(13) a. O Juan va al centro comercial o le compra a su mujer el regalo más caro.
or Juan goes to-the center commercial or CL buys to his wife the present more expensive
'Either Juan goes to the mall or he buys his wife the most expensive present.'
b. O Juan se va de vacaciones o escala la montaña más alta.
or Juan CL goes of holidays or climbs-he the mountain more high
'Either Juan goes on vacation or he climbs the highest mountain.'

Groenendijk, Stokhof, and Veltman (1995) claim that an additional presupposition has to be accommodated to derive the context sets in (14), namely, that all the objects under consideration are not equally expensive. Consider (14):

(14) a. Compré treinta libros el mes pasado. No debí haber comprado el más caro.
bought-I thirty books the month last. not must-I have bought the more expensive
'I bought thirty books last month. I shouldn't have bought the most expensive one.'

b. Le compré diez regalos de Navidad a mi hija. Solo le gustó la muñeca más cara.
CL bought-I ten presents of Christmas to my daughter. only CL liked the doll more expensive
'I bought my daughter ten Christmas presents. She only liked the most expensive doll.'

Nevertheless, this is precisely part of the descriptive content of the superlative operator, as defined in (8) above: not all degree properties are equal. Therefore, no additional mechanism to deal with their observation is needed. For example, the context set of the superlative description in (14b) is the set of Christmas presents in the preceding sentence.

4. Comparison and contexts sets

Heim (1996) claims that the context set restricts the superlative operator. The members of the context set are degree properties. Her proposal appears to conflate the contribution of two elements that are claimed in Gutiérrez-Rexach (2006b, 2011) to be syntactically and semantically different: the definite determiner and the superlative operator. In order to assign differential roles to the definite determiner and the superlative operator, their individual separate contribution has to be elucidated. This would require distinguishing between the restricting role of the context set, as described in the previous section, and the role of the scope or frame of the comparison, which is standardly claimed to restrict comparative elements. Context sets only restrict determiners, as originally proposed by Westerståhl (1985). Superlative operators may be restricted by an expression denoting the frame of the comparison. Syntactically, the PP acting as the frame of the comparison adjoins to the maximal projection containing the superlative operator. Consider the following discourse:

(15) Ismael fue a la tienda. Le compró a su mujer el regalo más caro de la sección de deportes.
Ismael went to the store CL bought to his wife the present more expensive of the section of sports
'Ismael went to the store. He bought his wife the most expensive present in the sports section.'

The Logical Form (LF) representation of the superlative description *el regalo más caro de la sección de deportes* 'the most expensive present in the sports section' in (15) is the following:

(16) [$_{DP}$ el [$_{DegP}$ [$_{DegP}$ regalo más caro] [$_{PP}$ de la sección de deportes]]]

The adjunct PP *de la sección de deportes* 'in the sports section' provides the scope of the comparison. It restricts the domain of the superlative operator. Its effect is that the operator is restricted from unrestricted comparison to comparing objects in the sports section. On the other hand, the context set restricts the definite determiner and is different from the scope or frame of the comparison. In (15) the context set is retrieved from the set of potential locations at the store ($\lambda p[Store(p)]$) by accommodating the function $f_p(w)(p)$ *(In)* and adding the associated set as the context set: the set of objects in the store ($\lambda x[In\_Store(x)]$). The frame of comparison restricts the denotation of the superlative further to the set of objects in the sports section ($\lambda x[In\_sports\_section(x)]$). Consider now the following discourses:

(17) a. Hay siete estudiantes de MA y diez de PhD en el programa. El mejor es Rudy.
there-are seven students of MA and ten of PhD in the program the best is Rudy
'There are seven MA and ten PhD students in our program. The best is Rudy.'
b. Hay siete estudiantes de MA y diez de PhD en el programa. El mejor en socio es Rudy.
there-are seven students of MA and ten of PhD in the program the best in socio is Rudy
'There are seven MA and ten PhD students in our graduate program. The best in Sociolinguistics is Rudy.'

The determiner *el* 'the-masc-sg' in (17a, b) is restricted by the same context set: the students in the MA or PhD program ($\lambda x[MA\_student(x)] \lor PhD\_student(x)]$). In (17a) there is no comparison frame. In (17b) the presence of the PP adjunct triggers the introduction of a condition restricting the comparison class of the superlative. There is a second difference between these two sentences: the presupposition triggered by the superlative. This presupposition is a non-equality condition: the rest of the individuals under consideration in the Socio class are not good to degree *d*, the degree to which

Rudy is good. Thus, there is a two-step restriction taking place. The comparison is first restricted to the individuals in the context set of the higher definite determiner and afterwards the comparison is further restricted to the comparison frame. The consequence of this stepwise process is that it is not possible for the individual satisfying the superlative definite description to be a member of the set of those in the Sociolinguistics class but not a member of the set of MA or PhD students.

5. Focus interpretation and superlatives

Recall that at the beginning of this chapter we mentioned Szabolcsi's (1986a) observation on the dependence of superlative interpretation on focus assignment. Depending on which element of the sentence is focused, different "comparative" readings may arise. This is illustrated by the contrast in (18):

(18) a. [Lola]$_F$ compró a Luisa el libro más largo.
[Lola]$_F$ bought to Luisa the book more long
'[Lola]$_F$ bought Luisa the longest book.' →
'Lola bought Luisa a book longer than the books that anybody else bought Luisa.'
b. Lola compró a [Luisa]$_F$ el libro más largo.
Lola bought to [Luisa]$_F$ the book more long
'Lola bought [Luisa]$_F$ the longest book.' →
'Lola bought Luisa a book longer than the books that she bought anybody else.'

One important observation with respect to these data is that the effect of focus on superlative interpretation seems to be local to the sentence in which the focused constituent occurs, as the following discourses show:

(19) a. [Ana]$_F$ fue al centro comercial. Le compró a Lorena el mejor regalo.
[Ana]$_F$ went to-the center commercial. CL bought to Lorena the best present
'[Ana]$_F$ went to the mall. She bought Lorena the best present.'
b. Cuando [Ana]$_F$ va al centro comercial, le compra a Lorena el mejor regalo.
when [Ana]$_F$ goes to-the center commercial CL buys to Lorena the best present

'Whenever [Ana]$_F$ goes to the mall she buys Lorena the best present.'

In the discourse in (19a), the focused element occurs in the first sentence. The superlative description that would be affected by contrastive focus is in the second. In (19b), the focused constituent is in the restriction of a tripartite quantificational structure: the adverbial clause introduced by *cuando*. The superlative expression is in the nuclear scope or main clause of the sentence. The focus-related comparative reading becomes unavailable in both cases. In other words, (19a) lacks the reading 'Ana bought Lorena a present better than the presents anybody else bought her'. The second sentence in (19b) also lacks this comparative reading. Assuming that comparative readings are focus-related, what this fact shows is that the focused element has to be in the same clause as the superlative description.

Thus, it seems obvious that there is a structural restriction on the availability of the comparative reading: Focus has to occur on the local domain of the superlative. In order to explain this restriction, the mechanism by which focus conditions the comparative reading has to be determined first. Following the proposal in Gutiérrez-Rexach (2006b, 2011), we claim that the context set is determined by the focus value (Rooth 1985, 1992b) of the sentential constituent (or TP) where the focused constituent occurs after the operation of Quantifier Raising (QR) has applied to the superlative description. This entails that the determination of superlative readings is subject to an interface condition, since it is sensitive to Logical Form operations.

Let us go back to sentence (18a) and look at the steps determining how the comparative reading is derived at the syntax/semantics interface. There are several operations that need to be applied. First, QR applies to the superlative description (superlative DP) and adjoins it to IP.

(20) [$_{TP}$ [$_{DP}$ el libro más largo]$_i$ [$_{TP}$ Lola compró a Luisa t$_i$]]

This would be required to determine the scope of comparison at LF. In a second step, the remnant TP constituent moves to the specifier of Focus Phrase (Brody 1990; Zubizarreta 1998; etc.) The moved constituent contains the focused expression:

(21) [$_{FocP}$ [$_{TP}$ Lola compró a Luisa t$_i$]$_j$ [$_{TP}$ [$_{DP}$ el libro más largo]$_i$ t$_j$]]

The focus value of the remnant TP in the specifier of Focus Phrase has to be calculated in order to determine the set of entities actually being contrasted. The focus value of this constituent in the specifier of FocusP is the set of contextually relevant alternatives y to the individual denoted by *Lola* in the model such that *y* bought *x* for Luisa:

(22) FV([Lola]$_F$ compró a Luisa x) =
λy[**PAST**(**Buy**(y, **Luisa**, x)) & y ∈ ALT(**Lola**)]

The focus value of the remnant TP will be the set that can be contextually used to establish comparisons or contrast with other elements. In the present case, this set will act as the context set for the definite determiner heading the superlative description. What this entails from an operational point of view is that this set is substituted for the context set variable of the determiner. In Gutiérrez-Rexach (2006b, 2011), the following calculation is proposed:

(23) Let C be the context set variable of the definite determiner and A the variable representing the focus value of the IP. Then C = λx[∃y[**A**(x, y)]].

Notice that the type of y is the type of the members of A. In our example, the context set has the following value:

(24) C = λx[∃y [**PAST**(**Buy**(y, **Luisa**, x)) & y ∈ ALT(**Lola**)]].

Summarizing, the focus value of the TP will act as the context set of the superlative description. Raising of the TP to FocusP is necessary in order to check the focus feature and activate the final interpretive step. It is also necessary because the focus value of the TP would not be accessible for the context set otherwise. Let us now consider the problematic (19a). Here the focus value of the first TP would be the set of individuals, alternatives to Ana, who went to the mall:

(25) FV([Ana]$_F$ fue al centro comercial) =
λz[**PAST**(**Go**(z, **to_the_mall**)) & z ∈ ALT(**Ana**)]

Then, if we choose FV to provide the context set of the superlative description, we have a problem because there is no object variable in FV corresponding to the content of the description. The relevant generalization seems to be that the focus value of an expression can provide the context set of a superlative description only if the remnant TP contains a variable (trace) of the superlative description. This automatically entails that the focused constituent and the superlative DP have to be in the same scopal domain. The locality of the focus-affected comparative reading follows without additional stipulations.

Let us consider the effect of focusing other sentential constituents. For example, in (26) the temporal adverb *ayer* 'yesterday' is focused:

(26) Pedro compró el libro más caro [ayer]$_F$.
Pedro bought the book more expensive yesterday
'Pedro bought the most expensive book [yesterday]$_F$.'

When the temporal adverb *ayer* 'yesterday' in (26) is focused, a "comparative" interpretation emerges in which the context set is the set of books purchased in the period under consideration, namely the set of alternatives to *ayer*. In this case we have to calculate the focus value of (27a), which is (27b), where M is a modifier variable.

(27) a. Pedro compró x [ayer]$_F$.
Pedro bought x yesterday
'Pedro bought x [yesterday]$_F$.'
b. $\lambda M\ [M(\textbf{Buy}(j, x))\ \&\ M \in \text{ALT}(\textbf{yesterday})]$

Notice that (27a) has a variable, as the result of the displacement of the superlative quantifier to the position where it takes scope. The resulting focus value of the open proposition is the set of alternative circumstances potentially making the proposition 'Pedro bought *x*' true, as shown in (27b). The context set restricting the superlative definite description is (28), which derives the intended meaning.

(28) $C = \lambda x[\exists M\ [M(\textbf{Buy}(j, x))\ \&\ M \in \text{ALT}(\textbf{yesterday})]]$

6. Questions and the comparative reading

It is a well-known fact that in interrogative sentences, the *wh*-word constitutes the focus of the sentence. If our hypothesis that comparative readings are intrinsically focus-dependent is correct, it should follow that interrogative sentences only allow comparative readings where the source of the comparison is the *wh*-word/phrase. This is exactly the case. In other words, a superlative DP occurring in an interrogative expression can only have a comparative reading where the comparison class is drawn from alternatives in the domain associated with the *wh*-element. As a consequence, comparative readings such as the ones in (29) normally arise:

(29) a. ¿Quién le dio a Juan el regalo más caro?
'Who gave Juan the most expensive present?' →
'Who gave Juan a present more expensive than the presents that anybody else gave Juan?'
b. ¿A quién le dio Juan el regalo más caro?
'To whom did Juan give the most expensive present?' →
'To whom did Juan give a present more expensive than the presents he gave to anybody else?'

The LF derivation providing the intended readings is as follows. First, the superlative description adjoins to IP, as shown above. The remnant IP moves to the specifier of the Focus Phrase, and finally the *wh*-word moves to the specifier of CP to check its [+wh] feature, leaving a trace in the specifier of FocusP. This trace is necessary in order to associate the interrogative expression with focus—the interrogative expression has to check two features: [+focus] and [+wh]. This LF feeds the semantic interpretation.

(30) [$_{CP}$ quién$_k$ [$_{FocusP}$ [t$_k$ le dio a Juan t$_i$]$_j$ [$_{IP}$ [el regalo más caro]$_i$ [$_{IP}$ t$_j$]]]]

The focus value of the remnant-IP expression ([t$_k$ le dio a Juan t$_i$]) in the specifier of FocusP is calculated as shown before. I assume that interrogative quantifiers are also restricted by context sets (Gutiérrez-Rexach 1997). The set of alternatives evoked by the *wh*-word *quién* corresponds to its descriptive content, namely, the set **PERSON** ∩ A, where A is the context set of the interrogative quantifier. The focus value of the remnant IP in the specifier of FocusP is (31), the set of alternative individuals who gave something to Juan:

(31) FV(PAST(**Give**(y, j, x))) = λz[PAST(**Give**(z, j, x)) & z ∈ PERSON ∩ A]

This set becomes accessible to the superlative description and the context set of the determiner *el* becomes (32), the set of things that where given by somebody to Juan:

(32) λx[∃y [PAST(**Give**(y, j, x)) & y ∈ **PERSON** ∩ A]

When the *wh*-phrase has a restriction, there are two comparative interpretations, depending on whether the context set consists only of individuals in the denotation of the restriction or also includes other individuals. In example (33) the two different interpretations would depend on whether the context set consists of Scandinavians or of Scandinavians and non-Scandinavians, as shown in (34).

(33) ¿Qué escandinavo recibió el premio más preciado?
'Which Scandinavian received the most valuable award?'

(34) a. Which Scandinavian received an award more valuable than the awards any other Scandinavian received?
b. Which Scandinavian received an award more valuable than the awards any other individual under consideration (including non-Scandinavian) received?

There are three potential derivations as candidates to generate the proper context set. Let us examine them. In the first derivation, the *wh*-phrase (interrogative quantifier) *qué escandinavo* 'which Scandinavian' moves to the specifier of CP, after adjunction of the superlative DP to IP and movement of the remnant IP to the specifier of FocusP:

(35) [$_{CP}$ qué escandivo$_k$ [$_{FocusP}$ [t$_k$ recibió t$_i$]$_j$ [$_{IP}$ [el premio más preciado]$_i$ [$_{IP}$ t$_j$]]]]

In the second alternative derivation, only the interrogative determiner *qué* 'which' moves in the last step, leaving its restriction in the specifier of FocusP.

(36) [$_{CP}$ qué$_k$ [$_{FocusP}$ [t$_k$ escandinavo recibió t$_i$]$_j$ [$_{IP}$ [el premio más preciado]$_i$ [$_{IP}$ t$_j$]]]]

Finally, in the third potential derivation, the restriction of the *wh*-determiner stays "in situ" within the IP and does not move with the remnant IP to the specifier of FocusP.

(37) [$_{CP}$ qué$_k$ [$_{FocusP}$ [t$_k$ recibió t$_i$]$_j$ [$_{IP}$ [el premio más preciado]$_i$ [$_{IP}$ escandinavo t$_j$]]]]

Let us now consider the context sets resulting from the interpretation of the three alternative LFs above. The context set in (38) is the one corresponding to the LF (35); the context set (39) corresponds to (36); and (40) corresponds to (37).

(38) C = λx[∃y [PAST(**Receive**(y,x)) & y ∈ SCANDINAVIAN ∩ A]]

(39) C = λx[∃y [PAST(**Receive**(y,x) & **Scandinavian**(y)) & y ∈ A]]

(40) C = λx[∃y [PAST(**Receive**(y,x)) & y ∈ A]]

The differential composition of the context set is related to the position of *escandinavo* 'Scandinavian' at LF. Interestingly, the first and the second context sets are equivalent, so the LF derivations render the same readings. In other words, whether the restriction moves to the specifier of CP or stays within FocusP does not trigger any difference in the semantic computation of the context set. Only when the restriction of the interrogative quantifier stays *in situ*, the context set includes alternative individuals of any nationality, not only Scandinavians.

When the superlative is in an embedded question, an interesting contrast arises depending on the nature of the embedding verb. In the examples in (41) only the reading in which the embedding verb is not part of the context set of the definite determiner is possible.

(41) a. ¿Quién sostienes que recibió el regalo más caro?
'Who do you claim got the most expensive present?'
b. ¿Quién dices que escaló la montaña más alta?
'Who do you say climbed the highest mountain?'

Sentence (41a) lacks the comparative reading 'Who are you claiming got a present more expensive than the presents you are claiming any other people got?'. It has, on the other hand, the comparative reading 'Who are you claiming got a present more expensive than the presents any other people got?'. In the former reading, the verb *sostienes* 'claim' would be part of the context-set restriction of the definite determiner. In the latter, it is not. Similarly, (41b) lacks the comparative reading 'Who do you say climbed a mountain higher than the mountains you said any other individual climbed?'. The comparative reading in which *dices* 'say' is not part of the context set of the determiner is possible: 'Who do you say climbed a mountain higher than the mountains any other individual under consideration climbed?'.

Contrastingly, in the examples of (42) both comparative readings are possible: a reading in which the embedding verb is part of the context set, and a reading in which the embedding verb is not part of the context set:

(42) a. ¿Quién crees que recibió el regalo más caro?
 'Who do you believe got the most expensive present?'
 b. ¿Qué estudiante piensa que leyó el libro más largo?
 'Which student thinks that he read the longest book?'

Sentence (42a) has two comparative readings. In the first one, the verb *crees* 'believe-you' is part of the context set of the determiner: 'Who do you believe got a present more expensive than the presents you believe any other people got?'. In the second reading, the verb is not part of the context set restricting the definite determiner: 'Who do you believe got a present more expensive than the presents any other people got?'. In a parallel fashion, both comparative readings are obtained in (42b): 'Which student thinks that he read a book longer than the books any other student thinks he read?', 'Which student thinks that he read a book longer than the books any other student read?'.

The difference between the verbs in (41) and (42) is that the former are speech-act verbs (*decir* 'say', *sostener* 'claim') whereas the latter are propositional attitude verbs (*creer* 'believe', *pensar* 'think'). I am going to assume, following Davidson (1968), that the complements of the verbs of the first type are not structured and they would stand for *that*-demonstratives. On the other hand, verbs of the latter type embed propositional complements which are syntactically structured. Then, the computation of the context set does not have access to the embedding verb in (41), whereas that possibility is available in the examples in (42).

Why- and *how*-questions exhibit an asymmetric behavior in comparison with the rest of argument and adjunct questions. Consider the following interrogative sentences:

(43) a. ¿Por qué leíste el libro más largo?
 'Why did you read the longest book?'
 b. ¿Cómo escalaste la montaña más alta?
 'How did you climb the highest mountain?'

The above sentences lack comparative readings based on the *wh*-term. In other words, in the case of (43a), the relevant alternatives cannot be calculated taking *why* as a basis. Thus, the superlative lacks the comparative reading

'For what reason did you read a book longer than the books you read for any other reason?'. The only comparative reading possible is 'For what reason did you read a book longer than any other book?'. This reading may fit the conditions for the superlative reading as well. The interrogative sentence (43b) lacks the comparative reading 'In which manner did you climb a mountain higher than the mountains you climbed in any other manner?', which would be the one based on alternatives related to *how*. The comparative/absolute reading that is available is 'In which manner did you climb a mountain higher than any other mountain?'.

The problem in the above sentences seems to be that the context set cannot be formed taking as a basis the set of alternatives in the sets **MANNER** or **REASON**. Szabolcsi and Zwarts (1993) claim that the set of manners and reasons has the structure of a join semi-lattice. Therefore, it is not closed under complements or meets. Yet the computation of the set of alternatives requires precisely taking into consideration the complement of a certain entity x, i.e. the set of alternatives to it: $ALT(x) = -x$.

7. The problem of existential constructions

Szabolcsi (1986a) also observes that in existential-*there* constructions only the comparative reading is allowed, as shown by the contrast in (44).

(44) a ??Ayer hubo la menor cantidad de invitados.
         '*Yesterday there were the fewest guests'
     b. La menor cantidad de invitados la hubo ayer.

Existential sentences obligatorily introduce non-dependent or free discourse referents (Kamp and Reyle 1993). As a consequence, the context set of the description is empty in (44a) and the description fails to refer—the intersection of the denotation of the descriptive part with the empty set is always empty. The corresponding representation is not well-formed. In (44b), *ayer* 'yesterday' occurs in a clefted focus position. The content of the context set is provided not by the previous discourse but by accommodation of the content of *there were x [yesterday]*$_F$ as above. This yields the context set (45), which is the set of individuals under consideration in ALT(**yesterday**):

(45) $C = \lambda x[\exists M \ [M(\textbf{Thing}(x)) \ \& \ M \in ALT(\textbf{yesterday})]]$

8. Conclusion

In this chapter I have addressed the ambiguities that arise in the interpretation of superlatives in Spanish and argued that they can be better understood as a byproduct of the context dependence of definite determiners. I have shown that the readings associated with superlatives are the compositional result of the combination of several factors: (i) the meaning of definite determiners, understood as determiner functions restricted to a context set; (ii) the comparative operator *más* 'more'; and (iii) the dynamics of context sets in discourse as they interact with focus interpretation. Using a basic and straightforward model for the dynamic interpretation of syntactically analyzed LF-structures, I have also defended that there are structural or interface constraints which also condition the availability of a certain context set. In sum, well-known factors related to context, focus, and the syntax/semantics interface conspire to produce an apparent multiplicity of readings. If this is correct, we have a powerful argument for a simpler account of the semantics of comparatives and superlatives.

9
The Dimensions of Modal Discourse Particles

1. Introduction

Discourse particles, and discourse markers or connectives in general, have been mostly the focus of attention of pragmatic, communicative and discourse-functionalist studies, with a variety of explanatory goals. The following issues are among those typically addressed: How these particles contribute to the overall coherence/cohesion of discourse; How they connect discourse segments; How they serve different argumentative functions; How they indirectly reflect or directly express speaker-oriented strategies or they trigger implicatures of different sorts; etc. Nevertheless, there still remain important properties and issues that cannot be properly accounted for using a pragmatic or communicative approach exclusively. The following questions seem to be relevant if we want to gain a comprehensive understanding of the meaning of discourse particles: What is the categorial ascription of these expressions?; Do they interact or determine other constituents at the subsentential level?; What do they tell us about the composition of meaning? In other words, what seems to be missing so far in most studies on this empirical domain is a clear connection between grammatical properties of a systematic nature and intentional or communicative functions. This connection is critical for our purposes, since it seems to clearly belong to one linguistic interface or more, namely, the interfaces between structure and meaning and the interface between semantics and pragmatics.

Recent formal perspectives on the analysis of discourse particles seem to point in the direction of a reassessment of how meaning is structured and how potentially different dimensions are articulated. Discourse particles can be seen as expressions connecting descriptive meaning and expressive meaning (Kratzer 1999; Potts 2003), as presupposition triggers (Zeevat 2002), as context markers (Zeevat 2004), as rhetorical-relation indicators bringing new points of attachment in discourse (Urgelles-Coll 2010), or as multi-dimensional semantic elements (Gutiérrez-Rexach 2006a; Zulaica-Hernández and Gutiérrez-Rexach 2012).

Following recent trends in the formal analysis of discourse particles, in this chapter a group of Spanish discourse particles is analyzed as a structured class comprising three types of adverbs of quantification, with universal, existential or negative force. These particles have the pragmatic function of conveying counter-argumentative or reformulative intentions. Nevertheless, the former aspect, namely their semantic content and structure, is claimed to be fundamental in determining their pragmatic meaning. Several arguments are presented in support of this hypothesis, as well as of the claim that these particles are associated with distinctive constraints at different levels of meaning. Such levels are characterized as the levels or dimensions of descriptive and expressive meaning.

From an empirical viewpoint, we will focus only on a small class of Spanish complex discourse markers or particles. This seems to be the best strategy, because the landscape of discourse markers is quite extensive—cf. Briz (2000). Nevertheless, some of the claims made in this chapter could easily be extended to particles in other subclasses. The particles considered in this chapter instantiate the following schema: "de + Q + N_{pl}," where Q stands for a quantifier expression, and N is a plural noun denoting manner, way or form. We call these particles complex to contrast them to those of simple lexical nature (*además, pues,* etc.). There are several particles instantiating the following structural arrangement: *de Q formas/maneras/modos* 'lit. of Q form(s)/way(s)/manner(s)/case(s)/event(s)'). For example, we have the particles, *de todas maneras/formas, de todos modos* ('anyway; lit. of all manners/forms/ways'); *de alguna manera/forma, de algún modo* ('somehow; lit. of some manner/form/way'); *de ninguna manera/forma, de ningún modo* ('not at all; lit. of no manner/form/way'); etc. In all of these complex particles, an initial prepositional element (*de* 'of') is followed by a determiner plus a noun denoting manner. It will be shown that determiner variation is significant, since it radically changes the meaning of the complex expression and is associated with quantificational variability. It will also be defended that these operators should be treated as adverbs of quantification (Lewis 1975; Heim 1982; etc.) with a systematic contrasting semantic behavior. Finally, there is evidence suggesting that the manner nouns involved in the construction (*formas, maneras,* and *modos*) also contribute to the interpretation of the discourse marker. Thus, it becomes obvious that the make-up of these complex discourse particles is compositional.

Overall, if a similar strategy were to be applied to other classes of discourse particles, a more fine-grained picture of their meaning would emerge, leading to a reconsideration of at least some of these expressions as operators with distinctive properties at the grammatical interfaces (semantics/pragmatics and syntax/semantics). If this were correct, even the descriptive label organizing them as discourse particles or markers would prove to be somewhat inadequate, inasmuch as their role in grammar would not only be to indicate discursive functions or textual structuring strategies. They would also have a significant quantificational role, one involving a speaker's attitudes and manner of evaluating a statement. This chapter builds on some of the evidence presented in Gutiérrez-Rexach and Howe (2003) and Gutiérrez-Rexach (2006a).

2. Particles with universal quantificational force

The discourse markers *de todas maneras/de todas formas/de todos modos* ('anyway, anyhow, in any case, in any event') are said to convey a relation of opposition or correction between propositions in a discourse, and they are usually characterized as counter-argumentative or reformulative particles— cf. Ferrara (1997); Portolés (1998); Montolío (2001); etc. In the discourse in (1), the proposition introduced by *de todas maneras* corrects, is opposed to, or contrasts in some fashion with what is stated in the previous statement.

(1) No sé por qué Juan estudia tanto. De todas maneras, suspenderá el examen.
not know-I by what Juan studies such of all manners will-fail-he the exam
'I do not know why Juan studies so much. Anyway/In any event, he will fail the exam.'

This standard behavior can be described assessing the primary counter-argumentative or contrastive use of this particle. It is also true that this complex particle can be used to reinforce an entailment or implicature of the preceding discourse. This latter use is usually descriptively characterized as a "reformulative" use, illustrated in (2):

(2) Las hamburguesas son demasiado grasientas y el pollo frito también.
the hamburgers are too greasy and the fried chicken too
De todas formas, nunca me ha gustado la comida rápida.
of all manners never CL have-I liked the food fast
'Hamburgers are greasy and fried chicken too. In any case, I never liked fast food.'

The use of *de todas maneras/de todas formas* 'anyway, in any case/event' in (1) and (2) is warranted by presuppositions previously introduced in discourse. These background presuppositions are not necessarily congruent with what the actual speaker believes, but serve as the basis to introduce the assertion following the complex particle. According to Fuentes Rodríguez (1996), reformulation is a communicative operation used by a speaker to reiterate the communication of an intended content that was not transmitted initially in a fashion adequate for his communicative intentions. Montolío (2001) notes that discourse markers with a reformulative function indicate the existence of a previous argument but instruct the addressee to discard it as relevant and consider only the argument or proposition they introduce. This type of account needs to be supplemented by a theory taking into consideration the differential effects of syntactic position in interpretation and how the semantics of these particles is linked to other related expressions with which they form a natural class.

First, a particle of this sort connects the preceding discourse—a proposition or conjunction of propositions P—with the proposition that it introduces explicitly (Q). The force of the quantifier in the '*de* + quantifier + manner-noun' sequence determines the relationship that is established between these two propositions, as will be argued below. Thus, it can be claimed that the particle should be treated as a quantificational operator with a tripartite structure of the form in (3):

(3) **every manner** $[_R\ P\ ][_{NS}\ Q]$.

The restriction ($[_R\ P\ ]$) of this operator is the relevant propositional discourse fragment: a proposition or the conjunction of several propositions.

This restrictive propositional content has been previously asserted or can alternatively be derived by presupposition accommodation (Lewis 1979; von Fintel 1994; Partee 1995; Kadmon 2000; etc.). Thus, *P* can be viewed as the conjunction of the propositional assertions or presuppositions available in the common ground determining the evidence underlying the assertion of the nuclear scope ($[_{NS}\ Q]$). There are important cross-linguistic differences that will not be dealt with in this chapter. For example, in English, the difference between *in any event* and *anyway* is that the latter does not need *P* (the restriction) to be related necessarily to previous propositions stated or presupposed. As we will see below, when we substitute Spanish *alguna/algún* 'some' or *ninguna/ningún* 'no' for *todas* 'all/every,' we have a similar tripartite structure that privileges the argument in the nuclear scope, although in the case of *ninguna/ningún* an overt nuclear scope is not required:

(4) a. ¿Vas a ir al cine?
    go-you to go to-the cinema
    'Are you going to the movies?'
  b. De ninguna manera.
    of no manner
    'Not at all.'

Second, the discourse particles under consideration exhibit a contrasting behavior as a function of their syntactic position. They behave like speaker-oriented adverbials (Jackendoff 1972) when in left-detached, sentence-initial position, as exemplified in (1) and (2). They may alternative behave as standard event modifiers (manner adverbials), when they occur in non-detached sentence-internal or sentence-final position. This contrast is linked to a difference in quantificational properties. Particles occurring in a detached position are selective adverbs of quantification and bind a contextual "manner" variable in their restriction, associated with the relevant assertions/presuppositions in the common ground of discourse (Gutiérrez-Rexach 2006a). They do not bind individual variables in their restriction or nuclear scope. In sentence internal or final (non-detached) position, however, these adverbs have a completely different interpretation as unselective operators.

We are using the selective and unselective terms in the fashion originally intended by Lewis (1975) and his followers (Kamp 1981; Heim 1982; etc.). Their idea is that quantificational elements are not expressions associated with a single variable in their logical representation uniformly. Those expressions behaving in such standard fashion are considered selective binders. On the other hand, other terms have the ability to bind more than one variable within the domain they have scope over. Those variables are typically introduced by indefinite expressions, which consequently inherit the quantificational force of the binding operator. In other words, the easiest way to recognize an unselective binder at work is to verify whether the indefinites occurring within its domain lack their default existential value and have the force of such an operator (universal, generic, etc.).

Let us consider the variant of a reformulative statement in which the particle occurs in a peripheral left-detached position first, as in (5):

(5) a. De todas maneras, Juan es inteligente.
of all manners Juan is smart
'In any case (no matter what alternative scenarios you consider), John is intelligent.'
b. De todas maneras, Juan beberá una cerveza.
of all manners Juan will-drink a beer
'In any case (no matter what alternative scenarios you consider), John will drink a beer.'

Notice that there are apparently no variables to be bound in the scope of the operator *de todas maneras* in (5a), given that *inteligente* 'intelligent' is an individual-level predicate and *Juan* is an individual constant. Recall that Kratzer (1995) claims that this class of predicates, denoting permanent or characterizing properties, lack event variables. Thus, the representation of the predication relation would be *Intelligent(j)*. If *de todas maneras* were an unselective adverb of quantification, it would quantify vacuously, so that an ill-formed logical representation would be derived, as in (6):

(6) *every manner$_{x, e}$ [P(x, e)] [**Intelligent(j)**]

Vacuous quantification emerges here because the quantifier does not bind a variable both in the restriction and the nuclear scope. There are no instances of the variables *x* and *e* in the nuclear scope, so this scopal domain is quantified over "vacuously." We have thus to conclude that (5a) only has a reading in which the "manner" variable pertains to accommodated information in the common ground that becomes relevant to the intended conclusion.

(7) every$_m$ [P(m)] [P(m) & **Intelligent**(j)]

Following (7), (5a) would express that there is information in the common ground pertaining to the "manner" of evaluation or evidence from which it can be concluded that Juan is intelligent. The information in the restrictor (*P(m)*) is copied in the nuclear scope by the property of conservativity (Keenan and Stavi 1986) as applied to adverbs of quantification—The relevant process would be similar to the mechanism and property of "dynamic conservativity" (Chierchia 1995). This selective variant of *de todas maneras* 'in any case' has been represented as (*every$_m$*). The variable *m* denotes a contextually determined and salient circumstantial/situational parameter: a context variable, possibly of shifting type, which expresses what we will be calling an "m-case". The importance of m-cases is that they determine how the quantifier is evaluated, i.e. how the variable *m* receives the proper assignment. Since it is a special designated variable for manners of evaluation, it ranges over m-cases: ways of evaluating a proposition. Formally, the truth conditions for (7) would be as in (8):

(8) Let P be the conjunction of the relevant propositions in the common ground, then **every**$_m$ [P(m)][P(m) & **Intelligent**(j)] is True if and only if every m-case satisfying P can be extended to an m-case satisfying [P & **Intelligent**(j)].

In this respect, the relevant presupposed propositions expressing the information in *P* serve as the basis for the inference in the nuclear scope. What (8) states is that all those propositions share a contextual parameter. This parameter is a "manner" or way of evaluating such propositions. Under any possible value of that parameter (any possible circumstance), the proposition in the nuclear scope holds. For example, with respect to (5a), let us assume a common ground in which it is presupposed that Juan has received poor grades, he has not been admitted to the university which was his first choice, his performance has been erratic in the last few years, etc. A speaker, when uttering this sentence, may express that he still regards Juan as an intelligent individual. This opinion may hold no matter what our opinion about all those propositions is—in other words, under any possible perspective or attitude we might adopt towards those facts or opinions. In this respect, it can be said that *todas* 'every' in *de todas maneras* 'in any case' indicates how the speaker evaluates the circumstances supporting his assertion: the nuclear scope of the operator.

Sentence (5b) poses a different problem: Both the event variable of the predicate and the individual variable of the indefinite *a party* can be bound. However, the universal event-dependent reading of (5b), where *de todas maneras* binds the manner, event and individual variables, is difficult or impossible to obtain.

(9) every$_{m, e, x}$ [P(m)] [P(m) & **Beer**(x) & FUT(**Drink**(e, j, x))]
i.e. '*In any m-case Juan will drink all the beers.'

Clearly, (5b) does not mean that Juan will drink all the beers, all circumstances considered. This leads again to the conclusion that the adverbial particle must also be a selective binder in (5b). Consider now (10), where the indefinite indeed has universal force.

(10) De todas maneras, un estudiante nunca llega tarde.
of all manners a student never arrives late
'In any case, a student never arrives late.'

It seems that the universal reading of (10) is due to *never* and not to *in any case*. Thus, this adverb of quantification would behave as an unselective binder of universal force providing such a force to the indefinite *estudiante* 'student'. On the other hand, the complex particle would be a binder only for the covert manner of evaluation variable. Since *every$_m$* seems to be consistently selective in left-detached position, any individual variables occurring in its scope should be bound by other means. For example, in (11a) below the variable *x* is bound by existential closure of the nuclear scope, i.e. the insertion of an existential quantifier to bind a variable at the appropriate scopal point in the representation (Heim 1982). Alternatively, the proposition may receive its force from other unselective quantifier, such as *nunca* 'never' in (10), yielding (11b). *Nunca* would decompose as *not some* applied to event and individual variables.

(11) a. every$_m$ [P(m)] [some$_{e, x}$ [P(m) & **Beer**(x) & FUT(**Drink**(e, j, x))]]
'In every m-case under consideration, John will drink a beer.'
b. every$_m$ [P(m)] [not some$_{e, x}$ [P(m) & **Arrive**(e, x) & **Late**(e)]]
'In every m-case under consideration, no student ever arrives late.'

Let us now consider the scenario where these adverbials occur in a sentence-internal or final position, of a non-detached nature. The resulting sentences are ambiguous. For example, (12) and (13) have two readings, depending on whether the indefinite has existential force or universal/generic force:

(12) Un estudiante aplicado aprobará el examen de todas maneras.
a student dedicated will-pass the exam of all manners
'A dedicated student will pass the exam no matter what' or
'Every dedicated student will manage to pass the exam.'

(13) Un elefante odiará a un ratón de todos modos.
an elephant will-hate ANIM a mouse of all modes
'An elephant will hate a mouse in any case' or
'Every elephant will hate a mouse anyway.' →
'It is always the case that an elephant will hate a mouse . . .'

The first reading is the one that we have characterized before and, for most speakers, it would not be available unless the adverbial is right-detached. In this reading, the complex particle is a selective quantifier binding a manner of evaluation variable. In the second and most prominent reading, the particles *de todas formas/de todas maneras/de todos modos* have universal or generic force and unselectively bind the individual, temporal, and modal variables in the sentence. Furthermore, these particles are incompatible with other unselective quantifiers in sentence-final, non-detached position, as the contrast between (14a) and (14b) shows:

(14) a. *Un elefante odia a un ratón siempre de todas formas.
an elephant hates ANIM a mouse always of all forms
'*An elephant always hates a mouse in any case.'
'*Every elephant hates a mouse.'
b. Un elefante siempre odiará a un ratón, de todas formas.
an elephant always will-hate ANIM a mouse of all forms
'In any case, an elephant always hates a mouse.'

Sentence (14a) is ungrammatical under the intended interpretation in which both adverbs are construed unselectively. Nevertheless, if an intonational break is inserted between the two adverbs of quantification or *de todas formas* is right-detached, as in (14b), then the sentence has the reading in which *de todas formas* is selective. In this reading, this complex particle binds the covert manner of evaluation variable and *siempre* behaves as an unselective adverb of quantification with universal force, binding the individual variables contributed by the indefinites *un elefante* and *un ratón*.

Further evidence of the differential selectivity of this discourse marker comes from the fact that only the selective, canonically left-detached variant allows cross-sentential anaphora of indefinites:

(15) a. De todas maneras, un ladrón se escapó. Pro$_{sg}$ era astuto.
of all manners a thief CL escaped pro was astute
'Anyway/In any event, a thief escaped. He was clever.'
b. *Un ladrón se escapa de todas maneras. Pro$_{sg}$ es astuto.
a thief CL escapes of all manners pro is astute
'A thief always escapes (no matter what). He is astute.'

In (15a), the complex particle is selective, and the indefinite is bound by existential closure, thus, it refers to a specific individual. This individual is also the entity referred to by the null pronoun in the second sentence of the discourse. This coreferential behavior follows the standard equation operation across discourse markers introduced by an existential quantifier and a pronoun. This equation can cross sentential boundaries (Kamp and Reyle 1993). On the other hand, the complex particle is unselective in (15b). The null subject pronoun of *is astute* in (15b) cannot be referring to the thief generically/universally invoked in the preceding sentence. This is so because universal/generic quantifiers are "externally static", i.e. they cannot bind beyond their scope (Chierchia 1995). Thus, cross-sentential anaphora is prohibited in this case because the complex particle blocks it. Note that cross-sentential anaphora is possible when the null pronoun occurring in the second sentence is plural, as in (16):

(16) Un ladrón se escapa de todas maneras. Pro$_{pl}$ son siempre muy astutos.
a thief CL escapes of all manners pro are always very astute
'A thief always escapes (no matter what). They are always very smart.'

This anomaly is only apparent, since it can be claimed that the reference of the plural pronoun is resolved by a "bridging" mechanism in this case (Asher and Lascarides 1999), among other pragmatic resources. From the discourse referent introduced in the first sentence, the bridging mechanism generalizes to thieves able to escape in general.

The evidence presented thus far strongly suggests a connection between the syntax and semantics of *de todas formas/maneras/modos*. The two resulting options can be represented as shown below:

(17) *Selective:*
every$_m$ [Ψ][Φ], where the adverb of quantification binds a "manner" variable in [Ψ].
Unselective:
every [Ψ][Φ], where all the variables in [Ψ], [Φ] are bound by the adverb of quantification.

Syntactically, it has been argued extensively during the last decade that elements occurring in the left periphery of the clause (Rizzi 1997) occupy positions related to informational-structure features. Assuming this line of reasoning, it is easy to conclude that occurring in such peripheral positions would block the relevant scopal configuration for unselective binding to take place. Recall that the essential condition for unselectivity to take place is that the unselective binder has to have scope over the indefinite expressions to be bound. What we can conclude from the evidence presented so far in this chapter is that displacing an element to topic/focus/force related positions is incompatible with unselective behavior. This claim is clearly true for discourse particles. Nevertheless, caution is in order before extending the generality of the claim to any operator, since operators participating in *wh*-constructions, of an exclamatory or interrogative nature, also have to be generated or displaced in the force layer of the left periphery and it is not clear that unselectivity is blocked in these cases.

3. The multidimensionality of particles: Descriptive and expressive content

In work by Kratzer (1999) and Potts (2003), among others, discourse particles are viewed as multidimensional expressions articulating a descriptive and an expressive meaning. The nature of the latter is not sufficiently clear yet, following David Kaplan's (1989) landmark insights, and will probably be subject to further debate in the coming years (Potts 2005). Expressive meaning can be viewed as comprising conventional implicatures in the sense of Grice

(1989), appropriateness conditions in a given context, or even more generalized constraints of a pragmatic nature (Potts 2007). Without committing to any particular theory on this matter for the moment, let us now summarize the essential ingredients of the meaning of universal counter-argumentative and reformulative discourse particles. The descriptive or truth-conditional content of the corresponding selective adverbial operator is as follows:

(18) every$_m$ [Ψ][Φ] iff every m-case satisfying [Ψ] can be extended to a m-case satisfying [Φ].

The notion of what counts as an "m-case" or satisfying circumstance is determined contextually. As indicated above, it is normally linked to the speaker's perspective: his evaluative judgment of what makes the propositions in the restrictor "relevant" or salient for the intended conclusion.

The expressive meaning of this operator can be divided in two components. First, it establishes a rhetorical relation between discourse segments, in the sense of Asher and Lascarides (2003). As accurately described in the literature, this rhetorical relation may be either contrastive/adversative or reformulative in nature. In the first case, given the well-known difficulty in characterizing the notion of contrast (de Hoop and de Swart 2004) or even in reducing it to a single rhetorical relation, I will assume the existence of a family of contrastive relations (*Contrast*$_i$, for 1≤ i ≤ n). Within this family, there might be relations with differential informational status, deriving the difference between contrastive topics and contrastive focus for example. There is also a family of elaboration relations (*Elaboration*$_i$, for 1≤ i ≤ n), with members of different informational and pragmatic status. What is of interest for our purposes here is that a rhetorical relation *Contrast*$_i$ or *Elaboration*$_i$ has to hold between the restrictor and the nuclear scope of the particle. Formally, the disjunctive constraint in (19) has to be satisfied—where CG stands for the conversational common ground and ⊧ is not the logical entailment relation but a weaker relation of contextual entailment or inference:

(19) CG ⊧ **Contrast**$_i$ ([Ψ][Φ]) or CG ⊧ **Elaboration**$_i$ ([Ψ][Φ])

What (19) states is that from the common ground it can be inferred that a contrastive or an elaborative relation holds between the discourse propositional fragments Ψ and Φ. The inference relation is not logical entailment. In other words, it does not necessarily follow from the content of such propositions *per se*. It requires a critical role from the discourse participants (speaker, addressee), who contribute their respective communicative intentions. Contrast and elaboration relations require the identification of a discourse topic or "question under discussion" in Ψ (Roberts 1996; Büring 2003). This topic is the element that becomes contrasted in some fashion with the nuclear scope of the particle (Φ) or is elaborated by it. The determination of the precise nature of the topic or question under discussion and of how the relevant contrastive or elaboration relation arises requires additional inferences on the part of the hearer. In this respect, particles might signal or serve to navigate through a "strategy" (Eckardt 2004).

The second ingredient in the expressive or non-descriptive meaning associated with the discourse particle is related to the speaker's attitude towards the expressed content. As was stated before, the speaker expects Φ to be the case, and expects so to a high degree. He is committed to the soundness of his expectations and he believes that the circumstances in question (the supporting "m-cases") warrant the intended inference. Thus, the following also holds:

(20) CG + [Ψ] $\models$ **Expect**(s, [Φ], δ) & **High**(δ)

Informally, updating a given common ground with the relevant assertion or presupposition expressed by Ψ contextually entails that the speaker s expects Φ to a high degree δ. Consider (21):

(21) De todas formas, te quedas castigado en casa esta noche.
      of all forms CL stay-you grounded in house this night
      'In any event, you are grounded at home tonight.'

A speaker may utter (21) in a situation in which he is upset about his adolescent son's behavior and, given the circumstances surrounding such behavior and his son's not very convincing excuses, he utters (21) to verbalize the intended punishment. From (21), not only it can be inferred that no matter what attenuating circumstances his son is presenting to justify his behavior he will be punished. It can also be inferred that the speaker has an expectation to a high degree of the soundness of his decision, the outrage motivating it, etc. The addressee, his son, has to understand that his father commitment for (21) to hold is high. Obviously, the addressee does not have to share the same degree of commitment for the proposition to hold.

Finally, the selective adverbial particle does not seem to interact scopally with other discourse particles or expressive elements, something that is not unexpected given what was stated in the previous section. Kratzer

(1999) notes that "other expressives in the scope of a discourse particle are ignored in the computation of the expressive meaning contributed by that particle". In this respect, they can all be treated as scope independent at the level of expressive content. For example, *de todas maneras* does not interact with the expressive *ahora que lo pienso* 'now that I think about it' in (22):

(22) a. De todas maneras, ahora que lo pienso, tendrás que llegar a tiempo a la reunión.
of all manners now that it think-I will-have-you that arrive at time at the meeting
'In any case, now that I think about it, you will have to be at the meeting on time.'
b. Ahora que lo pienso, de todas maneras tendrás que llegar a tiempo a la reunión.
now that it think-I of all manners will-have-you that arrive at time at the meeting
'Now that I think about it, in any case, you will have to be at the meeting on time.'

At first sight, it seems that the order of the expressive modifiers *de todas maneras* and *ahora que lo pienso* does not alter the expressive meaning of the sentence. The reformulative (contrastive or elaborative) content contributed by the universal manner particle remains identical. The same can be said with respect to the content of the actualizing idiom *ahora que lo pienso*. Its expressive role is to convey that the process leading to the assertion of the introduced proposition has just being culminated, adding immediacy to the relevant deliberation process. These two expressive inferences are not incompatible with each other and do not interact quantificationally, so it can be concluded that they are scope independent. Nevertheless, this generalization is not completely accurate. Interaction or lack thereof seems to be dependent on whether there is compatibility between the relevant particles in regard to their respective expressive meaning. For example, the assertion of the sentences in (23) requires a high degree of expectation or commitment by the speaker. Thus, *de todas maneras* is compatible with other high-commitment particles such as *por supuesto* 'of course':

(23) a. De todas maneras, por supuesto que tendrás que llegar a tiempo a la reunión.
of all manners by supposed that will-have-you that arrive at time at the meeting

b. Por supuesto, de todas maneras tendrás que llegar a tiempo a la reunión.
by supposed of all manners will-have-you that arrive at time at the meeting
'Of course, in any event you will have to be at the meeting on time.'

As it was the case with (22), the order of the modifiers does not make them interact in a scopal fashion at the level of expressive meaning. The point that we are arguing here is different, namely, that they are both alike in such expressive dimension and as a consequence they become compatible. On the other hand, other expressives such as *cualquiera sabe* 'who knows' or *no estoy seguro* 'I am not certain' do indeed interact with *de todas maneras,* since they explicitly mark the speaker's commitment to the proposition as not very high. By consequence, they become incompatible with the selective adverbial:

(24) Esta oportunidad es única para el negocio. Así que de todas maneras (*cualquiera sabe si/*no estoy seguro si) tendrás que llegar a tiempo a la reunión.
this opportunity is unique for the business so that of all manners anyone knows if/not am-I certain if will-have-you that arrive at time at the meeting
'This is a unique opportunity for our business. Thus, in any event (*who knows whether/*I am not sure whether) you will have to be on time at the meeting.'

What (24) clearly illustrates is that a potential interaction at the expressive dimension or level of meaning turns out to be more a matter of compatibility or not of the inferences associated with each expressive term. It is not a matter of scope. This conclusion would also follow from our claim that expressive connectives are normally selective and, if they bind variables, they are associated to such expressive content.

4. Existential and negative contractors or reformulators

The complex particles *de alguna manera/de alguna forma/de algún modo* 'somehow' ('lit. in some way/form/case') also exhibit the contrasting selective or non-selective behavior just attested for universal contrastive/reformulative adverbials. In the left-detached non-selective variant, they relate previous assertions/presuppositions with their nuclear scope by adding epistemic evidential content in which the speaker evaluates low probability (Kaufman 2001) or low expectation. Consider (25):

(25) De alguna manera, esto no me gusta.
 of some manner this not CL like
 'Somehow, I do not like this.'

What this sentence expresses is that there is a (salient) circumstance or "manner" of evaluating the relevant presuppositions in the common ground that grants my inference: 'I do not like this.' Formally:

(26) **some**$_m$ [P(m)] [**not**(Like(I, it))] iff there is an m-case satisfying [P] that can be extended to an m-case satisfying [**not**(Like(I, it))].

Notice that the main contrast with universal reformulative markers is that the force of the particle is existential in this case: it is only necessary to find one satisfying circumstance or m-case for the sentence to be true. For example, with respect to (25), the restriction may be constituted by several propositions regarding a recent business deal: a few shady characters were involved, it took place at night, we made too much money, etc. The relevant circumstantial parameter (m-case) could be a negative perception or evaluation on the part of the speaker about these facts. It is this perception that justifies the assertion in the nuclear scope.

Following recent trends in the semantics of indefinites, we may represent the existential force of the indefinite through the use of choice functions in the metalanguage (Winter 1997; Reinhart 1997; chapter three of this book). This seems to be the correct option, given that the indefinite in (25) always has a specific or wide-scope reading. In other words, the speaker is referring to a salient circumstance justifying his inference. This explains why existential contrastive or reformulative particles of the sort considered here can only be built in Spanish using the specific determiner *algún* 'some' and not the non-specific *un* 'a' (Gutiérrez-Rexach 2003): *de una manera 'lit. of a manner', *de un modo, 'lit. of a way', etc. The indefinite determiner *algún* introduces a special kind of choice function, namely an intensional choice function, given that what is selected is one of the circumstances or validating cases in the common ground:

(27) Let M-case be the set of potentially relevant contextual circumstances, and f(M-case) the member of this set selected by the choice function f. Then, some$_m$ [Ψ][Φ] iff there is a choice function f such that f(M-case) satisfies [Ψ] and f(M-case) can be extended to an m-case satisfying [Φ].

In sentence internal or final non-detached position, the adverbial has the already-mentioned event-related manner interpretation. It behaves as a non-selective existential quantifier binding an event variable and the individual variable corresponding to the indefinite. The manner noun is translated as a predicate of events, à-la Davidson (Parsons 1990). Sentence (28a) would be interpreted as 'There is an escaping event and that event was performed in a certain fashion by a thief', as represented in the logical form (28b).

(28) a. Un ladrón se escapó de alguna manera.
a thief CL escaped of some manner
'A thief escaped somehow.'
b. some$_{e, x, y}$ [$_R$ Thief(x)] [$_{NS}$ Escape(e) & Agent(e, x) & Manner(e, y)]

In the representation in (28b), thematic roles are decomposed in a Neo-Davidsonian fashion (Parsons 1990), as predicates of events or relating events and individuals (the relevant participants). The existential quantifier corresponding to the complex particle binds an event variable (e) and two individual variables (x, y). The expressive or non-descriptive content of this subclass of existential discourse markers seems to be similar to the expressive content of the universal particles. First, they trigger a rhetorical relation of contrast or elaboration in the common ground. Second, they are also associated with an expectation relation between the speaker and the content of the nuclear scope. We are not talking about a strong commitment or a high degree of expectation on the part of the speaker. Rather, the speaker's commitment can be described as sufficient but not high, in consonance with the existential force of the quantifier—only one circumstance of evaluation validates the inference, not all of them, so the speaker cannot be absolutely certain about the validity of his conclusion:

(29) CG + [Ψ] ⊨ Expect(s, [Φ], δ) & not(High(δ))

Consider (30):

(30) De alguna forma, aprobaré el examen.
of some form will-pass-I the exam
'Somehow, I'll pass the exam.'

What the speaker is asserting with (30) is his belief that he will pass the exam. Nevertheless, his degree of commitment toward the proposition is not high. There is a way in which he will be able to pass the exam, but he is not too confident about it either. The fact that not all possible courses of events validate his inference makes it considerably weaker than in the case of universal particles analyzed above.

Finally, the same syntactic and semantic distinction holds with *de ninguna manera/forma/de ningún modo* 'no way/in no case'. In its left-detached, selective position, *de ninguna manera* is a refutation operator that gives zero evidential support to the presuppositions in its restriction. Sentence (31) would be translated as (32):

(31) De ninguna manera, no creas que vas a ganar.
of no manner not believe-you that go-you to win
'No way, don't think that you are going to win.'

(32) **not some**$_m$ [P(m)] [P(m) & **not think(you, that you will win)**]

As it was proposed with existential particles, we can claim that the quantifier introduces a choice function that selects none of the m-cases potentially validating the propositions in the restriction and the nuclear scope. The relevant semantic satisfaction clause would be as follows:

(33) Let M-case be the set of potentially relevant contextual circumstances, and f(M-case) the member of this set selected by the choice function f. Then, **not some**$_m$ [Ψ][Φ] iff there is no choice function f such that f(M-case) satisfies [Ψ] and f(M-case) can be extended to an m-case satisfying [Φ].

Applying (33), sentence (31) would be interpreted as: 'There is no circumstance (m-case) that warrants the inference that you will win (from the available presuppositions in P)', as expected. Since we are treating negative particles as the negation of existential ones, the associated expressive content would also be the negation of the expressive content in (29):

(34) $\text{CG} + [\Psi] \models \textbf{Expect}(s, [\Phi], \delta)\ \&\ \textbf{not}(\text{not}(\textbf{High}(\delta))) =$
$\text{CG} + [\Psi] \models \textbf{Expect}(s, [\Phi], \delta)\ \&\ \textbf{High}(\delta)$

As expected, this turns out to be the expressive content of universal reformulative particles. In other words, these negative reformulative particles also express a high degree of commitment to the asserted proposition. For example, sentence (35), as asserted by a senator, expresses his strong belief that the law will not pass, for example because there is no way in which they will get the votes needed to do so, etc.

(35) De ningún modo, la ley no pasará.
of no mode the law not will-pass
'No way, the law will not pass.'

Since the semantics based on m-cases actually states that no m-case or validating circumstance exists making the relevant proposition true, it is predicted that only negative propositions are introduced by this type of markers. Thus, the correlate of (35) with positive polarity is not grammatical:

(36) *De ningún modo, la ley pasará.
of no mode the law will-pass
'No way, the law will pass.'

It is clearly obvious that it would be contradictory to assert that a proposition will hold and at the same time express that there are no circumstances making this possible. We see then that the expressive content of these particles is able to interact with its truth conditional content. On the other hand, when *de ninguna manera/forma/modo* occurs in sentence-final, non-detached position, the negative complex particle behaves as an unselective adverb of quantification whose restriction becomes a negative polarity item of a minimizing nature. Sentence (37) would have the representation in (38):

(37) Un león amaestrado no atacará de ningún modo.
a lion tamed not will-attack of no mode
'No tamed lion ever attacks at all.'

(38) **not some**$_{x,e}$ [**Lion**(x) & **Tamed**(e, x)] [**Attack**(e, x)]

5. Conclusion

In this chapter it has been argued that the members of a particular class of contrastive and reformulative discourse particles, represented in Spanish by expressions instantiating the structural pattern '*de* + quantifier + noun', should be treated as adverbs of quantification. In this respect, they give rise to a tripartite structure (quantifier-restriction-nuclear scope) and vary in terms of their binding relationships as a function of their syntactic position. When they occur in left-detached position, as the result of base generation in the left periphery of the sentence, they are selective binders. In this position, the variable that becomes bound by the adverbial is one corresponding to a contextually dependent circumstantial parameter related to "manner" of perception or evaluation by the speaker. On the other hand, when these particles occur in a non-detached position, they behave as non-selective operators. Several other properties follow from this characterization. Sentence-final, non-detached reformulative particles are normally incompatible with other unselective quantifiers that may occur in the sentence. They are also able to unselectively bind free variables and give rise to collateral effects, such as external anaphoric statism, etc. The distinction between descriptive and expressive meaning is used to fully characterize the contribution of this class of discourse particles to discourse integration and interpretation.

Obviously, not all discourse markers are amenable to a compositional analysis and it is expected that some of them will lack most, if not all, quantificational properties of the sort discussed here. In this respect, it would be interesting to consider whether there is a historical relationship or development by which more complex and semantically stronger discourse particles get "bleached" or lose their quantificational properties in time and become standard discourse connectors. This issue remains as an open question for further research.

Final Thoughts on Quantity, Structure, and Meaning

THE STUDY OF QUANTIFICATION and quantifiers has proven to be central to the concerns of many disciplines and areas of knowledge whose subject matter is the structure and articulation of symbolic systems. Quantification is a core component of natural language as well as of many other semiotic systems, independently of whether they are natural or artificial in nature. Whereas it is difficult to deny the centrality of quantification, it is also apparent that defining and articulating the boundaries and methods for its study has remained an elusive task for centuries. In other words, even if it were not difficult to explain why to undertake this task, many would still consider problematic its very possibility. How to do so and what to include are prominently controversial issues. In a well-known distinction articulated by Charles Morris, semantics was separated from syntax and pragmatics. Semantics, we were told, studies the relationship between a sign and its meaning, as opposed to syntax, which studies the relationship of signs to each other, and pragmatics, devoted to the relationship between signs and their users.

Nevertheless, there is no *a priori* general agreement on how to tackle this interconnection problem. Different assumptions may also be related to certain methodological choices: the desiderata for a higher level of formalization, the incorporation of structural phenomena, the willingness to consider data from different languages, etc. In sum, several potential alternative approaches may arise as a function of foundational or methodological choices. The diversity of problems and approaches that can be envisioned and undertaken could have seemed in the past to seriously cripple any potential development. Nevertheless, from our current perspective, one is forced to conclude that the actual result has been probably the opposite. The study of quantification is nowadays almost generally viewed as an interdisciplinary enterprise, where contributions from linguistics, philosophy, logic, psychology, and computer science converge. The results from different approaches are sometimes combined in unexpected ways. There have also been many efforts to integrate potentially different theories and consider the problems or prospects of such integration.

The rapid development of generative grammar in the fifties and sixties, after pioneering work by Noam Chomsky, forced a re-evaluation of earlier pessimistic diagnoses. During the late sixties and early seventies, several linguists and philosophers envisioned the possibility of a formal theory of meaning. Once the enterprise of characterizing the structure of natural language with recursive devices was contemplated not only as possible but also as surprisingly simple, the idea of specifying a semantic theory for a structurally analyzed language was within reach. The last two decades witnessed a definitive maturation of the field and also exposed some of the challenges it currently faces. On the one hand, a still ongoing debate emerged on how to integrate quantification into grammatical architectures. Ultimately, this debate has been superseded by the increasing sophistication of theoretical proposals and paradigms. For example, the emergence of the Minimalist Program during the mid-nineties stresses the importance of semantic properties in grammar, a fact sometimes overlooked by those adhering to the Autonomy of Syntax hypothesis. Currently it is believed that the only necessary levels of linguistic representation are the "interface" levels, namely those serving as input to semantic or phonological interpretation, and a great deal of evidence has been provided for this hypothesis in the present book. Overall, a change in focus seems to be taking place at the beginning of the new millennium. This change partially erases the traditional boundaries across phonology, syntax, semantics, and pragmatics, and seeks to explore the interfaces and relations between sound and meaning, structure and meaning, and meaning and context.

Another challenging area is related to how to incorporate the obvious (and complex) reality of linguistic diversity. There are more than six thousand languages in the world. One can legitimately wonder whether there are deep semantic universals, common to all language families. If this is found to be correct, then we will have opened a window into the workings of the human mind. In this sense, from an initial almost exclusive focus on English data and phenomena, current research on quantification is moving toward a genuine cross-linguistic perspective and toward the consideration of true universals (Keenan and Paperno 2012). The hidden laws of language indeed illuminate the universal laws of thought, a project that would have satisfied the logician George Boole.

The research presented in this monograph has been shaped to a great extent by the above-mentioned challenges: the need to integrate structure and meaning; the use of formal tools incorporating recent developments in neighboring areas of grammatical analysis; and the challenge of cross-linguistic diversity, including the proper description and explanation of phenomena that have received little of no attention in the literature. For obvious reasons, this latter aspect has mostly focused on the analysis of the Spanish language.

In general, the real measure of the strength and success of a scientific endeavor is its ability to improve our understanding of empirical phenomena. The expression of quantity and quantification in natural language is a complex but fascinating area in which the conspiracy of different resources becomes more than apparent. The most salient words expressing quantity and measure are the so-called articles or, more generally, determiners. Nevertheless, these determiners interact with other elements in an interesting fashion. In chapter two, it has been characterized how ellipsis blocks or allows certain scopal interactions, whereas chapter three argues for a more sophisticated treatment of the interplay of modality and quantification. Similarly, indefiniteness is connected in chapter four to the attribution of essential properties, a connection that takes place through the verb *tener* 'have'.

Let us look now at the empirical domain of *wh*-expressions. In English, if we compare a sentence such as *Which student came to the party* with *Some student came to the party*, probably we would not see any apparent or compelling reason to establish a connection between them, given the obvious fact that one is a question and the other is a declarative statement. Nevertheless, in many languages *which* and *some* are expressed by the same word, concretely the correlate of the determiner *some*. For example in Chinese the sentence *John mai le shenme* (lit. 'John bought something/what') would be interpreted either as a statement or a question depending on different intonational patterns. In other words, *shenme* means both *something* and *what*. In a parallel fashion, the sentence *Shei kanjian le shenme* can mean 'someone bought something' or the question 'who saw what.' This connection is intriguing and most descriptive and theoretical grammars ignore it when they ascribe *some* and *which* to different syntactic and semantic categories. Nevertheless, a proposal for a unification of declarative and *wh*-determiners can be formulated. It would be based on the idea that they both instantiate or have the same semantics properties, i.e. they denote very similar generalized quantifier functions. This unification is not without problems. As chapters five and six show, the analysis of relative clauses requires looking at additional layers of complexity, especially related to the expression of reference to degrees. The expression of quantity is not restricted to the category of determiners. Degree expressions such as *too, so, such* or *much* can also be considered quantifiers. Many of these are used in exclamative sentences to express a speaker's attitude toward the high degree of a property: *How tall you are!, What a smart person he is!,* etc. In this case, the conspiracy of structural and semantic resources can also be attested. In Spanish, determiners and other categories allow quantification over degrees whereas in English the range of categories expressing degree quantification is more restricted. This contrastive semantic property, in conjunction with the structural properties of relative clauses of different sorts (free relatives and correlatives), predicts the attested data, and illustrates how apparently arbitrary or meaningless differences hide the key to the understanding of deep universal mechanisms that determine the grammatical encoding of meaning.

Chapters seven and eight move away from *wh*-structures but keep their focus on the analysis of degree terms and reference to degrees. Concessive statements of the conditional variety are argued to be quantifiers over degrees with specific scalar properties in chapter seven, integrating structural considerations with others belonging to the semantics/pragmatics interface. A similar connection is argued for in chapter eight, and several degree-based readings of superlative descriptions are shown to interact with the interface property of focus.

In the last two decades, several authors have advocated the idea that context should be integrated as a syntactic/semantic parameter that can be built-in when computing determiner denotations. I believe that it can be convincingly argued that the implementation of this proposal allows us to understand some unexplained facts about context-dependent expressions. Chapter nine focuses on discourse particles or markers, which have traditionally viewed as pragmatic markers of context dependence in discourse. What has been argued here is that this connection with context is dependent on linguistic expression and structure, and also on the ability to articulate quantificational meaning.

Looking at the interplay of syntactic, semantic and pragmatic factors seems to be a very rewarding strategy in the analysis of quantificational expressions of all sorts. Structural facts and contrasts hide or, more properly, become the expression of subtle semantic distinctions. With this brief tour of the landscape of certain marginalized expressions of quantity in Spanish, I hope to have shown that the problems, paradoxes and intriguing data patterns that emerge when we study this concrete aspect of grammar seem to be telling us an even more intriguing story. A story that only now we can start to understand in the new theoretical landscape where quantification is viewed as a dynamic notion, whose study shows results that are very similar in nature to those obtained in current debates in neighboring areas of linguistic inquiry. We can no longer be satisfied with classifying words and expressions, in the taxonomic spirit of descriptive grammars. We can no longer be content either with merely deriving the structure of complex expressions from simpler ones, in the spirit of derivational syntactic approaches. Finally, we can no longer consider sufficient the sketchy empirical idealizations of the logical analysis of meaning. Getting one's hands dirty with the complexities and paradoxes of linguistic data from a variety of sources is not a distraction form the enterprise of building a solid theoretical foundation. Quite the contrary, if we assume that linguistic utterances are not arbitrary or the by-product of an individual speaker's decision at a single point in time, then they must be the manifestation of a hidden logic. This hidden structure might be one that we do not understand at this point in time. It might be even be one that we will never understand. Nevertheless, it is still worth to use the tools at our disposal to uncover new evidence and cross-domain connections.

Bibliography

Abusch, Dorit. 1994. The scope of indefinites. *Natural Language Semantics* 2: 83–135.
Alarcos, Emilio. 1994. *Gramática de la lengua española*. Madrid: Espasa Calpe.
Alonso-Ovalle, Luis, and Paula Menéndez-Benito. 2003. Some epistemic indefinites. *Proceedings of the North East Linguistic Society* 33: 1–12.
———. 2010. Modal indefinites. *Natural Language Semantics* 18: 1–31.
Arregi, Karlos. 2004. The *have/be* alternation in Basque. MS. University of Illinois, Urbana.
Arregui, Ana. 2006. *Cualquier*, exception phrases and negation. In *Romance Languages and Linguistic Theory 2004*, ed. J. Doetjes and P. González, 1–22. Amsterdam: John Benjamins.
Asher, Nicholas, Daniel Hardt, and Joan Busquets. 1998. Discourse parallelism, scope and ellipsis. *Proceedings SALT 7*. 19–36.
Asher, Nicholas, and Alex Lascarides. 1999. Bridging. *Journal of Semantics* 15: 83–113.
———. 2003. *Logics of Conversation*. Cambridge: Cambridge University Press.
Asudeh, Ash, and Richard Crouch. 2002. Derivational parallelism and ellipsis parallelism. *Proceedings WCCFL* 21. 1–14.
Baker, Mark. 1988. *Incorporation*. Chicago: University of Chicago Press.
Barker, Chris. 2002. Continuations and the nature of quantification. *Natural Language Semantics* 10: 211–42.
Barker, Chris, and Pauline Jacobson. 2007. *Direct Compositionality*. Oxford: Oxford University Press.
Barwise, John, and Robin Cooper. 1981. Generalized quantifiers and natural language. *Linguistics & Philosophy* 4: 159–219.
Bauer, Brigitte. 1996. Residues of non-nominative syntax in Latin: The *mihi est* construction. *Historische Sprachforschung/Historical Linguistics* 109: 241–56.
Beck, Sigrid. 1997. On the semantics of comparative conditionals. *Linguistics & Philosophy* 20: 229–71.

Beghelli, Filippo. 1995. The syntax of quantifier scope. PhD diss., UCLA.

———. 1998. Mood and the interpretation of indefinites. *Linguistic Review* 15: 277–300.

Bennett, Daniel. 1969. Essential properties. *Journal of Philosophy* 66: 487–99.

Bennett, Jonathan. 1982. Even if. *Linguistics & Philosophy* 5: 403–18.

Benveniste, Emile. 1971. *Problems in General Linguistics*. Coral Gables: University of Miami Press.

Berman, Steven. 1991. The semantics of open sentences. PhD diss., University of Massachusetts, Amherst.

Bhatt, Rajesh. 2003. Locality in correlatives. *Natural Language & Linguistic Theory* 21: 485–541.

———. 2006. Relativizing in space and time. MS, University of Massachusetts, Amherst.

Bianchi, Valentina. 1999. *Consequences of Antisymmetry*. Berlin: Mouton de Gruyter.

Boeckx, Cedric. 2011. *Oxford Handbook of Linguistic Minimalism*. Oxford: Oxford University Press.

Bosque, Ignacio. 1980. *Sobre la negación*. Madrid: Cátedra.

———. 1994. La negación y el PCV. In *Gramática del español*, ed. V. Demonte, 167–201. Mexico, DF: El Colegio de Mexico.

———. 1995. On degree quantification and modal structure. In *Aspects of Romance Linguistics*, ed. H. Campos et al., 87–106. Washington, DC: Georgetown University Press.

———. 1998a. Sobre la gramática de los contextos modales: Entornos modales y expresiones inespecíficas en espa ñol. *Actas del XI Congreso de Alfal*, ed. J. A. Semper and M. Troya. Las Palmas de Gran Canaria: Universidad de Las Palmas y Librería Nogal, 43–57.

———. 1998b. Sobre los complementos de medida. In *Estudios en honor del profesor Josse de Kock*, ed. Nicole Delbecque and Christian de Paepe, 57–72. Leuven: Leuven University Press.

———. 2001. On the weight of light predicates. In *Features and Interfaces in Spanish and French: Essays in Honor of Heles Contreras*, ed. J. Herschensohn, E. Mallén, and K. Zagona, 23–38. Amsterdam: John Benjamins.

———. 2012. Mood: Indicative vs. subjunctive. In *Handbook of Spanish Linguistics*, ed. J. I. Hualde and A. Olarrea, 373–94. Oxford: Blackwell.

Bosque, Ignacio, and Javier Gutiérrez-Rexach. 2009. *Fundamentos de sintaxis formal*. Madrid: Akal.

Brasoveanu, Adrian, and Donka Farkas. 2011. How indefinites choose their scope. *Linguistics & Philosophy* 34: 1–55.

Briz, Antonio. 2000. *Diccionario de partículas discursivas del español*. http://www.dpde.es/.

Brody, Michael. 1990. Some remarks on the focus field in Hungarian. *UCL Working Papers in Linguistics* 2: 201–25.

Brucart, Josep María. 1986. *La elisión sintáctica en español*. Bellaterra: Universitat Autònoma.

———. 1992. Some asymmetries in the functioning of relative pronouns in Spanish. *Catalan Working Papers in Linguistics* 7: 113–43.

———. 2004. Adición, sustracción y comparación: Un análisis composicional de las construcciones aditivo-sustractivas del español. In *Actas del XXIII Congreso de Lingüística y Filología Románica*, ed. A. Sánchez Miret, 11–60. Tübingen: Max Niemeyer.

Bruening, Daniel. 2001. QR obeys superiority: Frozen scope and ACD. *Linguistic Inquiry* 32: 233–73.

Brugger, Gerhard, and Mario D'Angelo. 1995. Movement at LF triggered by mood and tense. *Folia Linguistica* 29: 195–221.

Büring, Daniel. 2003. On D-trees, beans and B-accents. *Linguistics & Philosophy* 26: 511–45.

Cameron, Ross P. 2010. The grounds of necessity. *Philosophy Compass* 5: 348–58.

Caponigro, Ivano. 2001. On the semantics of indefinite free relatives. In *Proceedings Console 10*, ed. M. van Koppen, 49–62. Leiden: Sole.

———. 2003. Free not to ask: On the semantics of free relatives and wh-words cross-linguistically. PhD diss., UCLA.

———. 2004. The semantic contribution of *wh*-words and type shifts: Evidence from free relatives. In *Proceedings SALT* 14, ed. R. Young, 38–55. Ithaca, NY: CLC Publications.

Caponigro, Ivano, and Maria Polinsky. 2011. Relative embeddings: A Circassian puzzle for the syntax/semantics interface. *Natural Language & Linguistic Theory* 29: 71–122.

Carlson, Greg. 1977a. Amount relatives. *Language* 53: 520–42.

———. 1977b. Reference to kinds in English. PhD diss., University of Massachusetts, Amherst.

———. 1981. Distribution of free choice *any*. *Chicago Linguistics Society* 17: 8–23.

———. 2001. Weak indefinites. In *From NP to DP*, ed. Martine Coene and Yves de Hulst, 195–210. Amsterdam: John Benjamins.

———. 2006. The meaningful bounds of incorporation. In *Non-Definiteness and Plurality*, ed. S. Vogeleer and L. Tasmowski, 35–50. Amsterdam: John Benjamins.

Carnap, Rudolf. 1956. *Meaning and Necessity: A Study in Semantics and Modal Logic.* 2nd ed. Chicago: University of Chicago Press.

Carpenter, Bob. 1998. *Type-Logical Semantics.* Cambridge, MA: MIT Press.

Castroviejo, Elena. 2008. Deconstructing exclamations. *Catalan Journal of Linguistics* 7: 41–90.

Chierchia, Gennaro. 1995. *Dynamics of Meaning.* Chicago: University of Chicago Press.

———. 1998. Reference to kinds across languages. *Natural Language Semantics* 6: 339–405.

———. 2004. Scalar implicatures, polarity phenomena, and the syntax/pragmatics interface. In *Structures and Beyond*, ed. Adriana Belletti, 39–103. Oxford: Oxford University Press.

———. 2006. Broaden your views: Implicatures of domain widening and the 'logicality' of language. *Linguistic Inquiry* 37: 535–90.

Chomsky, Noam. 1957. *Syntactic Structures.* The Hague: Mouton.

———. 1965. *Aspects of the Theory of Syntax.* Cambridge, MA: MIT Press.

———. 1981. *Lectures on Government and Binding.* Dordrecht: Foris.

———. 1993. A minimalist program for linguistic theory. In *The View from Building 20*, ed. K. Hale and S. J. Keyser, 1–52. Cambridge, MA: MIT Press.

———. 1995. *The Minimalist Program.* Cambridge, MA: MIT Press.

———. 1998. Some observations on economy in generative grammar. In *Is the Best Good Enough?*, ed. P. Barbosa et al., 115–28. Cambridge, MA: MIT Press.

———. 2000. Minimalist inquiries: The framework. In *Step by Step: Essays on Minimalist Syntax in Honor of Howard Lasnik*, ed. R. Martin, 89–115. Cambridge, MA: MIT Press.

———. 2001. Derivation by phase. In *Ken Hale: A Life in Language*, ed. Michael Kenstowicz, 1–52. Cambridge, MA: MIT Press.

Chung, Sandra, and William Ladusaw. 2003. *Restriction and Saturation.* Cambridge, MA: MIT Press.

Cinque, Gughlielmo. 1994. On the evidence for partial NP-movement in the Romance DP. In *Paths towards Universal Grammar*, ed. G. Cinque and J. Koster, 85–110. Washington, DC: Georgetown University Press.

———. 1999. *Adverbs and Functional Heads: A Cross-Linguistic Perspective.* Oxford: Oxford University Press.

———. 2010. *The Syntax of Adjectives.* Cambridge, MA: MIT Press.

Collins, Chris. 1997. *Local Economy*. Cambridge, MA: MIT Press.

———. 2008. Economy conditions in syntax. In *The Handbook of Contemporary Syntactic Theory*, ed. M. Baltin and C. Collins, 45–61. Oxford: Blackwell.

Comorovski, Ileana, and Klaus von Heusinger, eds. 2007. *Existence: Semantics and Syntax*. New York: Springer.

Contreras, Heles. 1986. Spanish bare NPs and the ECP. In *Generative Studies in Spanish Syntax*, ed. I. Bordelois, H. Contreras, and K. Zagona, 25–49. Dordrecht: Foris.

Cooper, Robin. 1983. *Quantification and Syntactic Theory*. Dordrecht: Kluwer.

Copestake, Ann, Dan Flickinger, Carl Pollard, and Ivan Sag. 2006. Minimal recursion semantics: An introduction. *Research on Language and Computation* 3: 281–332.

Cormack, Annabel. 1984. VP Anaphora: Variables and scope. In *Varieties of Formal Semantics*, ed. F. Landman and F. Veltman, 81–102. Dordrecht: Reidel.

Corver, Norbert. 1997. The internal syntax of the Dutch extended adjectival projection. *Natural Language & Linguistic Theory* 15: 289–368.

Cresswell, Max. 1996. *Semantic Indexicality*. Dordrecht: Kluwer Academic Publishers.

Crevels, Mily. 2000. Concessives on different semantic levels: A typological perspective. In *Cause-Condition-Concession-Contrast, Cognitive and Discourse Perspectives*, ed. E. Couper-Kühlem and B. Kortmann, 313–40. New York: Mouton de Gruyter.

Culicover, Peter. 1999. *Syntactic Nuts: Hard Cases, Syntactic Theory, and Language Acquisition*. Oxford: Oxford University Press.

Culicover, Peter, and Ray Jackendoff. 1999. The view from the periphery: The English comparative correlative. *Linguistic Inquiry* 30: 543–71.

———. 2005. *Simpler Syntax*. Oxford: Oxford University Press.

Dalrymple, Mary. 1991. Against reconstruction in ellipsis. MS. CSLI, Stanford University.

Dalrymple, Mary, Stuart Shieber, and Fernando Pereira. 1991. Ellipsis and higher-order unification. *Linguistics & Philosophy* 14: 399–452.

Davidson, Donald. 1968. On saying 'that'. *Synthese* 19: 130–46.

Dayal, Veneeta. 1997. Free relatives and *ever*: Identity and free-choice readings. Proceedings *SALT* 7: 99–116.

———. 1999. Bare NP's, reference to kinds, and incorporation. In *Proceedings SALT* 9, ed. T. Matthews, 34–51. Ithaca, NY: CLC Publications.

———. 2004. Number marking and indefinites in kind terms. *Linguistics & Philosophy* 27: 393–450.

———. 2011. Hindi pseudo-incorporation. *Natural Language & Linguistic Theory* 29: 123–67.

de Hoop, Helen. 1992. Case configuration and NP interpretation. PhD diss., University of Groningen.

de Hoop, Helen, and Peter de Swart. 2004. Contrast in discourse. *Journal of Semantics* 21: 87–93.

Dekker, Paul. 1993. Transsentential meditations. PhD diss., University of Amsterdam.

———. 2012. *Dynamic Semantics*. New York: Springer.

den Dikken, M. 2005. Comparative correlatives comparatively. *Linguistic Inquiry* 36: 497–532.

Diesing, Molly. 1992. *Indefinites*. Cambridge, MA: MIT Press.

Doron, Edit. 1983. Verbless predicates in Hebrew. PhD diss., University of Texas, Austin.

Dowty, David. 1979. *Word Meaning and Montague Grammar*. Dordrecht: Reidel.

———. 1994. The role of negative polarity and concord marking in natural language reasoning. *Proceedings SALT* 4: 114–44.

Drubig, Hans B. 2001. On the syntactic form of epistemic modality. MS. University of Tübingen.

Eckardt, Regine. 2004. Particles and strategies. *Sprache und Datenverarbeitung* 28: 79–86.

Elvira, Javier. 1986. Quanto en español antiguo. *Anuario de Estudios Filológicos* 9: 101–17.

Español-Echevarría, Manuel. 1997. Inalienable possession in copulative contexts and the DP structure. *Lingua* 101: 211–44.

Espinal, Maria Teresa. 2001. Property denoting objects in idiomatic constructions. In *Romance Languages & Linguistic Theory 1999: Selected Papers from Going Romance 1999*, ed. Yves D'Hulst, Johan Rooryck, and Jan Schroten, 117–41. Amsterdam: John Benjamins.

Espinal, Maria Teresa, and Jaume Mateu. 2010. On classes of idioms and their interpretation. *Journal of Pragmatics* 42: 1397–411.

Espinal, Maria Teresa, and Louise McNally. 2009. Characterizing 'have' predicates and indefiniteness. *Proceedings of the IV NEREUS International Workshop, Fachbereich Sprachwissenschaft der Universität Konstanz Arbeitspapier* 124: 27–32.

———. 2011. Bare singular nominals and incorporating verbs in Spanish and Catalan. *Journal of Linguistics* 47: 87–128.

Farkas, Donka. 1985. *Intensional Descriptions and the Romance Subjunctive Mood*. New York: Garland.

———. 1992. Two types of 'world-creating' predicates. In *The Joy of Grammar*, ed. Diana Brentari, 35–63. Amsterdam: John Benjamins.

———. 1993. Modal anchoring and NP scope. Linguistics Research Center Working Paper 93–08, Linguistics Research Center, University of California, Santa Cruz.

———. 1996. Dependent indefinites. Linguistics Research Center Working Paper 96–04, Linguistics Research Center, University of California, Santa Cruz.

———. 1997. Evaluation indices and scope. In *Ways of Scope Taking*, ed. Anna Szabolcsi, 183–215. Dordrecht: Kluwer.

Farkas, Donka, and Kathalin Kiss. 2000. On the comparative and absolute readings of superlatives. *Natural Language & Linguistic Theory* 18: 417–55.

Farkas, Donka, and Henriette de Swart. 2003. *The Semantics of Incorporation*. Stanford, CA: CSLI Publications.

Fauconnier, Gilles. 1979. Implication reversal in natural language. In *Formal Semantics of Natural Language*, ed. F. Guenthner, 289–301. Dordrecht: Reidel.

Ferrara, Kathleen. 1997. Form and function of the discourse marker *anyway*. *Linguistics* 35: 345–78.

Fine, Kit. 1994. Essence and modality. In *Philosophical Perspectives* 8, ed. J. Tomberlin, 1–16.

———. 1995. The logic of essence. *Journal of Philosophical Logic* 24: 241–73.

Flamenco García, Luis. 1999. Las construcciones concesivas y adversativas. In *Gramática descriptiva de la lengua española*, ed. I. Bosque and V. Demonte, 3805–78. Madrid: Espasa.

Fodor, Janet, and Ivan Sag. 1982. Referential and quantificational indefinites. *Linguistics & Philosophy* 5: 355–98.

Fodor, Jerry. 1983. *The Modularity of Mind*. Cambridge, MA: MIT Press.

Fox, Danny. 1995. Economy and scope. *Natural Language Semantics* 3: 283–341.

———. 2000. *Economy and Semantic Interpretation*. Cambridge, MA: MIT Press.

Frampton, John, and Sam Guttman. 2000. Agreement is feature sharing. Unpublished manuscript, http://www.math.neu.edu/ling/pdffiles/agrisfs.pdf.

Freeze, Ray. 1992. Existentials and other locatives. *Language* 68: 553–95.

Fuentes Rodríguez, Catalina. 1996. *La sintaxis de los conectores supraoracionales.* Madrid: Arco Libros.

Gallego, Ángel. 2011. *La elipsis.* Madrid: Arco Libros.

Geis, Michael, and Arnold Zwicky. 1971. On invited inferences. *Linguistic Inquiry* 2. 561–66.

Giannakidou, Anastasia. 1998. *Polarity Sensitivity as (Non)-Veridical Dependency.* Linguistik Aktuell 23. Amsterdam: John Benjamins.

Gil, David. 1995. Universal quantifiers and distributivity. In *Quantification in Natural Language,* ed. E. Bach et al., 321–62. Dordrecht: Kluwer Academic Publishers.

Giorgi, Allessandra, and Giuseppe Longobardi. 1991. *The Syntax of Noun Phrases.* Cambridge: Cambridge University Press.

Giorgi, Allessandra, and Fabio Pianesi. 1997. *Tense and Aspect: From Semantics to Morphosyntax.* Oxford: Oxford University Press.

González-Rivera, Melvin. 2010. On the internal structure of Spanish verbless clauses. PhD diss., OSU.

Gorman, Michael. 2005. The essential and the accidental. *Ratio* 18: 276–89.

Graf, Thomas. 2010a. How economic is global economy: A survey of reference set computation. MS. UCLA.

———. 2010b. A tree transducer model of reference-set computation. *UCLA Working Papers in Linguistics* 15: 1–53.

Grice, Herbert. 1989. *Studies in the Way of Words.* Cambridge, MA: Harvard University Press.

Grinstead, John, ed. 2009. *Hispanic Child Languages: Typical and Impaired Development.* Amsterdam: John Benjamins.

Groenendijk, Jeroen, Martin Stokhof, and Frank Veltman. 1995. Coreference and contextually restricted quantification. *Proceedings SALT* 5: 112–29.

———. 1996. Coreference and modality. In *Handbook of Contemporary Semantic Theory,* ed. Shalom Lappin, 179–214. Oxford: Blackwell.

Groos, Anneke, and Henk van Riemsdijk. 1981. Matching effects in free relatives. *Theory of Markedness in Generative Grammar,* ed. A. Belletti, L. Brandi, and L. Rizzi, 171–216. Pisa: Scuola Normale Superiore.

Grosu, Alexander, and Fred Landman. 1998. Strange relatives of the third kind. *Natural Language Semantics* 6: 125–70.

Guéron, Jacqueline. 2003. Inalienable possession and the interpretation of determiners. In *From NP to DP,* vol. 1, ed. M. Coene and Y. D'Hulst, 189–220. Amsterdam: John Benjamins.

Gutiérrez-Rexach, Javier. 1996. The scope of universal quantifiers in Spanish interrogatives. In *Grammatical Theory and Romance Languages,* ed. K. Zagona, 87–98. Amsterdam: John Benjamins.

———. 1997. Questions and generalized quantifiers. In *Ways of Scope Taking,* ed. A. Szabolcsi, 409–52. Dordrecht: Kluwer Academic Publishers.

———. 1999a. Cláusulas de relativo y operaciones de forma lógica. *Revista de Lingüística Teórica y Aplicada* 37: 67–93.

———. 1999b. The formal semantics of clitic doubling. *Journal of Semantics* 16: 315–80.

———. 1999c. Neuter relatives and the degree operator. In *Semantic Issues in Romance Syntax,* ed. E. Trevio and J. Lema, 69–88. Amsterdam: John Benjamins.

———. 1999d. The quantificational variability of free relatives. In *Chicago Linguistics Society (CLS)* 35, pt. 1: *The Main Session,* ed. Sabrina J. Billings et al., 109–23. Chicago: Chicago Linguistics Society, University of Chicago.

———. 1999e. The structure and interpretation of Spanish neuter degree constructions. *Lingua* 109: 35–63.

———. 2000. Generalized minimalist grammars. In *Issues in Mathematical Linguistics*, ed. C. Martín-Vide, 19–52. Amsterdam: John Benjamins.

———. 2001a. Adverbial weak pronouns: Derivation and interpretation. In *Current Issues in Spanish Syntax and Semantics*, ed. J. Gutiérrez-Rexach and L. Silva-Villar, 143–74. Berlín: Mouton De Gruyter.

———. 2001b. The semantics of Spanish plural existential determiners and the dynamics of judgment types. *Probus* 13: 113–54.

———. 2001c. Spanish exclamatives and the semantics of the left periphery. In *Romance Languages & Linguistic Theory 1999: Selected Papers from Going Romance 1999*, ed. Yves D'Hulst, Johan Rooryck, and Jan Schroten , 167–94. Amsterdam: John Benjamins.

———. 2003. *La semántica de los indefinidos*. Madrid: Visor.

———. 2004. *Semantics: Critical Concepts*. London: Routledge.

———. 2006a. Discourse particles, quantification and multi-dimensional meaning. *SDV, Sprache und Datenverarbeitung: International Journal for Language Data Processing* 29: 35–46.

———. 2006b. Superlative quantifiers and the dynamics of context dependence. In *Where Semantics Meets Pragmatics*, ed. K. von Heusinger and K. Turner, 237–66. New York: Elsevier.

———. 2008. Spanish root exclamatives at the syntax-semantics interface. *Catalan Journal of Linguistics* 7: 117–33.

———. 2009. Correlativization structures and degree quantification in Spanish. In *Romance Linguistics 2007: Structure, Interfaces, and Microparametric Variation*, ed. P. Masullo, E. O'Rourke, and Chia-Hui Huang, 121–41. Amsterdam: John Benjamins.

———. 2010. Varieties of indefinites in Spanish. *Language & Linguistics Compass* 4: 680–93.

———. 2011. Characterizing superlative quantifiers. In *Adjectives: Formal Issues in the Analysis of Adjectives*, ed. P. Cabredo-Hoffher and O. Matushansky, 187–231. Amsterdam: John Benjamins.

———. 2012. Quantification. In *Handbook of Spanish Linguistics*, ed. J. I. Hualde, A. Olarrea, and E. O'Rourke, 307–32. Oxford: Blackwell.

Gutiérrez-Rexach, Javier, and Chad Howe. 2003. Selective and unselective manner operators. In *Romance Linguistics: Theory and Acquisition*, ed. A. T. Pérez-Leroux and Y. Roverge, 131–48. Amsterdam: John Benjamins.

Gutiérrez-Rexach, Javier, and Sandro Sessarego. 2011. A minimalist approach to gender variation in the Afro-Bolivian DP: Variation and the specification of uninterpretable features. *Folia Linguistica* 45: 465–88.

Gutiérrez-Rexach, Javier, and L. Silva-Villar. 1998. Locative and temporal weak proforms. In *Theoretical Research on Romance Languages*, ed. J. Lema and E. Treviño, 205–26. Amsterdam: John Benjamins.

Harbert, Wayne. 1983. On the nature of the matching parameter. *Linguistic Review* 2: 237–84.

Hardt, Daniel. 1993. Verb phrase ellipsis. PhD diss., University of Pennsylvania.

———. 1999. Dynamic interpretation of verb phrase ellipsis. *Linguistics & Philosophy* 22: 187–221.

Harris, Randy. 1995. *The Linguistic Wars*. Oxford: Oxford University Press.

Heim, Irene. 1982. The semantics of definite and indefinite NPs. PhD diss., University of Massachusetts, Amherst.

———. 1985. Notes on comparatives and related matters. MS. University of Texas at Austin.

———. 1996. On the logical syntax of degree operators. MS. MIT.

———. 2006. Remarks on comparative clauses as generalized quantifiers. MS. MIT.
Heim, Irene, and Angelika Kratzer. 1998. *Semantics and Generative Grammar*. Oxford: Blackwell.
Hendricks, Herman. 1993. Studied flexibility. PhD diss., ILLC, University of Amsterdam.
Higginbotham, James, and Robert May. 1981. Questions, quantifiers and crossing. *Linguistic Review* 1: 41–79.
Higgins, Roger. 1973. The pseudo-cleft construction in English. PhD diss., MIT.
Hinterwimmer, Stephan. 2008. *Q-adverbs as Selective Binders: The Quantificational Variability of Free Relatives and Definite DPs*. Berlin: De Gruyter.
Hinzen, Wolfram. 2012. Minimalism. In *Handbook of Philosophy of Linguistics*, ed. R. Kempson, T. Fernando, and N. Asher, 93–142. New York: Elsevier.
Hirschbühler, Paul. 1982. VP-deletion and across the board quantifier scope. *Proceedings NELS* 12: 132–39.
Hoekstra, Teun, and René Mulder. 1990. Unergatives as copular verbs: Locational and existential predication. *Linguistic Review* 7: 1–79.
Hopper, Paul, and Elizabeth Traugott. 2003. *Grammaticalization*. Cambridge: Cambridge University Press.
Horn, Larry. 1972. On the semantic properties of logical operators in English. PhD diss., UCLA.
Hornstein, Norbert. 1995. *Logical Form: From GB to Minimalism*. Oxford: Blackwell.
Hornstein, Norbert, Sara Rosen, and Juan Uriagereka. 2002. Integrals. In *Derivations: Exploring the Dynamics of Syntax*, ed. J. Uriagereka, 179–95. London: Routledge.
Iatridou, Sabine. 1991. Topics on conditionals. PhD diss., MIT.
———. 2013. Looking for free relatives in Turkish. MS. MIT.
Iatridou, Sabine, and Spirodoula Varlokosta. 1996. A crosslinguistic perspective on pseudoclefts. *Proceedings NELS* 26: 117–31.
Izvorsky, Roumyana. 1997. Syntax and semantics of correlative proforms. *Proceedings NELS* 26: 133–47.
———. 1998. The present perfect as an epistemic modal. *Proceedings SALT* 7: 222–39.
Jackendoff, Ray. 1972. *Semantic Interpretation in Generative Grammar*. Cambridge, MA: MIT Press.
———. 2002. *Foundations of Language*. Oxford: Oxford University Press.
———. 2007. Linguistics in cognitive science: The state of the art. *Linguistic Review* 24: 347–401.
Jacobson, Pauline. 1995. On the quantificational force of English free relatives. In *Quantification in Natural Language*, ed. E. Bach et al., 451–86. Dordrecht: Kluwer.
Johnson, David, and Shalom Lappin. 1997. A critique of the minimalist program. *Linguistics & Philosophy* 20: 272–333.
———. 1999. *Local Constraints vs. Economy*. Stanford, CA: CSLI Publications.
Johnson, Kyle. 2008. *Topics in Ellipsis*. Cambridge: Cambridge University Press.
Kadmon, Nirit. 2000. *Formal Pragmatics*. Oxford: Blackwell.
Kadmon, Nirit, and Fred Landman. 1993. Any. *Linguistics & Philosophy* 16: 353–442.
Kamp, Hans. 1981. A theory of truth and semantic representation. In *Truth, Interpretation and Information*, ed. J. Groenendijk and M. Stokhof, 1–41. Dordrecht: Foris.
Kamp, Hans, and Uwe Reyle. 1993. *From Discourse to Logic*. Dordrecht: Kluwer.
Kaplan, David. 1989. The meaning of *ouch* and *oops*: Explorations in the theory of meaning as use. MS. UCLA.
Kaufman, Stephan. 2001. Probabilities of conditionals. *Proceedings SALT* 11: 248–67.

Kayne, Richard. 1993. Toward a modular theory of auxiliary selection. *Studia Linguistica* 47: 3–31.

———. 1994. *The Antisymmetry of Syntax*. Cambridge, MA: MIT Press.

———. 2005. *Movement and Silence*. Oxford: Oxford University Press.

———. 2008. Expletives, datives and the tension between morphology and syntax. In *The Limits of Syntactic Variation*, ed. T. Biberauer, 175–218. Amsterdam: John Benjamins.

Keenan, Edward. 1985. Relative clauses. *Language Typology and Syntactic Description*, ed. T. Shopen, 141–70. Cambridge: Cambridge University Press.

———. 1987. On the semantic definition of 'indefinite NP'. In *The Representation of (In)definiteness*, ed. E. Reuland and A. ter Meulen, 286–319. Cambridge, MA: MIT Press.

———. 1989. Semantic case theory. In *Semantics and Contextual Expression*, ed. R. Bartsch, J. van Benthem, and P. van Emde Boas, 33–57. Dordrecht: Foris.

———. 1996. The semantics of determiners. In *Handbook of Contemporary Semantic Theory*, ed. S. Lappin, 41–64. Oxford: Blackwell.

Keenan, Edward, and Leonard Faltz. 1985. *Boolean Semantics of Natural Language*. Dordrecht: Reidel.

Keenan, Edward, and Denis Paperno, eds. 2012. *Handbook of Quantifiers in Natural Language*. New York: Springer.

Keenan, Edward, and Baholisoa Ralalaoherivony. 2000. Raising from NP in Malagasy. *Lingvisticae Investigationes* 23: 1–34.

Keenan, Edward, and Ed Stabler. 2003. *Bare Grammar: Lectures on Invariants*. Stanford, CA: CSLI Publications.

———. 2009. Language variation and linguistic invariants. MS. UCLA.

Keenan, Edward, and Jonathan Stavi. 1986. A semantic characterization of natural language determiners. *Linguistics & Philosophy* 9: 253–326.

Keenan, Edward, and Dag Westerståhl. 1997. Generalized quantifiers in linguistics and logic. In *Handbook of Logic and Language*, ed. J. van Benthem and A. ter Meulen, 837–94. Cambridge, MA: MIT Press.

Kelepir, Meltem. 2007. Copular forms in Turkish, Turkmen and Noghay. *Proceedings of the 2nd Workshop on Altaic Formal Linguistics*. Distributed by MIT Working Papers in Linguistics, Cambridge, Massachusetts. 83–100.

Kennedy, Chris. 1997. Projecting the adjective. PhD diss., UC Santa Cruz.

———. 2007. Vagueness and grammar: The semantics of relative and absolute gradable adjectives. *Linguistics & Philosophy* 30: 1–45.

Kobele, Greg. 2012. Ellipsis: computation of. *Wiley Interdisciplinary Reviews: Cognitive Science* 3: 411–18.

Koenig, Ekkehard. 1986. Conditionals, concessive conditionals and concessives: Areas of contrast, overlap and neutralization. In *On Conditionals*, ed. E. C. Traugott et al., 229–46. Cambridge: Cambridge University Press.

———. 1992. From discourse to syntax: the case of concessive conditionals. In *Who Climbs the Grammar-Tree?*, ed. R. Tracy, 423–33. Tübingen: Max Niemeyer.

Koenig, Ekkehard, and Johan van der Auwera. 1988. Clause integration in German and Dutch conditionals, concessive conditionals and concessives. In *Clause Combining in Grammar and Discourse*, ed. J. Haiman and S. Thompson, 101–33. Amsterdam: John Benjamins.

Koenig, Ekkehard, and Peter Siemund. 2000. Causal and concessive clauses: Formal and semantic relations. In *Cause-Condition-Concession-Contrast, Cognitive and Discourse Perspectives*, ed. E. Couper-Kuhlem and B. Kortmann, 341–60. New York: De Gruyter.

Koizumi, Masatoshi. 1995. Phrase structure in minimalist syntax. PhD diss., MIT.

Koktova, Eva. 1999. *Word-Order Based Grammar*. Berlin: De Gruyter.

Koopman, Hilda. 2000. *The Syntax of Specifiers and Heads*. London: Routledge.

Kornfilt, Jacklyn. 2005. Free relatives as light-headed relatives in Turkish. In Organizing Grammar: Linguistic Studies in Honor of Henk van Riemsdijk, ed. N. Corver et al., 340–49. Berlin: De Gruyter.

Kratzer, Angelika. 1981. On the notional category of modality. In *Words, Worlds and Context*, ed. H. J. Eikmeyer and H. Rieser, 38–74. Berlin: De Gruyter.

——. 1986. Conditionals. *Chicago Linguistics Society* 22: 3–15.

——. 1991. The representation of focus. In *Semantics: An International Handbook of Contemporary Research*, ed. A. von Stechow and D. Wunderlich, 804–25. Berlin: De Gruyter.

——. 1995. Individual-level and stage-level predicates. In *The Generic Book*, ed. G. Carlson and F. Pelletier, 125–75. Chicago: University of Chicago Press.

——. 1998. Scope or pseudo-scope? Are there wide-scope indefinites? In *Events and Grammar*, ed. Susan Rothstein, 163–96. Dordrecht: Kluwer.

——. 1999. Beyond ouch and oops: How descriptive and expressive meaning interact; A comment on David Kaplan's paper. MS, Cornell Conference on Theories of Context Dependency. Ithaca, NY: Cornell University.

——. 2012. *Modals and Conditionals*. Oxford: Oxford University Press.

Kratzer, Angelika, and Junko Shimoyama. 2002. Indeterminate pronouns: The view from Japanese. *Proceedings of the Third Tokyo Conference on Psycholinguistics* ed. Y. Utso, 1–25. Tokyo: Hituzi Syobo.

Ladusaw, William. 1979. *Polarity Sensitivity as Inherent Scope Relations*. New York: Garland.

Lahiri, Utpal. 1991. Embedded interrogatives and predicates that embed them. PhD diss., MIT.

——. 2002. *Questions and Answers in Embedded Contexts*. Oxford: Oxford University Press.

Laka, Itziar. 1990. *Negation in Syntax: On the Nature of Functional Categories and Projections*. PhD diss., MIT.

Lakoff, George. 1970. Repartee. *Foundations of Language* 6: 389–422.

——. 1971. On generative semantics. In, *Semantics: An Interdisciplinary Reader in Philosophy, Linguistics and Psychology*, ed. D. Steinberg and L. A. Jakobovits, 232–96. Cambridge: Cambridge University Press.

——. 1987. *Women, Fire, and Other Dangerous Things*. Chicago: University of Chicago Press.

Lascarides, Alex, Jo Calder, and Keith Stenning. 2006. *Introduction to Cognition and Communication*. Cambridge, MA: MIT Press.

Lasnik, Howard, Juan Uriagereka, and Cedric Boeckx. 2005. *A Course in Minimalist Syntax*. Oxford: Blackwell.

Lees, Robert. 1972. The Turkish copula. In *The Verb Be and Its Synonyms*, vol. 5, ed. J. Verhaar, 64–73. Dordrecht: Reidel.

Leonetti, Manuel. 2012. Indefiniteness and specificity. In *Handbook of Spanish Linguistics*, ed. J. I. Hualde and A. Olarrea, 285–306. Oxford: Blackwell.

Lewis, David. 1968. Counterpart theory and quantified modal logic. *Journal of Philosophy* 65: 113–26.

——. 1975. Adverbs of quantification. In *Formal Semantics of Natural Language*, ed. E. Keenan, 3–15. Cambridge: Cambridge University Press.

——. 1979. Score keeping in a language game. In *Semantics from Different Points of View*, ed. R. Bäuerle et al., 172–87. Berlin: Springer.

Liu, Feng Hsi. 1998. *Scope and Specificity*. Amsterdam: John Benjamins.

Longobardi, Giuseppe. 1994. Reference and proper names. *Linguistic Inquiry* 25: 609–65.

———. 2001. How comparative is semantics? A unified parametric theory of bare nouns and proper names. *Natural Language Semantics* 9: 335–69.

López-Carretero, Luis. 2009. *A Derivational Syntax for Information Structure*. Oxford: Oxford University Press.

———. 2011. Objetos indefinidos: La intersección entre morfología, semántica y sintaxis. *Cuadernos de la ALFAL* 3: 124–37.

———. 2012. *Indefinite Objects*. Cambridge, MA: MIT Press.

López Palma, Elena. 1999. *La interpretación de los cuantificadores: Aspectos sintácticos y semánticos*. Madrid: Visor Libros.

Mahajan, Anoop. 2000. Relative asymmetries and Hindi correlatives. In *The Syntax of Relative Clauses*, ed. A. Alexiadou, P. Law, and C. Wilder, 201–29. Amsterdam: John Benjamins.

Manzini, Rita. 2000. Sentential complementation: The subjunctive. In *Lexical Specification and Insertion*, ed. P. Coopmans, 241–68. Amsterdam: John Benjamins.

Marantz, Alec. 1995. The minimalist program. In *Government and Binding Theory and the Minimalist Program*, ed. G. Webelhuth, 349–82. Oxford: Basil Blackwell.

Martins, Ana M. 1994. Enclisis, VP deletion and the nature of Sigma. *Probus* 6: 173–206.

Martí, Luisa. 2007. Restoring indefinites to normalcy: An experimental study on the scope of Spanish *algunos*. *Journal of Semantics* 24: 1–25.

———. 2009. Contextual restrictions on indefinites: Spanish *algunos* vs. *unos*. In *Quantification, Definiteness, and Nominalization*, ed. A. Giannakidou and M. Rathert, 108–32. Oxford: Oxford University Press.

Massam, Diane. 2001. Pseudo noun-incorporation in Niuean. *Natural Language & Linguistic Theory* 19: 153–97.

Masullo, Pascual. 1992. Incorporation and case theory in Spanish: A crosslinguistic perspective. PhD diss., University of Washington.

Matthewson, Lisa. 1999. On the interpretation of wide-scope indefinites. *Natural Language Semantics* 7: 79–134.

Matushansky, Ora. 2002. Movement of degree/degree of movement. PhD diss., MIT.

May, Robert. 1977. The grammar of quantification. PhD diss., MIT.

———. 1985. *Logical Form*. Cambridge, MA: MIT Press.

McCawley, James. 1988. The comparative conditional construction in English, German and Chinese. *Proceedings Berkeley Linguistic Society*, 176–87.

McNally, Louise. 1995. Bare plurals in Spanish are interpreted as properties. In *Proceedings 1995 ESSLLI Formal Grammar Conference*, ed. G. Morril and R. Oehrle, 197–212. Barcelona: UPC. (Also *Catalan Journal of Linguistics* 3 [2004]: 115–33).

———. 1998. Existential sentences without existential quantification. *Linguistics & Philosophy* 21: 353–92.

———. 2013. Semantics and pragmatics. *Wiley Interdisciplinary Reviews: Cognitive Science* 4: 285–97.

Menéndez-Benito, Paula. 2010. On universal free choice items. *Natural Language Semantics* 18: 33–64.

Merchant, Jason. 2001. *The Syntax of Silence*. Oxford: Oxford University Press.

Milsark, Gary. 1977. Toward an explanation of certain peculiarities in the existential construction in English. *Linguistic Analysis* 3: 1–29.

Moltmann, Friederike. 1992. Coordination and comparatives. PhD diss., MIT.

Montague, Richard. 1975. *Formal Philosophy.* New Haven, CT: Yale University Press.

Montolío, Estrella. 2001. *Conectores de la lengua escrita.* Barcelona: Editorial Ariel.

Moreno Cabrera, Juan Carlos. 2003. *Semántica y gramática: Sucesos, papeles semánticos y relaciones sintácticas.* Madrid: Antonio Machado Libros.

Moro, Andrea. 1997. *The Raising of Predicates.* Cambridge: Cambridge University Press.

Morrill, Glyn. 1994. *Type Logical Grammar.* Dordrecht: Kluwer.

———. 2012. Logical grammar. In *Handbook of Philosophy of Linguistics,* ed. R. Kempson, T. Fernando, and N. Asher, 63–92. New York: Elsevier.

Navarro Tomás, Tomás. (1918) 1982. *Manual de pronunciación española.* 8th ed. Madrid: CSIC.

Neeleman, Ad, Hans van de Koot, and Jenny Doetjesl. 2004. Degree expressions. *Linguistic Review* 21: 1–66.

Nunes, Jairo. 2004. *Linearization of Chains and Sideward Movement.* Cambridge, MA: MIT Press.

Ogihara, Toshiyuki. 1989. Temporal reference in English and Japanese. PhD diss., University of Texas, Austin.

O'Grady, William. 1998. The syntax of idioms. *Natural Language & Linguistic Theory* 16: 279–312.

Oltra-Massuet, Isabel, and Isabel Pérez-Jiménez. 2011. La interacción contabilidad-gradabilidad en los SSPP escuetos. *Cuadernos de la ALFAL* 3: 138–58.

Pancheva, Roumyana, and Rakesh Bhatt. 2004. Late merger of degree clauses. *Linguistic Inquiry* 35: 1–45.

Papafragou, Anna. 2006. Epistemic modality and truth conditions. *Lingua* 116: 1688–702.

Parsons, Terence. 1990. *Events in the Semantics of English.* Cambridge, MA: MIT Press.

Partee, Barbara. 1986. Ambiguous pseudoclefts with unambiguous *be. Proceedings NELS* 16: 354–66.

———. 1995. Quantificational structures and compositionality. In *Quantification in Natural Languages,* ed. E. Bach et al., 1–11. Dordrecht: Kluwer.

———. 1999. Weak NPs in HAVE sentences. In *Van Benthem Feitschrifft, ed.* J. Gerbrandy, M. Marx, M. de Rijke, and Y. Venema. Amsterdam: ILLC. (Available online: http://www.illc.uva.nl/j50/contribs/partee/).

Partee, Barbara, and Fred Landman. 1987. Weak NPs in HAVE sentences. MS.

Pastor, Alberto. 2008. Split analysis of gradable adjectives in Spanish. *Probus* 20: 257–99.

Paul, Ileana. 2006. Bare nouns in Malagasy. Talk, NIK, University of Ottawa.

Pesetsky, David. 1987. *Wh-in-situ:* Movement and unselective binding. In *The Representation of Indefiniteness,* ed. E. Reuland and A. ter Meulen, 98–129. Cambridge, MA: MIT Press.

Pesetsky, David, and Esther Torrego. 2007. The syntax of valuation and the interpretability of features. In *Phrasal and Clausal Architectures,* ed. S. Karimi and V. Samiian, 262–94. Amsterdam: John Benjamins.

Peters, Stanley, and Dag Westerståhl. 2006. *Quantifiers in Language and Logic.* Oxford: Oxford University Press.

Pietroski, Paul. 2008. Minimalist meaning, internalist interpretation. *Biolinguistics* 2: 317–41.

Plantinga, Alvin. 1974. *The Nature of Necessity.* Oxford: Clarendon Press.

Pollard, Carl. 2008. An introduction to convergent grammar. MS. OSU.

Portolés, José. 1998. *Marcadores del discurso.* Barcelona: Editorial Ariel.

Potts, Chris. 2003. Expressive content as conventional implicature. *Proceedings of NELS* 33: 303–22.

———. 2005. *The Logic of Conventional Implicatures*. Oxford: Oxford University Press.

———. 2007. Into the conventional-implicature dimension. *Philosophy Compass* 2: 665–79.

Prüst, Hub, Remko Scha, and Martin van der Berg. 1994. Discourse grammar and verb phrase anaphora. *Linguistics & Philosophy* 17: 261–327.

Pustejovsky, James. 1995. *The Generative Lexicon*. Cambridge, MA: MIT Press.

Quer, Josep. 1998. Mood at the interface. PhD diss., University of Utrecht.

———. 2009. Twists of mood: The distribution and interpretation of indicative and subjunctive. *Lingua* 119: 1779–87.

———. 2010. On the (un)stability of mood distribution in Romance. In *Modality and Mood in Romance*, ed. M. Becker and E. Remberger, 163–80. Berlin: De Gruyter.

Ramchand, Gilian, and Charles Reiss, eds. 2007. *The Oxford Handbook of Linguistic Interfaces*. Oxford: Oxford University Press.

Ramos-Santacruz, Milagrosa. 1994. Silent heads of Spanish non-specific free relatives. *Proceedings SCIL* 6: 283–96.

Real Academia Española (RAE). 1972. *Esbozo de una nueva gramática de la lengua española*. Madrid: Espasa.

———. 2009. *Nueva gramática de la lengua española*. Madrid: Espasa.

Reinhart, Tanya. 1991. Elliptic conjunctions: Non-quantificational LF. In *The Chomskyan Turn*, ed. A. Kasher, 360–84. Oxford: Blackwell.

———. 1997. Quantifier scope: How labor is divided between QR and choice functions. *Linguistics & Philosophy* 20: 335–97.

———. 2006. *Interface Strategies. Optimal and Costly Computations*. Cambridge, MA: MIT Press.

Retoré, Christian, and Ed Stabler. 1999. Resource logics and minimalist grammars. INRIA Rapport de recherché 3780.

Reuland, Eric, and Alice ter Meulen, eds. 1987. *The Representation of (In)definiteness*. Cambridge, MA: MIT Press.

Rivero, Maria L. 1979. Referencia y especificidad. In *Estudios de gramática generativa del español*, 123–61. Madrid: Cátedra.

———. 1994. On indirect questions, commands, and Spanish quotative *que*. *Linguistic Inquiry* 25: 547–54.

———. 2011. *Cualquiera* posnominal: Un desconocido cualquiera. *Cuadernos ALFAL* 3: 40–60.

Rizzi, Luigi. 1990. *Relativized Minimality*. Cambridge, MA: MIT Press.

———. 1997. The fine structure of the left periphery. In *Elements of Grammar*, ed. L. Haegeman, 281–338. Dordrecht: Kluwer.

Roberts, Craige. 1996. Information structure in discourse: Towards an integrated formal theory of pragmatics. *OSU Working Papers in Linguistics* 49: 91–136. Columbus, OH: Ohio State University. (published in *Semantics and Pragmatics* 5 (2012):1–69).

———. 2003. Uniqueness in definite noun phrases. *Linguistics & Philosophy* 26: 287–350.

Robinson, John A. 1965. A machine-oriented logic based on the resolution principle. *Journal of the ACM* 12: 23–41.

Rodman, Robert. 1976. Scope phenomena, movement transformations, and relative clauses. In *Montague Grammar*, ed. B. Partee, 165–76. New York: Academic Press.

Roeper, Tom. 2011. Strict interfaces and three kinds of multiple grammar. In *The Development of Grammar*, ed. E. Rinke and T. Kupisch, 205–28. Amsterdam: John Benjamins.

Rooth, Matts. 1985. Association with focus. PhD diss., University of Massachusetts, Amherst.

———. 1992a. Ellipsis redundancy and reduction redundancy. *Proceedings of the Stuttgart Workshop on Ellipsis*, ed. S. Berman and A. Hestvik, 1–15.

———. 1992b. A theory of focus interpretation. *Natural Language Semantics* 1: 75–116.

Ross, John R. 1967. Constraints on variables in syntax. PhD diss., MIT.

Rothstein, Susan. 2004. *Structuring Events*. Oxford: Blackwell.

Rullmann, Hotze. 1995a. Maximality in the semantics of wh-constructions. PhD diss., University of Massachusetts, Amherst.

———. 1995b. Negative islands and maximality. *Proceedings WECOL 94*: 210–23.

Russell, Bertrand. 1905. On denoting. *Mind* 14: 479–93.

Ruys, Eddy. 1992. *The scope of indefinites*. PhD diss., OTS, Utrecht University.

Saebo, Kjell. 2009. Possession and pertinence: The meaning of *have*. *Natural Language Semantics* 17: 369–97.

Sag, Ivan. 1976. Deletion and logical form. PhD diss., MIT.

Sag, Ivan, Thomas Wasow, and Emily M. Bender. 2003. *Syntactic Theory: A Formal Introduction*. 2nd ed. Stanford, CA: CSLI Publications.

Sánchez López, Cristina. 2009. Las correlaciones comparativas de proporcionalidad en español. *Boletín de la Real Academia Española* 89: 161–92.

Sánchez-Valencia, Víctor. 1991. Studies on natural logic and categorial grammar. PhD diss., University of Amsterdam.

Sauerland, Uli. 2000. Syntactic economy and quantifier raising. MS. MIT.

Schwarzschild, Roger, and Karina Wilkinson. 2002. Quantifiers in comparatives: A semantics of degree based on intervals. *Natural Language Semantics* 10: 1–41.

Schwenter, Scott. 1999. *Pragmatics of Conditional Marking: Implicature, Scalarity and Exclusivity*. New York: Garland.

Sharvit, Yael, and Penka Stateva. 2002. Superlative expressions, context, and focus. *Linguistics & Philosophy* 25: 453–504.

Sher, Gila. 1991. *The Bounds of Logic*. Cambridge, MA: MIT Press.

Smith, Elizabeth. 2010. Correlational comparison in English. PhD diss., Ohio State University.

Sperber, Dan, and Deirdre Wilson. 2004. Relevance theory. In *Handbook of Pragmatics*, ed. G. Ward and L. Horn, 607–32. Oxford: Blackwell.

Sportiche, Dominique. 1998. *Partitions and Atoms of Clause Structure*, London: Routledge.

Srivastav, Veneeta. 1991. The syntax and semantics of correlatives. *Natural Language & Linguistic Theory* 9: 637–86.

Stabler, Ed. 1997. Derivational minimalism. In *Logical Aspects of Computational Linguistics*, ed. C. Retoré, 68–95. Berlin: Springer.

———. 2010. After GB. In *Handbook of Logic and Language*, ed. J. van Benthem and A. ter Meulen, 395–414. New York: Springer.

Stowell, Tim. 1993. Syntax of tense. MS. UCLA.

Stowell, Tim, and Filippo Beghelli. 1994. The direction of quantifier movement. MS. UCLA.

———. 1997. Distributivity and negation: The syntax of *each* and *every*. In *Ways of Scope Taking*, ed. A. Szabolcsi, 71–108. Dordrecht: Kluwer.

Suñer, Margarita. 1984. Free relatives and the matching parameter. *Linguistic Review* 3: 363–87.

———. 2009. Formal linguistics and the syntax of Spanish: Past, present and future. In *Selected Proceedings of the 11th Hispanic Linguistic Symposium*, ed. Joseph Colentine et al., 9–26. Somerville, MA: Cascadilla Press.

Szabolcsi, Anna. 1983. The possessor that ran away from home. *Linguistic Review* 3: 89–102.

———. 1986a. Comparative superlatives. *MIT Working Papers in Linguistics* 8: 245–65.

———. 1986b. From the definiteness effect to lexical integrity. In *Topic, Focus and Configurationality*, ed. W. Abraham and S. de Meij, 321–48. Amsterdam: John Benjamins.

———. 1997. *Ways of Scope Taking*. Dordrecht: Kluwer Academic Publishers.

———. 2004. Positive polarity—negative polarity. *Natural Language & Linguistic Theory* 22: 409–52.

———. 2010. *Quantification*. Cambridge: Cambridge University Press.

Szabolcsi, Anna, and Frans Zwarts. 1993. Weak islands and an algebraic semantics for scope taking. *Natural Language Semantics* 1: 235–84.

Tancredi, Chris. 1992. *Deletion, deaccenting and presupposition*. PhD diss., MIT.

Tomioka, Satoshi. 1995. [Focus]$_F$ restricts scope: Quantifier in VP ellipsis. *Proceedings SALT* 5: 328–45.

———. 2008. A step-by-step guide to ellipsis resolution. In *Topics in Ellipsis*, ed. K. Johnson, 210–28. Cambridge: Cambridge University Press.

Torrego, Esther. 1984. On inversion in Spanish and some of its effects. *Linguistic Inquiry* 15: 103–29.

Tredinnick, Victoria. 1994. On the interpretation and distribution of *-ever* in English free relatives. *Proceedings CONSOLE* 2: 253–68.

———. 2005. *On the semantics of free relatives with -ever*. PhD diss., University of Pennsylvania.

Urgelles-Coll, Miriam. 2010. *The Syntax and Semantics of Discourse Markers*. London: Continuum.

Uriagereka, Juan. 1996. Form being to having: Questions about ontology from a Kayne/Szabolcsi syntax. In *University of Maryland Working Papers in Linguistics 1996*, ed. J. C. Castillo, V. Miglio, and J. Musolino, 152–72. College Park, MD: Department of Linguistics, University of Maryland.

———. 1999. Multiple spell-out. In *Working Minimalism*, ed. S. D. Epstein and N. Hornstein, 251–82. Cambridge, MA: MIT Press.

———. 2012. *Spell-Out and the Minimalist Program*. Oxford: Oxford University Press.

Uribe-Echebarría, Miriam. 1994. *Interface licensing conditions on NPIs: A theory of polarity and tense interactions*. PhD diss., University of Connecticut.

van Benthem, Johan. 1984. Questions about quantifiers. *Journal of Symbolic Logic* 49: 443–66.

van Craenenbroeck, Jeroen. 2010. *The Syntax of Ellipsis: Evidence from Dutch Dialects*. Oxford: Oxford University Press.

van Geenhoven, Veerle. 1998. *Semantic Incorporation and Indefinite Descriptions: Semantic and Syntactic Aspects of Noun Incorporation in West Greenlandic*. Stanford, CA: CSLI Publications.

Vargas-Tokuda, Marissa, John Grinstead, and Javier Gutiérrez-Rexach. 2009. Context and the scalar implicatures of indefinites in Spanish. In *Hispanic Child Languages*, ed. J. Grinstead, 93–116. Amsterdam: John Benjamins.

Vergnaud, Jean R. 1974. *French relative clauses*. PhD diss., MIT.

Villalta, Elizabeth. 2008. Mood and gradability: An investigation of the subjunctive mood in Spanish. *Linguistics & Philosophy* 31: 467–522.

von Fintel, Kai. 1994. *Restrictions on quantifier domains*. PhD diss., University of Massachusetts, Amherst.

von Fintel, Kai, and Sabine Iatridou. 2003. Epistemic containment. *Linguistic Inquiry* 34: 73–198.

Ward, Greg, and Betty Birner. 1995. Definiteness and the English existential. *Language* 71: 22–74.

Westerståhl, Dag. 1985. Determiners and context sets. In *Generalized Quantifiers in Natural Language*, ed. J. van Benthem and A. ter Meulen, 45–71. Dordrecht: Foris.

———. 1989. Quantifiers in formal and natural languages. In *Handbook of Philosophical Logic*, vol. 4, ed. D. Gabbay and F. Guenthner, 1–131. Dordrecht: Reidel.

Williams, Edwin. 1977. Discourse and logical form. *Linguistic Inquiry* 8: 101–39.

———. 1983. Semantic vs. syntactic categories. *Linguistics and Philosophy* 6: 423–46.

Wiltschko, Martina. 1998. Free relatives as indefinites. *Proceedings of WCCFL* 17: 700–712.

Winter, Yoad. 1997. Choice functions and the scopal semantics of indefinites. *Linguistics & Philosophy* 20: 399–467.

Yalcin, Seth. 2006. A paradox of epistemic modals. Talk at *Sinn und Bedeutung* 11, Barcelona.

———. 2007. Epistemic modals. *Mind* 116: 983–1026.

Yang, Charles. 1997. Minimal computations. Master of Science. thesis, MIT.

Zalta, Edward. 2000. A (Leibnizian) theory of concepts. *Philosophiegeschichte und Logische Analyse/Logical Analysis and History of Philosophy* 3: 137–83.

Zanuttini, Raffaella, and Paul Portner. 1998. The interdependence of specifier and head of CP. Paper presented at LSRL 28. University of Michigan.

Zeevat, Henk. 2002. Explaining presupposition triggers. In *Information Sharing*, ed. K. van Deemter and R. Kibble, 61–87. Stanford, CA: CSLI Publications.

Zeevat, H. 2004. Particles: Presupposition triggers, context markers or speech act markers. In *Optimality Theory and Pragmatics*, ed. R. Blutner and H. Zeevat, 91–111. New York: Macmillan.

Zimmermann, Thomas E. 1993. On the proper treatment of opacity in certain verbs. *Natural Language Semantics* 2: 149–80.

Zubizarreta, Maria L. 1998. *Prosody, Focus and Word Order*. Cambridge, MA: MIT Press.

Zulaica-Hernández, I., and J. Gutiérrez-Rexach. 2012. A multidimensional semantics for discourse particles: Evidence from Spanish neuter demonstratives. *International Review of Pragmatics* 4: 29–57.

Index of Abbreviations

ANIM	animacy marker
AP	Adjective Phrase
CH(f)	f is a choice function
CL	clitic
CP	Complementizer Phrase
DP	Determiner Phrase
DegP	Degree Phrase
ELAT	elative
ESG	Ellipsis Scope Generalization
FR	free relative
FUT	future
GB	Government & Binding
iff	if and only if
IND	indicative mood
IP	Inflection Phrase
LF	Logical Form
NEUT	neuter
NOM	nominative
NP	Noun Phrase
NPI	negative polarity item
NumP	Number Phrase

PL	plural
PP	Prepositional Phrase
PRES	present
QP	Quantifier Phrase
QR	Quantifier Raising
REFL	reflexive
SC	Small Clause
SE	reflexive pronoun
SG	singular
SUBJ	subjunctive mood
t	trace (movement copy)
TP	Tense Phrase
VP	Verb Phrase

Logical symbols

$\exists$	existential quantifier
$\forall$	universal operator
λ	lambda (abstraction) operator
ι	iota operator
$\in$	set membership
$\vee$	disjunction
$\wedge$	conjunction
$\rightarrow$	if ... then
$\neg$	negation
$\leq$	less than or equal
$\cup$	set union
$\cap$	set intersection
$\subseteq$	set inclusion

Index

accommodation, 176–77, 188, 194
adverbs of quantification, 15–17, 104–5, 115–17, 125, 133, 155–57, 174, 191–92, 197–209
agreement, 18, 66–73
anaphora, 28, 35, 39, 109–10, 199
Asher, Nicholas, 36, 78, 199, 201

Barker, Chris, 19
Beghelli, Filippo, 18, 32, 42, 47–48, 56, 59, 64
Benveniste, Emile, 77
Berman, Steven, 104
Bhatt, Rajesh, 119, 126, 128, 142
Bosque, Ignacio, 17–18, 51, 60, 64–66, 88, 94, 104, 110, 128–29, 144, 160, 167, 173
Brucart, Josep María, 22, 115, 131

Caponigro, Ivano, 101–3, 134, 139
Carlson, Greg, 35, 82, 88, 108, 134, 139
categorial grammar, 10, 22, 28
Chierchia, Gennaro, 19, 64, 102, 115, 164, 176, 196, 199
choice functions, 3, 18, 52–58, 63, 69–72, 205–7
Chomsky, Noam, 7–9, 22, 25, 29, 30, 40, 49, 66, 211
Cinque, Gughlielmo, 66, 87, 173
collective, 36–37, 48, 113
common ground, 37, 88, 194–96, 201–06
comparative reading, 171–72, 175, 178, 180–88

complementizer, 101–2, 107, 110, 114, 141, 143, 159, 168
compositionality, 9, 19
concessive, 3, 124, 143–63
conditionals, 3, 132, 133, 143–60
context set, 79, 97, 98, 172–87
copula, 69, 76–80, 93–99, 111, 112
copy, 24, 30, 32, 38, 126, 128

definiteness, 3, 75–81, 85–89, 95, 97, 103, 113, 212
degrees, 3, 4, 17, 20, 41, 73, 97, 119, 123–34, 145, 149, 154, 156–60, 165–70, 171, 173, 178, 179, 183
demonstrative, 14, 120, 121, 136, 172, 187
derivation, 8–10, 22, 29–32, 45, 48, 68, 73, 121, 128, 130, 140, 145, 185, 214
Discourse Representation Theory, 11
distributive, 18, 34–37, 42, 47–49
Dowty, David, 152, 161

economy, 2, 22, 25, 27–31, 35, 39, 45
Espinal, Maria Teresa, 85, 99
events, 17, 25, 105, 134, 160, 206–7
existential, 12–16, 31, 32, 35, 54, 75–82, 84, 86, 91, 95, 99, 103, 106, 113, 115, 118, 134, 156, 172, 188, 195, 199, 204

Farkas, Donka, 53, 55, 61, 72, 91, 106, 170

233

feature, 10, 18, 28, 34, 40, 42, 45–49, 64, 68, 71, 86, 93, 122, 130, 161, 173, 182, 184, 200
focus, 6, 19, 39, 45, 50, 66, 80, 92, 137, 146, 150, 163, 168, 170–88

generalized quantifiers, 12, 15, 29, 43, 77, 92–100, 109, 112, 126, 132, 135, 172, 213
generative grammar, 7, 28, 211
genericity, 16, 65, 80, 91, 102, 104, 115–17, 133, 195–99
Government and Binding Theory, 8, 22

Heim, Irene, 9, 104, 112, 114, 128, 132, 170, 173, 178, 192, 194, 197

implicature, 19, 64, 89, 153, 159, 163, 168, 190, 193, 200
incorporation, 86, 87, 90–93, 168, 173, 210
indefinites, 16, 19, 34, 50–60, 75, 86, 91, 101–7, 114, 133, 138, 170, 195–99, 205, 212
intensional, 29, 32, 55, 59, 64, 69, 106, 205
interfaces, 7–9, 11, 22, 126, 143, 190, 211
interrogatives, 15, 34, 100, 105, 172, 183, 200, 220
intersectivity, 13, 15
islands, 51, 61, 71, 128,

Jackendoff, Ray, 7, 9, 19, 39, 121, 194

Kamp, Hans, 11, 177, 188, 194, 199
Kayne, Richard, 68, 77, 80, 130, 141
Keenan, Edward, 10, 12, 17, 19, 75–77, 91–97, 100, 115, 119, 172, 196, 212
Kratzer, Angelika, 9, 35, 53, 65, 114, 117, 136, 155, 156, 191, 195, 200, 202

Lewis, David, 56. 155, 192, 194
logic, 3, 11, 18, 53, 136, 143, 153, 195, 201
Logical Form, 8–18, 23, 39, 49, 70, 133–40, 164, 179, 181, 206

maximality, 101, 116–18
Minimalist Program, 8, 22, 25, 28, 66, 211
modal, 17, 51, 57–61, 66–73, 99, 104, 112, 117, 140, 155, 162, 190, 212
monotonicity, 13, 123
Montague, Richard, 12, 19

mood, 3, 28, 58–68, 72, 106–10

negation, 32–33, 64–68, 107–8, 129, 148, 150, 154, 166, 208

object, 14, 18, 23–30, 34, 43–49, 66, 70, 77, 79–84, 90–94, 101, 145, 159, 182

parallelism, 22, 27, 30, 35–41, 46–48
Partee, Barbara, 91, 111–12, 194
particles, 4, 190–94, 198–206
polarity, 64–65, 68, 104, 109, 166, 208
possession, 76, 83–85, 94, 97, 99
Potts, Chris, 191, 200, 201
predication, 79–84, 94, 96–99, 111, 195
presupposition, 55, 101, 112, 118, 134, 139, 158, 168, 177, 191, 193, 202, 205
Principles and Parameters, 28, 79, 99

quantificational variability, 3, 100–104, 133, 156, 191
quantifier raising (QR), 14, 15, 27, 170, 181

reconstruction, 24, 26, 67–73, 83, 165
relative clauses, 58–70, 101, 119–23, 129–33, 138, 141, 213
rhetorical relation, 78, 191, 201, 206
Rivero, Maria L., 58, 117, 141

scalar, 123, 129, 149, 157–60, 169, 213
scope, 7, 14, 20, 22–29, 39, 41–49, 52–60, 107, 115, 128, 136, 154, 164, 174, 178–83
specific, 35, 42, 52, 58–60, 68–73, 102, 113, 139, 199, 205
strong and weak determiners, 75, 80
subject, 11, 14, 18, 23, 27, 31–38, 43, 69, 77, 82–84, 90–97, 127, 165, 199
Suñer, Margarita, 20, 128, 130
Szabolcsi, Anna, 12, 17, 41, 50, 66, 77, 94, 108, 129, 138, 170, 180, 188

unification, 10, 22, 28, 40, 49, 92
universal quantifiers, 12–16, 27, 31–38, 56, 59, 65, 96, 101–18, 134, 156, 162, 191, 195–201
unselective binder, 16, 104
Uriagereka, Juan, 9, 66, 77, 81, 82

THEORETICAL DEVELOPMENTS IN HISPANIC LINGUISTICS
Javier Gutiérrez-Rexach, Series Editor

This book series aims to be an outlet for monographs or edited volumes addressing current problems and debates within Hispanic linguistics. The series will be open to a wide variety of areas and approaches, as long as they are grounded in theoretical goals and methodologies. Contributions from the disciplines of syntax, semantics, pragmatics, morphology, phonology, phonetics, etc. are welcome, as well as those analyzing interface issues or the historical development, acquisition, processing, and computation of grammatical properties. Research topics of interest are those dealing with Spanish or other Hispanic languages, in any of their dialects and varieties.

Interfaces and Domains of Quantification
   JAVIER GUTIÉRREZ-REXACH

www.ingramcontent.com/pod-product-compliance
Lightning Source LLC
Chambersburg PA
CBHW020123240426
43673CB00038B/575